JASPER JOHNS

PRIVILEGED INFORMATION

JILL JOHNSTON

THAMES AND HUDSON

First published in the United States of America in hardcover in 1996 by
Thames and Hudson Inc., 500 Fifth Avenue, New York, New York 10110

First published in Great Britain in 1996 by Thames and Hudson Ltd., London

Library of Congress Catalog Card Number 96-60331

British Library Cataloguing-in-Publication Data
A catalogue record for this book is available from the British Library

ISBN 0-500-01736-0

Designed by BTD/Robin Bentz

Printed and bound in the United States of America

CONTENTS

ACKNOWLEDGMENTS

When Elizabeth Baker, editor-in-chief of *Art in America,* asked me to write about the work of Jasper Johns in 1987, she unwittingly gave birth to this book. I have continued to enjoy her advice, support, and special interest in my critical work on the artist. Another progenitor is Nikos Stangos, an editor at Thames and Hudson in London. He enthusiastically backed the concept of the book and has provided invaluable encouragement and counsel throughout the arduous process of research and writing. I am indebted also to my editor in New York, Peter Warner, whose advocacy of the book has never waned, and whose assistance in many instances I cannot imagine having done without. His editing skills and careful attention to the manuscript have been very meaningful to me. I want to thank Laurance Rosenzweig of Thames and Hudson for his friendliness and esteemed services in the many aspects of production.

No hyperbole would be too strong to describe the indulgence of Ingrid Nyeboe, my partner and helper, a model of steadfastness through the innumerable trials, doubts, surges, and setbacks of an endeavor like this. She has spent many hours looking at Johns paintings with me, listening to my ravings about them, providing insights of her own, traveling to remote places with me on missions to discover sources of Johns's work and life, obtaining literature and information at libraries, setting up computer coding and filing systems, critically reading my writing in progress, managing somehow to maintain jobs and interests of her own while being a collaborator extraordinaire in a project not of her own devising. But for her, I believe this book would not exist.

My daughter, Winifred B. Lanham, has been a wonderful ally, taking a particular interest of her own in Johns's paintings and being a good friend and well-wisher in my undertaking.

I am especially grateful to my friends Warren Wynshaw, who contributed legal counsel beyond the call; George Walsh, who always responds with humor and intelligence to my issues of publishing intricacies and has been a stalwart in every time of trial; and Geoff Hendricks, a rock of support throughout my pursuit. Other friends have been both comforting and helpful to me: Charlotte Bellamy, Kate Berney, David Bourdon, Candace Chaite, Tony Delamothe, James Fowler, Lynn Fowler, Mary Gorham, Grace Gorham, Paul Gruber, the late Teeny Duchamp, James Lawson, Jackie Matisse Monnier, Ann Pollard, Vaughan Rachel, Elinore Standard, Michael Standard, Marianne Sturman, Ann Wilson.

I have benefited tremendously from conversations and correspondence with Johns scholars Fred Orton and Richard Shiff. Commentary on my manuscript by Richard Shiff was a great help to me. I owe thanks to Terry Myers, who provided me with copies of the immense artist file on Jasper Johns at the Museum of Modern Art library.

It is a pleasure to remember my conversations, in some cases correspondence, with the many other people who were willing to talk with me about Jasper Johns. I am grateful to all of them for their time and candor: Jean Basile-Bezrodnof, Roberta Bernstein, the late James E. B. Breslin, the late John Cage, Leo Castelli, Riva Castleman, Remy Charlip, Charlotte Christensen, Michael Crichton, Robert Delahanty, John Duff, Richard Elovich, Viola Farber, Rick Flores, the late Christian Geelhaar, John Giorno, Bill Goldston, Manuel Gonzalez, Maxine Groffsky, Agnes Gund, Jonathan Katz, Billy Kluver, Max Kozloff, Mark Lancaster, Margo Leavin, Margaret Leng-Tan, James Lord, Julie Martin, Robert Morris, Si Newhouse, Robert Rauschenberg, Barbara Rose, Mark Rosenthal, Rachel Rosenthal, Ethel Scull, Jim Self, David Shapiro, Ken Silver, Leo Steinberg, the late Paul Taylor, Calvin Tomkins, Kirk Varnadoe, Jonathan Weinberg, Wolfgang Wittrock, and the late Thomas Yingling.

Among those who brought me closer to the artist were some of his family members, friends, and past associates, along with informants, in the artist's home state of South Carolina. I wish to thank all of them for their memories and sufferance as they granted me their time to talk about a favorite son: Bruce Burch, J. R. Craft, Betty Ruth Crews, Jane Griffin, Katherine Grubbs, Robin H. Dial, Brent Holcomb, Bill and Mary Johns, Debbie Johns, P. M. Johns, Ann Lafitte, Thomas Lawton, Geraldine Lewis, Betty Lind, Robert Ochs, Moe Oswald, John Oswald, Edward Patterson Riley, Camille Sharpe, Charles Shealey, Jerry Sineath, Victor Spigner, Ernie Stevenson, Mary Terry, Diane van Hook, Professor Edmund Yaghian, and Mary Young. Joe Topper of Allendale, South Carolina, gave me extraordinary support by introducing me to people in his community who could help me. Emanuel, of Columbia, South Carolina, befriended me when I first arrived in those parts to do research. She was a great

*The publisher regrets that Jasper Johns has refused permission to repro-
duce his work in Jill Johnston's book. Such a decision is an obstacle to
the free exchange of ideas, interpretation, and critical response. We are
confident, however, that the author's representation of Johns's life and
work can stand on its own.*

But Johns was a *secret* autobiographer. His figures were not for public consumption. Once he began showing them, the year after our luncheon, nobody could "see" them because he had obscured their faithfully traced outlines with paint and pattern in various ingenious ways, so much so that the areas they occupied in his paintings appeared to be abstract or decorative. Critics began calling this work autobiographical not because they recognized the figures, but simply because they noted an accumulation of personal icons and potent images or signs of death. But a subject was missing. A narrative is difficult to construe without a protagonist. Then in 1987 Johns exhibited four big canvases called *The Seasons,* each featuring a figure, but it was only his shadow. His true subject—one of the figures he had been tracing and concealing since 1981—was buried as a detail in these four works.

At the time of this exhibition, I had been practicing criticism again for three years. In my new life as a critic, I enjoyed a certain freedom, unimaginable in the 1960s, to consider biographical aspects of the artists about whom I wrote, in relation to their work. Using biography to support or mirror an art object had come to seem to me a proper goal of criticism. Why should such a prerogative be left to the mostly posthumous medium of critical biography? The work artists make not only evolves from the traditions of their media but also arises directly from their lives and times. If their lives are important in their art, their lives should be meaningful to both scholars and viewers at large. I believe that the widespread critical practice of isolating art in its traditions, where intramural influences may be enthusiastically plied, has kept audiences aesthetically fulfilled while turning off other human responses. I would like to see the once autonomous, incorruptible art object, bereft of information outside itself other than its art-historical pedigrees and virtually a freak of culture, nudged into the open, no longer a fugitive from important truths.

Jasper Johns's public exposure of a "secret autobiography" was a special challenge. The twin concerns of this book are an account of the secret spaces in his paintings, where he has stashed the two figures emblematic of his story, and aspects of his life that I have sought out in an attempt to breathe life into the figures. Such a venture should, it seems to me, help fill a vacuum in the critical literature on Johns. The critical establishment has been largely occupied with the formalist and painterly aspects of Johns's work, while its iconographic features have been ignored, or presented in laundry-list fashion, or introduced to account for a titillating mystery factor in the work that has long been noticed and long been considered off-limits. Johns's personal absence from his work has not gone unremarked. And it is this absence that I have made the central question of my work on the artist.

The further question, Why did Johns construct his conundrum, an autobiography with a concealed subject? is a kind of engine of the book. Another question, which I ask indirectly of the reader, is whether art as exercised and commodified in our society, as seen through the prism of the most successful living artist in America today, is a good medium for encouraging human interpersonal development. Or does it provide an enclave for one class of people, artists, to dwell further on their alienation from society in general? Implicit in my linkages between art and life is a related question: Must we assume from the custom of leaving the lives of artists out of considerations of their art that we believe life, compared to art, is a degrading experience? That life is unimportant, chaotic, embarrassingly different because private, subject to forces beyond individual control, happily transcended or at least momentarily forgotten in the great enterprises of art? Or that only the dead merit our compassionate attention to their lives?

Although I have no evidence to support Jasper Johns's interest in my project and have no doubt that my venture has appeared at the very best dubious to him, I have also concluded that any autobiographer who, as insistently as Johns, simultaneously exposes and conceals himself publicly, is crying for recognition of more than his art. Once I had understood this and had been given the opportunity to explore it, my license to probe such a sensitive issue was never a serious question for me.

One quote of Johns's that I cherish because it seems to resonate with my point of view gives me a glimmer of faith in the mutuality, however unmanifest, of my enterprise. He said, "I feel that if all were right in the world that art would not be made. I see no point in it. Or if it were made it would have a very different function and physique."

Ironically, I suppose, the deeper my investigations took me, the more I began to admire Johns's art and to marvel at his command of so many artifices of his trade and his invention of so many new sleights and ruses. Not for nothing, obviously, is he a titan of art in our time. Frequently I have fallen, figuratively, off his terrace, astonished at the surprises he has devised for his unsuspecting audiences.

Not so surprising, in retrospect at least, has been the manner in which I have created in the artist a surrogate for my own autobiographical interests, which have been on hold since I undertook this study. Gradually it became clear to me that I had not really dropped anything; I had simply resumed my interests in a novel guise. I had been drawn toward an artist whose artistic concealments and vivid suppression of information about himself, telling of puzzles and enigmas in his past, reflected a mystery in my own background—the fact that had attracted me to autobiography.

With this book, in some ways I come full circle with the artist, from lunch that day in 1983 at his house in Stony Point. I know now that his jests were not gratuitous. His sparkling merriness at my expense has turned out to mark fears he has had for the protection of his own autobiography—either the real thing, or its "fictional" equivalent in covertly painted autobiographical subjects.

As I prepared to leave his house that afternoon, he enveloped me in his arms and held me tight in a long, unequivocally affectionate bear hug, as if to apologize for his qualms, even perhaps to quietly take responsibility for them.

INTRODUCTION

On February 14, 1989, I arrived at 157 East 70th Street in Manhattan for an 8 P.M. dinner appointment at Si Newhouse's townhouse. America's most celebrated artist—Jasper Johns—was going to be there, along with other wealthy and influential people, including architect Philip Johnson, with his longtime companion David Whitney, and Kirk Varnedoe, the new director of painting and sculpture at the Museum of Modern Art. Newhouse had invited me in the morning, when I called to ask him if I could see his collection of Johns paintings. Wanting to be a little bit late, I walked half a block west to Lexington to monitor the time on a store clock. Glancing downtown, I spied Johns walking to the party. His own townhouse was located seven blocks south on Sixty-third Street. I slipped inside a building recess and waited a few minutes before reapproaching Newhouse's door. An African-American maid ushered me in, took my scarf and jacket, and showed me upstairs to a tall-ceilinged bar-*cum*-den, where Johns and two other guests were already holding cocktails in their hands. Johns's 1959 *Out the Window* was on the wall to my right, Roy Lichtenstein's *Engagement Ring* on my left.

Mrs. Newhouse, sitting on a sofa, was talking about the two weeks she and her husband spend annually in Vienna going to the opera and the theatre. The women, who included Varnedoe's wife, Elyn, and Agnes Gund, a collector and a trustee at the Museum of Modern Art, wore conventional evening dresses. I had not owned a dress in decades, but I was dressed up by my standards—in navy blue Burberry blazer, black cord pants, white silk shirt, and neck jewels. I also wore an arm splint to protect my right hand, broken a few months earlier. Someone asked me how I did it and I said jokingly, "Oh, I punched somebody out." Since nobody smiled or laughed I added, "I fell down."

While I stood in the den before dinner holding my Perrier and talking to Jasper and Agnes Gund, I noted that his necktie, a bold orange, bore a motif that resembled one of his own—the so-called crosshatch pattern that he began painting in the 1970s. I asked him where he got the tie. He said a Japanese gallery sent it to him. When I wondered where I could get one, he said he'd give me one, adding, with a mischievous smile, "Unless you want something else."

At dinner I was seated on the left of my host, whose small stature and disarming chipmunk grin make him seem an unlikely co-owner of something called Advance Publications, an empire comprising twenty-nine newspapers, the Random House book publishing group, and many magazines, all said to add up to America's greatest concentration of wealth in private hands. Directly behind him hung the recently famous *False Start,* painted by Johns in 1959, one year after his historic overnight success at the age of twenty-seven. Newhouse had bought it at auction just three months earlier for the record-breaking price of 17.1 million dollars, the most ever paid for the work of a living artist. The tycoon was known for his "very precise collection," as Kirk

Varnedoe has put it, of Abstract Expressionism and early Pop art—the core of it early de Kooning, Kline, Oldenburg, and Rauschenberg.

Facing me and Newhouse at the other end of the long table were Johns and Mrs. Newhouse. Hanging on the wall directly behind Johns was his big, wide three-panel painting *Weeping Women* of 1975, his head framed by the blunt ends of two steam-iron imprints in the center panel. A huge David Salle hung on the west wall. The commodious and windowless room seemed to swarm with African-American maids serving dinner, though there may have been only two of them.

This Consummation ritual, as Tom Wolfe once described the meeting of a successful artist and his benefactors (curators, collectors, culturati) on shared sacred ground, had long been a commonplace event for Johns. But his recent acquisition of an Upper East Side townhouse of his own, from which he had to walk only seven blocks to have dinner with the cohead of the Advance empire, made him seem more indistinguishable from his hosts. His necktie, with its heraldic sign of his work, was token of at least an original difference. For Johns was once assuredly what Wolfe called the Boho artist—a downtown denizen, impoverished and unknown, living in a raw loft long before lofts became fashionable and gentrified. Once anointed, in 1958, Johns never looked out of place in Consummation settings. Just as he appeared now, turned attentively toward Mrs. Newhouse—impassive, polite, recessive, appropriately attired—he has appeared down the decades, his hair now thinner, his face rounder, his girth more considerable. He blended in nicely with the bankers and businessmen who made him what he is. At the Newhouse table he slipped once, if it could be called that, when he overheard me describe a mutual friend to our host.

Down the length of the table and barely raising his voice, he begged to differ. When I raised my own voice back in disagreement, causing all other conversation to cease, he lifted his hand instantly to restrain me. Philip Johnson, seated to my left (himself a longtime Johns collector), attempted to put me at ease. Gesturing toward *False Start,* he told me he didn't care for its "Ab-Ex" style. He went on to comment on the *t* in my name, the lack of it in his, and the superiority of the Scots (the Johnsons with the *t*s in their names), to the U.S. dirt farmers he said he comes from. (A biography of him published in 1994 makes very clear how well his ancestors did once they left their farms.)

Leaving the dinner table to go back upstairs we passed another big Johns, a 1960s grisaille with the title page from Ted Berrigan's *Sonnets* embedded in it, close by a Rauschenberg of the same size (the only Rauschenberg I saw in the house). Over demitasse in Newhouse's large front living room, the presence of work by Johns was overwhelming. The colossal 1964 *According to What* consumed the entire west wall of the room. On the wall opposite *According to What* was *Spring* from *The Seasons,* close to a Lichtenstein featuring Dick Tracy. Watching Johns appraise his *Spring* as if alone in a gallery space, I approached him and said, "I wish I were a painter, it must be great to see your pictures on someone's walls." "It's *easy* to be a painter," he replied. David Whitney, who had joined us, went in for higher flattery. "Is it easy to be a *great* painter?" Unhesitatingly Johns said yes, and Whitney responded, "I *knew* you were going to say that." I recognized a typical bit of art world banter. The complimentary put-on, the ironic affirmation, the collusive insider pretense of knowing the artist's mind. That could be the sum of this world, I thought. Once you've become a wealthy lionized artist, fully Consummated, you get to stand in the drawing room of someone who owns what might be called an empire, holding a demitasse, surrounded by admirers and your own work, moved by blandishments to mock its seriousness. But Johns is still a serious artist. And that came out next. Impressed by a volume he was reading of van Gogh's letters to his brother Theo, he re-marked sympathetically that Vincent had said that with more money he could paint more paintings. Imagine, I thought, what Vincent could have done with *his* fortune!

The evening ended, either by design or by accident, when Newhouse went over to his prize monster, the monumental *According to What,* bent down, and closed the small door or panel on the bottom left corner of the painting. By this gesture he put to bed, as it were, Marcel Duchamp, Johns's chief art hero through the 1960s, whose famous self-portrait profile is visible when the panel is open.

Near Newhouse's front door I said good-bye to Johns's de-parting back. When he swung round to reciprocate the farewell I pursued the exchange before he had a chance to turn away. "Let's get together soon . . . have lunch?" He nodded politely, perfunctorily, I thought. We had known each other better in for-mer days. A book now stood between us.

THE GRÜNEWALD CONNECTION

I.

What we cannot speak about we must pass over in silence.
—LUDWIG WITTGENSTEIN

We understand that what we cannot speak about (by saying it)
it is necessary to say (by silencing it).
—MARIE BALMARY

Two years earlier over lunch with Elizabeth Baker, editor-in-chief of *Art in America,* I had agreed to write a five-hundred-word review of the new Johns exhibition called *The Seasons.* Four tall rectangular paintings, *Spring, Summer, Fall,* and *Winter,* along with some thirty-three related drawings, were on view at the Leo Castelli Gallery on West Broadway. Published in October 1987, my review had ballooned into a jumbo cover article, which in turn had become the basis for a book project. Johns's assay into the traditional subject of the four seasons was not in itself cause for my critical enthusiasm, nor the fact that these new paintings

were the occasion for his first presentation of a whole human figure, nor even that this was the first time he included himself (the
figure) so openly in a work with obvious autobiographical associations. Most of the critics who reviewed the show soon after
it opened were unimpressed, some even hostile. There were of
course his loyal connoisseurs and followers, his establishment
minions, who respectfully noted the several innovations the work
entailed and through their familiarity with the artist were able to
identify in a couple of cases some of the sources for the plenti-
ful iconography crowded into his seasonal representations.

I fell into no particular camp myself, and had virtually come
upon the work fresh, with no prior critical experience of Johns's
work, and no special concern for his progress as an artist. Until
this moment he had been Jasper, a famous artist I happened to
know, though at points during the early and mid-1980s he was
an incipient friend. Entering the space of *The Seasons* that February 1987, I was also not handicapped by any attachment, as
many observers have been, to his early flags, targets, alphabets,
and numbers—work deemed to have constituted a defining moment in the development of postwar American art, shattering the
brief hegemony of Abstract Expressionism and helping to pre-
figure the Pop art movement. I simply liked the way *The Seasons* looked, and I responded with naive cheerfulness to the life-
size shadow images of the artist, which all tilted left at the same
angle and dominated each painting. But within a few months,
thanks to a chance discovery, I was no longer simply cheerful; I
was living a critic's dream.

While playing catch-up that spring on the Johns literature, an
obscure detail appearing in each *Season* captured my attention.
By May it had evolved into the opportune exposure of a secret
figure, its identity kept successfully hidden through a number of
painted versions over the previous six years. My windfall demanded a greater immersion in Johns than had seemed even re-

motely necessary at the outset of my venture. Ultimately it became the point of departure for locating a premise of autobiographical quiddity in all of Johns's oeuvre.

The four *Seasons* paintings are a cubist collage analogue of moving house. Johns was in fact moving house when he launched the series in 1984–85. He had just established a studio on the Caribbean island of St. Martin, and had bought a townhouse on the Upper East Side in Manhattan. He still owned the old Provident Loan Society building on Houston and Essex streets, where he lived and worked from the late 1960s to the early 1970s, as well as a country–house-*cum*-studio in Stony Point, New York, about forty miles north of the city. For *The Seasons* Johns used his own shadow as a template to trace his self-portrait on the floors of his four establishments, as represented by their materials—stone, brick, wooden planks, and terra-cotta tiles.

During 1985, he has said, he was "doing a lot of shifting of things from place to place," setting up a studio on St. Martin, switching his main New York place of work from Stony Point to his new Sixty-third Street townhouse, and also moving belongings there from his downtown bank, where he had paintings stored in old vaults. That year Johns's secretary of a decade, English artist Mark Lancaster, who had lived in the bank, left Johns's employ to return to Britain, and in 1988 the structure was sold.

He made *Summer* in 1984–85 as an independent work, not imagining that it would become part of a series. The painting remained nameless until it occurred to him to make it the basis for three additional images. Having been asked during this time to illustrate a special edition of the poems of Wallace Stevens, a memory of Stevens's poem "The Snow Man" made him think of winter, a thought that ignited the concept of doing four seasons. Since the painting that would become titled *Summer* was already about moving house, Johns extended the theme through the changes of the seasons, traditionally viewed as an allegory of the ages of man through childhood, adolescence, and maturity to old age, thus uniting an autobiographical subject with a motif of eternal relevance. This would be a work of a certain monumentality, reflecting his arrival at an age when people customarily begin to look back, take stock, and contemplate their position in the universal scheme of things.

Johns had always looked back artistically. His well-known habit of plundering his own storehouse of images and updating them in a great variety of contexts and mediums began with his breakthrough work, *Flag* of 1954–55. *Flag,* having waved through many paintings and prints from the mid-1950s on, appears as a detail in *Summer,* representing part of the baggage an artist naturally moves when transferring property from one house to another. Old icons in *The Seasons* are not just acknowledged casually; rather they seem to be the deposits of an artist making an ambitious display of possessions, as if to say, "I'm moving house, here's a goodly sample of what I own—these are the wages of success." He had arrived a long time ago; now he seemed convinced of it. Barring global economic collapse, his wealth and top standing in the world of art were assured.

Fittingly for a stocktaking, Johns appropriated two subjects by Picasso, the artist of the twentieth century with the grandest international reputation. In a book called *Picasso's Picassos* he had seen a small Picasso painting of 1936 called *Minotaur Moving His House* in which the artist, cast in one of his favorite roles as the mythological half-bull–half-man monster who feeds on human flesh, is pulling a cart containing plants, a parturient horse, a ladder, and a large painting secured by a rope. Johns said, "It was the subject matter more than the structure of the painting that interested me." He found it "very odd to see the cart before the horse," a kind of surprise and aberrancy that Johns almost congenitally finds appealing. "There was something very wonderful, very interesting in an unexpected way." Deferring to the mighty Spaniard, he concluded, "How did he have that thought? I wouldn't have that thought."[1]

For *The Seasons* Johns pirated every element in Picasso's work except the Minotaur, which he replaced with an idea from another Picasso painting—the self-portrait foreground shadow of Picasso regarding the contents of his studio or bedroom in a large 1953 painting called *The Shadow.* Framed by the outline of a door, Picasso's primitively rendered shadow image falls across the room's floor and rests against a painting of a recumbent nude. At top left is a small silhouette of a horse and cart, the horse here in the customary hauling position. In *The Minotaur Moving His House,* the horse giving birth is in the cart, its head horribly lolling out and scraping the ground. It represents his *maîtresse-en-titre* of the moment, Marie-Thérèse Walter, who had given birth to Maya, Picasso's second child, in 1935, a year before *Minotaur* was painted.

Johns's answer to Picasso's superfecund beast of burden in the *Minotaur* painting is his small seahorse just right of center in *Summer*—one of the few species where the male bears offspring. The elongated snout of the seahorse's grey shadow touches the edge of the grey painted shadow of the artist, uniting man and fish as monogenetic functionaries. Childless and unmarried, Johns identifies his own reproductive powers simultaneously with self-generation and with the production of paintings. He dilates upon this theme in *Spring,* where he places the centered shadow-form of a child (drawn from the cast shadow of the son of friends, one of his godsons) directly underneath his own shadow figure. The child's head, cut off just above the ears, slashes across Johns's body right below crotch and thigh. Father to the man, the child can be read as progenitor of the painting as well, his torso bedecked with the geometric symbol of construction that appears in each

Season—symmetrically disposed pairs of circles, triangles, and squares.[2]

With his love of compound and cross-correspondences, Johns matches Picasso's hybrid Minotaur with hybrids of his own: the miscegenated man and boy; and most delectably the bisexual, half-horse, half-fish seahorse. By making his own shadow in *Summer* contiguous with the seahorse's, Johns implies something centaurial for himself, a hidden analogy with Picasso's virile, lusting, very visible crossbreed brute. But the seahorse is of the sea and is capable of giving birth, which suggests a more androgynous association of the artist with this small mermaidlike creature.

While Johns gave each *Season* one or several elements unique to it and appropriate for the time of year it represents, such as the slanting streaks of rain across *Spring* and the snowflakes studding *Winter,* he made the series cohere by his large repeated shadow form that "moves" from painting to painting and by the reappearance in each work of Picasso's six features in *Minotaur Moving His House:* stars, ladder, rope, picture, branch, and cart wheel—altered to suit each *Season.* Johns's branch, which pends off different vertical dividing lines in each picture, sprouts in *Spring,* blooms in *Summer,* breaks in *Fall,* and withers in *Winter.* The stars similarly metamorphose, ripe and luscious in *Summer* for instance, and barely visible in *Fall.* The wheel of Picasso's cart in *Minotaur* is ingeniously transformed by Johns into a time piece, "rolling" along from painting to painting accompanying the human shadow, prime indicator of the temporal aspect of his subject. The conversion of the wheel-clock's hour or second hand into an imprint of the artist's own right forearm and hand tips us off that the circles refer not only to Picasso's *Minotaur* cart but to certain omnipresent circular images of Johns's own during the 1960s. *Device Circle* of 1959—the image of a perfect circle created compass-style by a stick that Johns left in the painting as evidence of how the circle was made—set off a flurry of "device circles" during the early 1960s, including *Good Time Charley,* which features a partial circle traced by a ruler used as a compass that remains in the painting. By 1963 Johns had incorporated his own forearm and hand as a circle-producing instrument, either literally or implied. It is this image, best remembered in *Periscope (Hart Crane)* of 1963, that he updated for his "clock" in *The Seasons.* From *Spring* through *Winter* Johns's forearm describes a movement of time from the twelve o'clock to the six o'clock position, a sweep of arrows within outermost perimeters indicating the direction he intends to have his hand perceived as moving, an artifice also familiar from "device circle" paintings and others of the 1960s.

The hand moves, the partial circle-clock itself shifts position from painting to painting, and so does everything else. From his original painting, *Summer,* Johns shifts his successive images by a quarter, to make one full rotation through the timeless cycle of decay and renewal, death and rebirth, or the "ages of man" from infancy to decrepitude. Thus in *Fall* his shadow figure is split in two and moved to the sides, all the objects appearing in the center. One more quarter turn for *Winter* shows his objects on the left, figure to the right; and finally, in *Spring,* divided like *Fall* into three parts, the objects on the sides flank the central figures of Johns and his putative child-shadow.

It's true that *The Seasons* are "well mannered, self-consciously 'artistic' " and "satisfied with the convention of representation to memorialize things that have passed".[3] And also "labored," though not certainly "to extinction," even perhaps too audaciously painted with the "appropriated . . . idea of being an Old Master."[4] But as is generally true with Johns, the existence here of much more than meets the eye makes the work as challenging as anything he had ever done. *The Seasons'* contents are so readable, so autobiographically superficial (a mere collection of possessions), that were it not for a mysterious empuzzled image appearing in each of the pictures, they might not transcend their function as a unique and personal postmodern variation on a traditional high art theme.

The mystery image in *The Seasons* leads autobiographically inward, to uncharted substantive territory, and presents a gauntlet to critics and art public extending beyond the merely personal to issues involving figuration and abstraction that continually shape art discourses.

II.

Stop, stop, I did not drag my father beyond that tree.
—GERTRUDE STEIN

I'm not going to tell you anything.
—JASPER JOHNS

The main attractions in *The Seasons,* in addition to Johns's shadow, are various "pictures" bound to a ladder by a rope, a figure he copied from the Picasso *Minotaur* painting. Moving house, Picasso as Minotaur most ostentatiously hauls the two items without which he would not be Picasso: one of his works, conspicuously framed, and his pregnant woman, represented as a horse. Johns actually "hauls" several pictures, framed and unframed, in his own complex allegory of moving house. His pictures partially obscure each other, the way stacked pictures can. They are also incompletely visible through being "slid behind" the vertical panels containing Johns's tilting shadow and the large dark wheel-clocks, with which they share the accompanying vertical spaces.

There, in his picture baggage, most visible in *Summer* and *Fall,* was the tantalizing image that increasingly arrested my attention during the spring of 1987. It was as if I had been a critic assigned to inventory and collate the belongings of some artist's house when I suddenly came upon a body in a trunk, turning me into an art PI. This image, more disguised in *Spring,* actually scumbled in *Winter,* consists of jigsaw-puzzle-like shapes at once fitted together yet differentiated by their directionally opposed stripes. In *Summer,* the image—bright, full, sharp—musters importance by lying flush to the Mona Lisa and two stacked American flags. The flag of course has a hallowed place in Johns's lexicon; and he has long admired Leonardo, whose Mona Lisa he once called "one of [his] favorite paintings"[5]—an idol he modestly appropriated in 1969, then again more visibly in 1984. Perhaps Johns felt about his three-in-one "picture" in *Summer* the way Picasso did about the particular painting shown being hauled in *Minotaur,* one he said he couldn't bear to leave behind.[6] As for Johns's cryptic image, he not only did not leave it behind; he had considerable uses for it in his work to come.

In packing up his belongings, the crosshatch or herringbone motif that so dominated Johns's work of the 1970s was a critical piece of luggage. Though Johns's admirers might have found a few favored icons from his history missing, his Ballantine ale or Savarin coffee cans for instance, the absence of some example of crosshatching would probably have seemed inconceivable, and in *The Seasons* their busyness plays nicely against the other plainer elements. Regarded at a glance, there's no reason to imagine the image to be other than an abstraction, the form all his crosshatchings during the 1970s assumed. Scrutinized more closely, in *Fall* certainly, the suspicion of something more could arise. In any event, several critics in February 1987 identified the image as a "fragment" from Mathias Grünewald's sixteenth-century Isenheim Altarpiece. Barbara Rose, a longtime authority on Johns, was more specific, saying it was a detail from the Resurrection panel of the Altarpiece.[7] I could only wonder what this

Resurrection source looked like, indeed what it *was*, for though I might once have seen reproductions of the Altarpiece, which hangs in the city of Colmar in the Alsace-Lorraine region of France, I had no memory of it whatsoever. The Altarpiece, completed between 1508 and 1516 and consisting of thirteen panels with predellas, was a "religious machine" commissioned by the Antonite monks of the Isenheim monastery as part of the healing program of the monastery hospital.[8]

At first the "detail" was an idle curiosity, but as time went on it became a more pressing desideratum. *Art in America,* not always in a hurry to cover exhibitions, and generally hopeful of what their writers can do, was willing to wait months, possibly longer, for my report. At length it became clear to me, from studying the literature on Johns's previous show in 1984, that Rose had updated allusions in that show to the fallen foreground soldier from Grünewald's Resurrection panel, identified most notably in the monumentally impressive *Perilous Night* (1982). Once I did get a look at a Grünewald reproduction and could match up a Johns soldier with the Grünewald Resurrection soldier, I still felt no reason to doubt that Johns, as Rose and others implied, had installed such a "fragment" from his previous work in *The Seasons.*

Then a review of descriptions of the image by several critics of the 1984 show yielded some striking discrepancies. While John Russell and Roberta Smith identified the soldier in Johns's *Perilous Night,* they also mistakenly placed him in *Ventriloquist, Racing Thoughts,* and an untitled painting.[9] English critic Richard Francis made similar assumptions in his book on Johns published that year.[10] John Ashbery correctly saw *two* soldiers.[11] Russell's description of the one he saw—"faint but distinct"—exactly fits the realization of both figures. Grünewald's foreground helmeted and armor-garbed body and its sword (having just fallen, his right leg still off the ground, left arm raised over head, turned toward us, shielding himself from the brilliant light of the rising Christ), along with the soldier hovering over him, are traced or outlined lightly by Johns in reddish purple, perfectly discernible floating in a dark sea of black, grey, and white paint. In *Racing Thoughts, Ventriloquist,* and the untitled work in question, the outlines of something or other are a lot more distinct, but with very dissimilar contours, impossible to confuse with the *Perilous Night* tracings.

Having noticed these differences, it seems hard to imagine how it was possible to avoid stumbling over that body-in-a-trunk stashed amongst the artist's belongings in *The Seasons,* which drew primarily on images from Johns's 1984 show. Once it became clear that the patterned detail in *The Seasons* had nothing in common with the soldier tracings in *Perilous Night,* it became equally clear that the motif was holding an unknown identity hostage. In *Summer* and *Fall* its jigsaw contours strongly suggest a concealed subject. Now it became additionally evident, from comparing the jigsawlike design in these two *Seasons* paintings to strange patterns in several untitled 1984 works as well as in the ground of the whole left side of *Racing Thoughts,* also 1984, that whatever was in the latter, misidentified in reviews as the soldier, was also in *The Seasons* detail. There were corresponding shapes, and in two works you could see the same "eyes." In one, these eye forms, surrounding a rendering of Johns's skull and crossbones, can be read as ghosts or scary night creatures. Momentarily I thought I might uncover a phantom. But I assumed that the missing identity could be found, like the soldier, somewhere in Grünewald's Altarpiece. The PI move suggested at this point was a meeting with the artist.

After several days of volleying phone calls back and forth, Jasper proposed lunch at Da Silvano, a restaurant on lower Sixth Avenue in Manhattan much frequented by artists and dealers. It was May 19—four days after his fifty-seventh birthday, and incidentally two days after my own fifty-eighth. I arrived first and was seated on the far side of a brick wall that partially divides the restaurant. I was unaware, as I waited and sipped coffee, that my lunch partner had taken a seat at a table on the side of the brick wall close to the entrance. In due time the maître d' approached me and said he thought perhaps the person I was waiting for was already there. I found him drinking a beer on the other side of the wall, about a foot away from where I had been sitting. While this was good for a laugh, I dimly suspected being a victim of a private symbolic joke, with Jasper meaning to underscore the barrier he intended to erect and maintain between us. Indeed, we were not even finished laughing over our little contretemps, and I had barely sat down next to him, when he interjected disarmingly, on the wave of our risibility, *"I'm* not going to tell you anything."

He told me things nonetheless, though he was unswervingly mum on what I had come specifically to find out. He didn't mind saying that he had first seen Grünewald's Altarpiece when a friend of his in Basel (an hour's drive from Colmar) was dying. Some time later Walter Wittrock, a German dealer in modern master drawings, sent him the gift of a big book of reproductions of the Altarpiece, which he "loved," prompting his first tracing. Having visited the Altarpiece in 1976 and again in 1979, Johns began appropriating details from it soon after receiving the portfolio of reproductions, and he presented his first effort to Wittrock.[12] It was a drawing called *Tracing* (1981, ink on plastic) based on a detail from the Crucifixion panel showing John the Evangelist supporting the swooning Virgin—an image by Johns as unreadable without source information as the Resurrection soldier, or as my mystery detail.

Perhaps because Johns found it difficult to believe that I was about to turn into one of his critics, having for so many years been a harmless art world compatriot, I was not treated on this occasion to his famously reticent, suspicious, intimidating, and self-protective interview style: "Questions are met by long silences, then answered with a precision that is . . . legalistic"; a "remoteness . . . makes all questions sound vaguely coarse and irrelevant."[13] Until I asked him directly about the detail in *The Seasons,* he was quite easy and communicative, even confidential—mentioning his "dying friend," imparting an intimate cameo profile of his father upon request, and sometimes erupting in raucous merriment, a spontaneous release at his own jokes that Johns rides recklessly, though only for a moment. Discussing what was "freely drawn" in the *Seasons* paintings, such as the tiny hummingbird he drew in *Spring,* he complained unembarrassedly that he still couldn't draw. But when he alluded to his appropriations, he admitted that he "resented" his "continuing dependence on preexistent forms."

"Isn't it fortuitous that . . ." I began hesitantly. He picked up the question and polished it off, laughing uproariously, "That I would pick up tracing?"

Our conviviality ended when finally I threw my "cards" on the table—various glossies, other pictures, postcards of the Altarpiece from Colmar—and more or less demanded to know if these patterns in certain untitled works and in *Racing Thoughts* were variations on the soldier.

He said no, they were not.

Well, what are they then?, I wanted to know. I tried running down the Altarpiece panels. Could they be from the Crucifixion, the Annunciation, the Nativity, or the Lamentation?

No response.

Could they be from The Temptation of St. Anthony?

He said he thought they were, though he wasn't sure.

I knew I was on the right track; indeed *something* was there, and that something was from the Altarpiece, as I had arbitrarily assumed. The postcard of the Temptation, along with its companion, the Meeting of St. Anthony and St. Paul in the Desert, were the only two Altarpiece images I had left at home, for some reason. Our lunch was over. I could hardly have asked for more than I got—one vague clue.

At home I spent an hour trying to locate a detail in the two Altarpiece pictures that might match the pattern in *Racing Thoughts* and five untitled works. I found nothing; the Temptation panel in particular is teeming with details, as are the Johns paintings. I called him at his Manhattan home.

Now he was busy and irritated. He couldn't remember, and the information was in the country.

I said, "Look, there's Anthony in the long white beard being hauled off . . ."

He interrupted with a diversion, recalling a Gertrude Stein line, "Stop, stop, I did not drag my father beyond that tree."

When I countered with the Stein title, *The Blood on the Dining Room Floor*, he said he had that book and he never read it. And I replied, "I have it too and haven't read it either." Then I pulled him back to Grünewald: "Is that it, is it in that particular panel—St. Anthony sprawled in purgatory?"

"Yes, but it's skin."

III.

[Johns] had gotten in somehow between the two monolithic notions that a painting either alluded to the real world, or referred to an invisible one that transcended or substituted itself for appearances.

—MAX KOZLOFF

Skin! I spent more time looking, turning my glossies and postcards and book reproductions this way and that. I opened Richard Francis's 1984 book on Johns to the untitled 1983–84 ink on plastic.[14] Here, the suspicious detail occupies the whole left side of the picture and lies unobstructed by any collage element as in other works. I turned it upside down and positioned the Temptation postcard right next to it, then focused on an outstanding feature in the corners of both the Grünewald and the Johns, a kind of three-pronged claw. Suddenly, in hardly more than a nanosecond, a complete figure from the bottom left corner of Grünewald's Temptation took shape before me in the Johns painting—like a picture in a darkroom being born out of emulsion. I have no idea what I had expected to find, but surely I must have intuited that Johns would not have gone to so much trouble and for so long to conceal anything very ordinary.

Nothing could have prepared me for the body that now appeared in his luggage.

It was a devastated creature, a human turning into an animal, apparently into one of the monsters who gang up on St. Anthony in the scene directly above him and haul him through hell by his white hair. The semihuman creature in the bottom foreground, his feet already webbed, witnesses the fate that awaits him above. His stomach is bloated and ballooned, his greenish skin (the *skin!*) is inflamed and marked with pocks, and an arm raised over his upturned head ends in a stump. With his right hand he grasps what appears to be a torn bag containing papers or books, symbols of some role in the world he is perforce about to leave.

It was the creature's striking three-pronged, webbed claw, swiveled around behind his body, that unlocked Johns's picture. The creature's stump echoes St. Anthony's left arm, which is raised in helpless defense above his face. Further identifying the two figures, Grünewald has St. Anthony clutching something of his own with his right hand—his rosary beads and the handle of his staff or cane, which he can be seen holding while talking to St. Paul in the desert in the companion panel, a not so deceptively pacific setting, full of threatening omens anticipating the horrors of the Temptation. Now fallen and ignominiously abducted by underworld beasts, St. Anthony grips symbols of his religious status—rosary and staff handle—against an attack on them by the open beak of a hideous armor-plated varmint that occupies ground just in front of the disease-ridden figure's bent right leg and faces the same direction, craning its neck around to close in on the old man's hand and its contents and suggesting a divestiture in progress. In Johns's tracing of the ill-fated creature, details of St. Anthony's voluminous robe—that part being seized and pulled possessively up and away by a horned monster directly above him—can be made out.

I quickly found the creature in a number of other untitled works, all upside down. I also found it upside down in *Racing Thoughts,* but here occluded in a couple of its parts by Johns's hanging ochre pants and a portrait photograph of Johns's dealer Leo Castelli as a young man, "tacked" *trompe l'oeil* style to the painting.[15] What I had seen as eyes while comparing various pictures and learning that more than one mysterious pattern existed now could be identified as the pocks or lesions on the victim's distended stomach.

Finally I turned to the *Seasons,* the origin of my search, where various details of the figure could now be picked out. When *Summer* and *Fall,* containing the two most readable fragments, are rotated a little more than a quarter turn to the right, details heave into view. In *Fall,* only the creature's bent right leg, with part of the pile of papers or books lying beside him, can be made out; the rest of him is hidden behind the wheel-clock. Traced folds of St. Anthony's robe rise above his knee to surround the perimeter of the wheel. *Summer* has more of the figure, hardly any robe. Here the figure is flopped, facing left, part of its bent leg obscured by a George Ohr pot, its stomach discoverable along with its arm and hand clutching books and its clawlike webbed foot. In *Win-*

ter the St. Anthony creature is scumbled, in keeping with the general obscurity of images brought on by snow. By contrast a small, practically unreadable, fragment in *Spring* merely represents the creature, its color stripe pattern exactly matching the larger display in *Summer*.

Johns's devices for disguising his St. Anthony victim are pointedly different from his methods for obscuring the Resurrection soldier. Outlines or tracings of the St. Anthony detail are filled in with opposing sections of stripes, making the whole figure look quite like a collection of interlocking picture-puzzle pieces, and readable only as abstractions or decorative patterns.

The body of Johns's creature in its original and many later forms is blocked into eleven different areas of opposed striation. The scrunched-up face alone is plotted in two sections—nose, eyes, and forehead forming a triangulated region, and the tiny bit of lower face or mouth and chin area set off by contrary markings. The largest distinct tracts consist of stomach, bent leg, right arm, and the victim's V-shaped garment covering his upper back. The garment is a kind of middy, and a long form that is part of a complex headdress hangs from it, ending bulbously.

The portrait of Leo Castelli, which is superimposed in *Racing Thoughts* on the upside-down creature, is actually a silkscreen of a photograph that was made into a jigsaw puzzle. By showing the portrait-puzzle fully assembled, Johns provides a clue to the fact that something unknown might exist "behind" and around the portrait. Indeed the "ground" of the Castelli portrait presents the conventional picture-puzzle form turned inside out. Starting with a whole intact figure, Johns decomposes it, makes it unrecognizable through interconnecting pieces of design—"resolved" as an abstract picture!

Picasso's transposition of cart and horse in *The Minotaur Moving His House*—which so impressed Johns—is nothing next to his own startling inversion of jigsaw-puzzle solving. When we reconstitute an image about which we have some prior knowledge, like the Castelli head, we of course deal only momentarily in abstractions. With his Grünewald puzzles, Johns systematically confuses abstraction and figuration, creating epistemological questions that equal in scope and significance the formalist enigmas invoked by *Flag* (1954–55). Once the figures in his Grünewald "abstractions" are seen, dilemmas of recognition parallel to those that preoccupied critics when dealing with *Flag* must be faced.

The famous enigma of *Flag* stemmed "from the paradoxical oneness of the picture as painting and image."[16] Johns "had gotten in somehow between the two monolithic notions that a painting either alluded to the real world, or referred to an invisible one that transcended or substituted itself for appearances."[17] The Grünewald details have added enigmatic dimensions. By deconstructing "private" images, Johns challenges our "right" to know what these puzzles are and our capacity to appreciate them as abstractions—both before we know that figures are being held "hostage" by them and after the figures are brought out of captivity, so to speak. We are dared as well to imagine what made him invent this complex conundrum. And defied to understand or interpret vital subject matter, once laid bare, in humane terms. This may be the greatest challenge of all. Postmodernist critics, whose hermeneutics tend decidedly toward the self-referentially abstract or theoretical, are not exactly noted for their kindly interests.

Discovery of the St. Anthony figure was delayed in large part through its very limited exposure in exhibition. Prior to 1987, when it appeared as a remaindered detail in *The Seasons,* it had been shown in 1984 and then only in *Racing Thoughts* and an untitled encaustic, and of these two, the obscuring designs are tremendously different. Without a clue the identical tracings were not detectable; an additional difficulty with the figure in the untitled painting was that the figure was reversed. By June 1988, even had I not exposed the figure in *Art in America* a half dience would tactfully ignore the expressive implications of his new subjects. When the Resurrection soldier was first identified in 1984, for instance, nothing was made of the fact that this was the first whole figure Johns had ever painted. The critics' choice, in any case, for his first-ever such figure became his later shadow in the *Seasons*. The soldier was allotted exactly a sentence by each of the five or six critics who identified him, and of these only John Ashbery noted that there were actually *two* soldiers, while only one other, Jeanne Silverthorne, perceived or at least wrote that *Perilous Night* held an additional representation of the pair.[19]

Matching the fully stretched out foreground Resurrection soldier by Grünewald with the Johns tracings, it can be seen that he included outlines of the helmet, shoulders, and arms of the soldier, who is hovering, falling, over the supine figure's midsection. Had this additional soldier been absent from Grünewald's picture, Johns would probably have traced folds of the sheet in which Christ had just been entombed, which the soldier blocks from view—paralleling his tracings of St. Anthony's robed folds directly above the victim in the Temptation panel. Dramatically unlike St. Anthony's robe, which is under seizure by netherworld demons, suggesting impending denudation, in the Resurrection panel Christ's sheet as it winds up out of the tomb with his re-vivified form is transformed into a glorious flaming red and yellow garment draped forward over his shoulders and covering his hitherto naked torso. Actually Johns traces just a piece of Christ's sheet, along with horizontal and diagonal lines of the opened tomb upon which the sheet lies, appearing off the back and left arm of his hovering soldier. Grünewald's third soldier, a small figure tumbling forward head over heels in the background of the Resurrection, completes a classical dramatis personae for resurrection scenes. He echoes the amazed and blown-away attitudes of the foreground soldier and of the "companion" who hovers and falls over him (the two traced by Johns), and he structurally reinforces the diagonal thrust of the figures toward the bottom left corner of the picture, in contranegative formation to the Christ pulling away above and beyond them, fully and frontally transfigured as he ascends to eternal life.

Johns's extra rendition of Grünewald's two soldiers in *Perilous Night* is more than half as small as the large version that consumes the whole left side of the diptychal canvas and no more identifiable. It is histrionically "presented" by the fingertips of two plaster cast forearms hanging down from the top right edge of the canvas that nearly touch the top edge of an interior painting within a painting in which the soldiers are traced and painted. A third cast forearm, smaller and to the left of the other two, hangs above the outline of a handkerchief "nailed" to a *faux bois* surface and helps fill in Johns's dark Christian narrative. The two hanging casts at the right belong somehow to the two men in armor, wrenched from their original redemptive context. In Grünewald's picture it's clear they are being blown away by the brilliance of Christ ascending above them in a glorious aureole of light. In Johns's picture, they are still overwhelmed by *some*thing, but the hovering one, instead of just falling as in the Grünewald over his foreground mate, can now be read as gently attending his plight.

The discolorations of John's painted forearm casts provide clues to an autobiographical intensity that arose in his work during the late 1970s, gaining momentum with his Grünewald venture. An arm cast similar to those in *Perilous Night* appears in Johns's 1982 *In the Studio*, painted in blotches of several alternating colors that match those of a sample of his crosshatch motif close by—another picture within a picture. The cast must be seen as the artist's hand at work as well as the use of the cast *for* the work. The fingertips of another such cast forearm hang vertically the same way in an untitled of 1983, nearly touching the tips of brushes planted in his well-known Savarin can, which lies superimposed on ghostly grey crosshatching. Again the artist at work is signified, but here emotionally shaded by the death imagery of skull and crossbones to the right, and a striped spread of sanguine purples and dark greys of the upside-down St. Anthony victim to the left.

Here it seems Johns secretly associated the "skin" of his forearm cast—painted dappled flesh and grey colors and hung between a death's head and the mortally ill (however disguised) human creature—with the garishly scarified skin of Grünewald's Temptation-panel sufferer. This coupling of self and victim redeemed by art, inspired by Grünewald, became a major theme for Johns by the early 1980s.

The divine victim, Christ, purged by Johns from his Resurrection appropriations, rises in the *Seasons* as the redemptive figure of Johns himself—the ascendant sacrificial artist, incorporeally transparent, surrounded by certain deathless signs of his craft. Accidental gaps left in the palms of his hands within the wheel-clocks by the imprint process can become hard not to see as stigmata.

IV.

*It's very impressive [the Isenheim Altarpiece], very big, it seems
to explode through the space. It has a quality that is very
glamorous, sort of like a movie.*
— JASPER JOHNS

*The shadow is never particularly active. Rather, . . . the
personage is more a victim of or witness to his own traditions
than a perpetrator.*
— MARK ROSENTHAL

*The function of the beholder is to be dominated and awestruck
by the work of art, ... recast as a simulacrum of the male
artist's autonomous, impenetrable self.*
— DAVID HICKEY

By tradition St. Anthony, patron of the Antonite brotherhood, was born around the year A.D. 251 in Middle Egypt and died at the age of one hundred and five in 356. He became a desert recluse and word spread of his thaumaturgic powers and his fearlessness against the devil, demons, and wild animals.

Over time he became associated with a plaguelike burning sickness variously called Hell's Fire, Holy Fire, St. Anthony's Fire,[20] Le Mal des ardents, or more technically *ignis plaga* or *pestilentia ignis*,[21] which first appeared in Europe in the eleventh century. The Antonite order, founded in 1093 by a nobleman whose son was cured of the burning sickness through the intercession of St. Anthony, was a hospital order, devoted to the care of the sick.[22] It spread rapidly through France and Germany in Grünewald's lifetime. Grünewald's Altarpiece, completed between 1508 and 1516, was designed to help sick inmates to meditate upon their salvation. In the thirteen panels of the work, portraits and narratives of the saint share pride of place with scenes from the life of Christ. Very little is known about the artist who created the Altarpiece, unlike his contemporary Albrecht Dürer. Grünewald's birthdate is uncertain, but his date and place of death are known to be in 1528 in Halle.

The symptoms of St. Anthony's Fire were caused by food poisoning. Some historians believe the source was unknown at the time.[23] Symptoms of the disease were often confused with epilepsy, leprosy, and especially syphilis. The offending food, bread, appears clearly in *The Meeting of Saints Anthony and Paul in the Desert*. Painted against a pale sky turning pink, high above the conversing saints, a raven flies down toward the two men with two small loaves of bread in its beak, omens of disease that overtakes the Temptation panel, where St. Anthony himself is implicated in sufferings he has been appointed to cure. A painting of the same subject by Diego Velázquez shows St. Paul, hands clasped in prayer, gazing upward at the bird carrying bread that is zooming down like a black bomber out of a turbulent sky. Hieronymous Bosch has also depicted the raven and bread in a painting of this subject. Like Velázquez, Grünewald's St. Paul is aware that the bird and bread signify an impending disaster; he casts his gaze skyward while he gestures toward St. Anthony, apparently warning him of what is to come.

Referred to as *historical ergotism* in modern times, the disease was contracted by eating bread baked from a contaminated flour, a spurred rye, or parasitic fungus that can grow on certain grains. Until a singular outbreak of the disease in southern France in 1951, historical ergotism was "thought to be a thing of the past, a relic of the Middle Ages," wrote John Fuller in *The Day of St. Anthony's Fire*.[24] By historical account "the sick utter that they are being destroyed by a burning fire."[25] Other symptoms include insomnia accompanied by convulsions and deliriums, hallucinations, and madness. A severe dehydration also occurs. There can be damage to the eyes and digestive upsets. Boils or lesions all over the victim's skin seem to be the result of "tumors that developed into incurable ulcers" when the "blood was affected by a poisonous inflammation [consuming] the whole body."[26] Gangrene of the extremities develops in some cases. Popular representations in Grünewald's time often show its victims with a crutch under one arm, the other arm going up in flames.[27] When the great epidemic struck Pont St. Esprit in 1951, residents would recall the portent of a storm just the previous day that fantastically ripped the left arm off the statue of their Virgin, who commanded a view of the countryside from a high tower near the village.[28]

The 1951 outbreak of St. Anthony's Fire in France became all the more fascinating in 1968 when Fuller's book on the subject was published, because of the chemical similarity of the fungus causing the disease to lysergic acid diethylamide, or LSD, first synthesized in 1938 in Basel, used experimentally during the

1950s, and consumed flagrantly by people at large as a mind-altering or mind-expanding drug during the 1960s. The dark visions in Grünewald's panels, the hallucinatory transformations, the rubescent colors, incandescent lights, dazzling associations, and engrossing attention to detail show a possible conflation of the actual psychoneural effects experienced by the Isenheim patients with effects well known to be sustained in Christian conversions—the subject of the Altarpiece.

Johns's admiration for Grünewald was recorded as early as 1967.[29] Judging from a remark Johns made in 1988—that he had "just learned food poisoning was the plague in Grünewald's time," he had not been academically interested in the work that bowled him over.[30] He was assuredly aesthetically and emotionally enamored of the Altarpiece, but it seems he also intuited its sacred purpose and entered into its plan, feeling at once benighted and uplifted by it. Like the two foreground figures he chose to trace, he was overcome by the scenes before him, on the one hand the workings of evil in the Temptation, on the other the radiant transcendence in the Resurrection—both the artistry and the humanity in the pictures. The two figures raise left arms against the events they fear will destroy them, the soldier obviously with more success—fully armored and turning away, he moves toward us out of the picture. The Temptation victim, mostly naked, feet webbed, and missing a hand, facing in toward the scene of St. Anthony's ordeal, is transitionally already a part of what he resists. Johns's project shows every indication of an attempt to save him by means of (his own) art.

This entailed making the Temptation victim invisible to those who would damn him if they saw him. Condemned by Grünewald, yet part of a vast narrative redemptive program as understood through the Resurrection, the victim would become the object of a unique rescue operation undertaken by Johns the twentieth-century postmodernist—in a singular performance, by way of the medium that had been his own salvation. Already decomposing, the figure is removed by Johns from his original context—the setting where he will be transfixed ultimately as a monster—and further broken down by having his parts analyzed for schematic abstractions. Now he belongs to Johns. Now he is held fast, inert, permanently arrested, immutably captured in gossamers of paint, untouchable or off limits, sanctioned in a sacred space of art alone. Moreover he is now *beautiful!* As an abstraction, at any rate, he can't be faulted. His contours quite flattened out according to the most basic modernist tenet, his gross imperfections absorbed into lines and stripes and a few tiny irregular circles and color stratagems, a portrait now resembling patchwork agrarian landscapes seen aerially, his transformation would be beyond the wildest imagination of Grünewald. With his victim mummified, Johns feels it fair, having been "attracted to the qualities conveyed by the delineation of the forms [in Grünewald] and [wanting] to see if this might be freed from the narrative,"[31] to claim that its interest should lie exclusively in its appearance as he devised it. "I got annoyed that pictures were being discussed in terms of imagery that could not be perceived. . . . I thought it was of no particular interest that [an image] was once one thing or another or something else."[32] It seems unlikely that he really has "finally simply dropped [his] reserve" as he asserted in 1978 when comparing his later stance to his early work, in which, he said, "I tried to hide my personality, my psychological state, my emotions."[33] When he made that comment of course he could have had no inkling that he would be painting (and concealing), three years hence, such intimately expressive figures as the Grünewald, in particular the stigmatized St. Anthony victim. What is Johns's limit or tolerance for what he would have us see once his "reserve" is dropped?

Going by the *Seasons,* he wants us to see the artist qua artist, and a very insubstantial one at that, a mere shadow next to his concrete productions crowding in around, beside and between him. On the surface, it's a simple autobiographical statement. Even while his primary identity may be as a painter, he invests his work itself with the most essential importance. In 1979 a critic called attention to Johns's "mask of anonymity," noting his "non-appearance, in a diverting strategy, the hiding of the . . . self, in a denial of authorship, dispossession."[34] His transparent shadow form in the *Seasons* is quite real. In life, as in art, Johns negotiates his own absence: introverted and reclusive, unable or unwilling to reveal himself. His dealer of three and a half decades has called him a "very enigmatic person."[35] One might imagine his etherealized form in the *Seasons* commenting on the act of making art the way Johns actually once did, as a "helpless statement," as something "you can't avoid saying." He is "more a victim or witness of his own traditions than a perpetrator."[36]

When asked why he introduced autobiography into his paintings, Johns replied, "They're not particularly autobiographical. Where is the autobiography?"[37] He is not, after all, really there, as his gauzy tilting shadow attests. This quite fits with his objections, when alluding to his Grünewald appropriations, over "pictures . . . being discussed in terms of imagery that could not be perceived." He thought it "was of no particular interest that an [image] was once one thing or another or something else." Like himself, the Temptation victim's figurative past (in Grünewald) is now an abstraction. And Johns became an artist—someone who can magically obliterate these histories.

He vividly identifies his shadow with the Isenheim Temptation victim in *Summer* by linking his shadow form at the wrist area with that of his seahorse. Here also he could be *holding* the "picture" containing the victim, a portion of it lying flush to the lower arm and hand, which it obscures. Johns unites his (covered) hand, the victim detail, the seahorse, the American flag, and the Mona Lisa in *Summer*. The hermaphroditic seahorse most aptly represents the self-generating (male) artist, whose breeding of paintings is his raison d'être—the patent subject of the *Seasons*. The submerged St. Anthony detail, unidentified for six years when the four paintings were shown in February 1987 and forsworn by the artist once the body was disinterred, strengthens the position assumed by its maker—a featureless shadow in a figurative painting with nobody home. "The shadow could be viewed as a double . . . a conceit that allows the artist to maintain his privacy and the secrecy of his intentions."[38]

Johns the autonomous artist closes the door firmly on his viewers; at the same time he lets you know it's not locked, in case you have the nerve to push it open and step through. You can't picture what is inside just by looking at the paintings, which at their best are awesome in their autarchic and gorgeous surfaces. Only outside information—art historical and biographical—will get you inside. And even then, once apparently there, what can one dare to see, much less understand? The critical community knows Johns's story—or the bare bones of it at least—and it can identify which of his "abstractions" are based on the Grünewald Altarpiece. But like the artist, critics at the end of the twentieth century are bound by a code of noncommunication, of silence on matters personal, of reverence for what meets the eye: the picture plane in all its formalist policies. The viewer, says David Hickey in one of his four brilliant "essays on beauty" called *The Invisible Dragon,* is cast "in the role of an irresponsible, alienated, elitist voyeur."[39]

While Johns has found a way to tell his story, to project powerful fictional self-portraits that he encapsulates in a secret space, he has maintained an objective front with his critics and public, as when he asked an interviewer, "Where is the autobiography?" Indeed it is only what he would have you see, something no more captivating than the universal condition of a man who makes products associated with a particular profession. For us his

Grünewalds are meant to be abstractions even after we see them "in the flesh" in the originals. And as such, of course, we can hardly see them play any narrative roles. In his most widely shown works featuring St. Anthony—the large 1983–84 drawings—it would be unseemly to imagine the victim as Johns originally saw him in Grünewald's Temptation picture. We are thus unable to recognize the figure as Johns recasts him: a hieroglyph of death, frequently coupled with the skull and crossbones; or an object of rescue, often "watched over" by an old crone omnipresent in Johns's work of the 1980s.[40]

Johns's earliest image, *Flag,* quoted and commemorated in *Summer,* has ironically become an urtext for the artist's personal origins, a linkup he suggested himself in 1977. Considering the powerful epistemological questions—the formalist enigmas—raised in common by *Flag* and the Grünewalds, a new autobiographical outlook on *Flag* might complete the connection with his first overt (however hidden) autobiographical projections inspired by the Isenheim Altarpiece. United in the image of the Resurrection soldiers, *Flag* and the Grünewalds demonstrate Johns's resolutely piecemeal advance through life and work—images diffused over large spans of time and space, established then recollected and updated, ever moved into novel, unexpected relations. Considered as a whole, the work can look like a giant collage of cross-references, of narratives inside narratives, or narratives completed by linkages from painting to painting, close or far in time—some guiding core story tied up secretly within.

THE PATERNITY OF FLAG

I.

*Using the design of the flag took care of a great deal for me
because I didn't have to design it. . . . So I went on to similar
things like the targets—things the mind already knows. That
gave me room to work on other levels.*

—JASPER JOHNS

*How does the flag sit with us, we who don't give a hoot for
Betsy Ross, who never think of tea as a cause for parties?*

—JOHN CAGE

*The habit of dissociating "pure painting" from content is so
ingrained, that almost no critic was able to see both together.*

—LEO STEINBERG

In 1963 Leo Steinberg wrote: "It remained the most interesting
point about Johns that he managed somehow to discover uninteresting subjects,"[1] referring of course to the flags, targets, and
numbers. This is probably how Johns wishes his much later

Grünewald subjects to be seen, if seen at all. In a 1990 interview, he gave a formalist justification for his flags and the Grünewalds, while glossing over any import attached to the wholesale concealment in his work beginning in the 1980s. The interviewer had confronted him: "The hidden motifs in your work these days seem to be in marked contrast to your paintings of flags." Johns replied, "No they aren't. In all cases, the outlines of particular forms are followed rather faithfully, but not entirely faithfully, and filled in with some variation in color and texture."[2]

Flag was of course Johns's first "uninteresting subject," though some critics were of a mind to think that the chief event in a Johns painting was "to render an overlooked subject suddenly recognized."[3] Robert Rosenblum wrote that "Johns first astonishes the spectator and then obliges him to examine for the first time the visual qualities of a humdrum object he had never before paused to look at."[4] John B. Myers saw Johns as "the Surrealist of naming things," making clear what things are—"like the small child who holds up an egg, having discovered such an object for the first time in a hidden nest, and cries, 'Egg!' "[5] Fairfield Porter agreed: "He looks for the first time, like a child."[6] Harold Rosenberg and Hilton Kramer conceived the recognition factor in political terms, seeing Johns as having abdicated from pure (formalist) concerns of art in order either to provoke or to soothe his viewers. Rosenberg had "Johns [sticking] the emblem he adores . . . right up against the gallery goer's nose," while Kramer had him unabashedly seeking "to please and confirm the decadent periphery of bourgeois taste."[7] Curiously, a number of years later Kramer reversed himself, saying, "Imagine painting the American flag! Wow! Dada—the very essence of the avant garde spirit, was reborn."[8] And later still he exclaimed, "I mean, basically what the Flag paintings were saying is to hell with the flag."[9]

Other writers of the early 1960s concluded that Johns chose

his subjects to make them disappear altogether, a view closer to Johns's own apparent intentions. To Kramer and Rosenberg he would have said, as he did in 1958, "I have no ideas about what the paintings imply about the world, I don't think that's a painter's business."[10] Or two decades later: "One doesn't set out to make a work which will have a certain effect in the society. I don't think that I have that kind of large grasp of society to begin with."[11] But he would hardly have disapproved of the critic who said, "Johns likes to paint objects so familiar that the spectator can cease to think about them and concentrate on the poetic qualities of the picture itself."[12] We assume that this is what Johns meant himself, in one of his most quoted statements: "Using the design of the flag took care of a great deal for me because I didn't have to design it. . . . So I went on to similar things like the targets—things the mind already knows. That gave me room to work on other levels."[13] Filling in predesigned entities has been an important stock-in-trade for him, an activity having something in common with the traditional coloring-book pleasures of children. "He is the realist for whom preformed subject matter is a condition of painting."[14] In a sense he *was* saying "to hell with the flag," if not in the political way Kramer imagined. For Johns, a flag is a flag is a flag, and the same for targets, letters, numbers, books, newspapers, shades, drawers, and thermometers, each of which he has used at least once. These objects are around us all the time; we handle them and casually take them for granted. While they may have been "interesting" to critics as Dada expressions, or as common objects never perhaps heretofore noticed, their ultimate interest to critics lay in how they were presented, in the brand-new twist Johns simultaneously put on figuration and abstraction. "Subject matter is back," said Leo Steinberg, "not as an adulteration, nor as a concession, nor in some sort of partnership, but as the very condition of painting, in which content and form, life and art, and the paint and the message are so much one and the same, that the distinction is not yet, or no longer intelligible."[15]

Johns had eliminated the "ground" that traditionally sets subjects off, depriving his figures of context. For him, a painting had to be what it represents. In its purest form, *Flag* of 1954–55, the outer edges of the image correspond to the perimeters of an actual flag. It frames itself, it could be said. It both represents its subject and is the subject represented. The famous question in the wake of *Flag* was, "Is it a flag or is it a painting?" With the ascendancy of abstraction in the twentieth century, "the habit of dissociating 'pure painting' from content" had become "so ingrained, that almost no critic was able to see both together." Flags had been seen in paintings before, waving somewhere in the middle of compositions, but never as the object itself, except in folk art or the crafts. "Johns doesn't give us the commonplace *in* a painting (transfigured by light, composition and style), but the commonplace *as* a painting. This is different." It distinguished him from figurative painters and abstractionists alike. Paint in his hands was no longer a medium of transformation. Steinberg placed him "at a point outside the crowded room, whence one suddenly saw how Franz Kline bundles with Watteau and Giotto. For they are all artists who use paint and surface to suggest existences other than surface and paint. The degree of nonfigurative abstraction has nothing to do with it. Existences other than those of paint are suggested, are implied, when dark nearing blacks block the openness of a white space; when pure color patches are allowed to locate themselves at varying distances from the picture plane; when painted canvas permits the illusion that form and space, figure and ground are not of one stuff."[16]

Johns's drive to eliminate both figure and ground by making one indistinguishable from the other is still at work nearly thirty years later, as he takes two figures painted by a Renaissance master and deprives them of their context, of their *reasons* for looking the way they do. Apart from rendering the figures as "details," one obvious strategy was to deprive the figures themselves of their look, to flatten them out like flags or targets, to turn them into designs. But could he say of the Grünewalds as he did of the flag that they took care of a great deal for him because he didn't have to design them? Not exactly. The flag is already a "design." He had to perform surgery on his figures to convert them to patterns; only then could he have "room to work on other levels," that is, with "variations in color and texture." Simply outlining the figures would suggest a "ground," if recognizable. He came perilously close to grounding them, perhaps inviting their discovery, with at least one rendition of the St. Anthony victim, whose contours stand out in an all-grey crosshatching field. Here he dodges the normal advantage he gives himself of color-contrasting areas that help to obscure his images.[17] The subject is quite obvious to anyone knowing the figure already.

In any event, Johns's goal, from *Flag* to the *Seasons,* has remained the same—to avoid positing "existences other than surface and paint"; even his own existence, as implied in the *Seasons,* is that of someone wholly immersed in surface and paint, and indistinguishable from them as their maker. Johns's shadow is meaningfully transparent; the "ground" leaks through its body, eating away at its legs. It has no ground even to stand on. Yet as such, it already implies or describes *some* kind of existence apart from its integration as collage component in surfaces of great formality. It has in fact been precisely as a collagist that Johns in his later work has undermined his original formalist program, by introducing images with references that could no longer be contained by or within themselves, "wherein paint and the message are so much one and the same," in which "a painting both represents a subject and is the subject represented."

This "corruption" in Johns's work, beginning in the late 1970s, maturing in the 1980s, dismayed many fans and observers who have followed his career. His Grünewald appropriation shows him going in two directions at once: back to *Flag* and its bedfellows, turning something very much not of their nature *into* them, through pattern and disguise; and away from them, because the heavy charge of emotion, of human vulnerability, is unmistakable once the source of the designs is recognized. Then figure and ground reemerge in all their preabstract glory. References outside the work overrun it. Images in the work now have histories. Leo Steinberg anticipated this in 1961, saying that "something [in the works] impressed me as the intensity of their solitude."[18]

Steinberg asked himself, "How improper is it to find poetic, metaphorical or emotional content in Johns's work?" He found a certain "solitude" regardless of the "deadpan materiality" of the paintings and "despite the artist's assurance that no emotional content was either overtly or implicitly present." When he told Johns that his early works seemed to be "about human absence," Johns replied "that this would mean their failure for him; for it would imply 'that he had been there,' whereas he wants his pictures to be objects alone." Steinberg concluded, "Well then I think he fails; not as a painter, but as theorist. For the assumption of a realism of absolute impersonality always does fail—if taken too seriously. That assumption is itself a way of feeling; it is the ascetic passion which sustains the youthful drive of a Caravaggio, Velázquez, or Courbet while they shake the emotional slop from themselves and their models."[19]

In the passivity of Johns's early pictures, Steinberg found "a sense of perpetual waiting—like the canvas face-to-the-wall that waits to be turned, or the empty coat hanger." But it is a "waiting for nothing, since the objects as Johns presents them, acknowledge no living presence; they imply human absence from a man-made environment. Only man's objects remain, overgrown by paint as by indifferent vegetation."[20]

The Grünewalds by contrast are waiting for *something*. Bodies submerged in paint, killed off, if you will, secreted only to be revealed, they lie suspended between death and discovery, marking time for two essential, inevitable outcomes: identification and the development of their histories, the latter of necessity including the artist's special interest in them. An equal desire to be hidden and to be found out adumbrates movement toward disclosure, conceivably imagined by Johns as a posthumous event. *Flag* itself awaits its history, its meaning as an icon to both artist and critics.

Early on, the artist provided a story about *Flag,* saying he dreamt one night of painting a large American flag and then got up and proceeded to do so. It seems probable that the critics didn't hear about this dream until 1964, a full decade after its supposed occurrence, when Alan Solomon brought it up in his catalogue essay for Johns's Jewish Museum retrospective that year. Harold Rosenberg embroidered on it the same year, saying Johns "dreamed one night that he had painted an enormous and beautiful [flag]."[21] The story was not cited by Steinberg, Rosenblum, Porter, Myers, Irving Sandler, or others in the literature between 1958 and 1963, and it isn't known when exactly and to whom Johns originally mentioned the dream. Calvin Tomkins once reported that Rachel Rosenthal, a close friend of Johns during the time he painted *Flag,* had been told by Johns that "he had dreamed he saw himself painting a large American flag," which he painted soon afterward.[22] I asked Rosenthal about this myself in 1991, but she had no memory of him mentioning it back then. I then asked her if he made it up later. At first she said yes, he made it up later. Then she said she didn't know.[23]

In the very first sentence of her 1975 book on Johns (a fount of information for critics and scholars), Roberta Bernstein coupled *Flag* with its source in the alleged dream, commenting that Johns had reiterated the story several times, and would "offer no other explanation for the appearance of this remarkable painting." She gave the dream a weight that no other observer had. "The revelation of Johns's initial, generative work in a dream is similar to the way solutions to problems or changes in thinking usually occur to creative individuals." Placing the dream on a par with sources of scientific discoveries, mindful evidently of the exalted place in modernist art accorded *Flag,* Bernstein quoted from Thomas Kuhn's *The Structure of Scientific Revolutions,* where he says that major changes in scientific thinking occur "not by deliberation and interpretation, but by a relatively sudden and unstructured event like the gestalt switch. Scientists . . . often speak of the 'scales falling from the eyes' or the 'lightning flash' that 'inundates' a previously obscure puzzle, enabling its components to be seen in a new way that for the first time permits its solution. On other occasions the relevant illumination comes in sleep."[24]

Max Kozloff, a leading exegete of Johns's work in the 1960s, minimized the importance of the dream, feeling it "hardly helped clarification." No Abstract Expressionist, Kozloff asserted, "ever claimed to have gotten his ideas from dreams, least of all ideas as irritatingly commonplace as these." He had no truck with dreams for Johns. "The suggestion of imagery that was received automatically and unconsciously had an implausibility that contrasted with the actual product; in essence nothing could be more ordinary."[25]

But the dream was completely congruent with Johns's general abdication of responsibility in his choice of subjects. "What Johns loves in his subjects," Steinberg observed, "is that they are nobody's preference; not even his own."[26] Going by the story of the dream, *Flag* was not a choice at all, except insofar as he decided to realize his dream by painting a flag when he woke up. It was something *given* to him, as potent as a destiny. And the product was far from "ordinary," considering both the impact it had on the art world and its role in establishing a remarkable career. But *Flag* also had questionable credentials as the great "commonplace" it was touted to be. The national emblem is a powerful symbol wherever it is flown, taken for granted yet a subconscious stimulus exciting community identification and underlying the whole cultural fabric of a country. It's difficult to imagine any other rectangular "commonplace" inciting artists, critics, and public the way *Flag* did when "flown" from the Castelli mast in January 1958. An artist, member of a chronically disaffected subcultural group, had captured the flag, so to speak, and at a most (inadvertently) climactic moment, coinciding— though of course the critics never said so—with the burgeoning realization that New York had replaced Paris as the capital of the Western art world.

Johns might have seemed an unlikely standard-bearer— young, unknown, an outsider to the group of Abstract Expressionists who had forged the very success in American art that he now suddenly and unexpectedly epitomized. But he had a private history, a driving force behind him, obscure at the time to others and seemingly to himself, that had catapulted him to the position. His artistry, his dream, his paternity and roots in the South, his family and personal circumstances during his mid- to late twenties, all converged in the image of *Flag,* powering an individual denouement that conflated with postmodernist needs in art for images reconciling abstraction and figuration.

In 1977, the year of Johns's second big retrospective in the United States, at the Whitney Museum of American Art, another piece of information about *Flag* entered the public record. Ancestral in nature, it gave body to the dream and created the beginnings of a myth for the artist, making it possible to get the national emblem off the gallery wall and stick it in the ground. Then with the addition of the Grünewald soldier in 1981, *Flag* could be further humanized, planted in our imaginations by an appearance as cogent as Armstrong taking the moon for America.

II.

Artistic production is a contract between fathers and sons.

— C R A I G   O W E N

I have not dreamed of any other paintings. I must be grateful for such a dream! The unconscious thought was accepted by my consciousness gratefully.

— J A S P E R   J O H N S

In 1976, the year of America's bicentennial, one year before Johns's Whitney retrospective, art critic and historian Charles Stuckey sent a letter to *Art in America* speculating on the origins of *Flag*. In the course of unrelated research Stuckey found references to one Sergeant William Jasper, the Revolutionary War hero of the South who twice recovered the fallen flag, dying young and gloriously in his second attempt. Freely associating the sergeant's last name with Johns's first, Stuckey wondered if "Jasper Johns [was not] in some way the namesake of the famous soldier, . . . whether the school books in South Carolina, where he spent his childhood, underlined for Johns the brave daring of the hero who kept our flag visible." Picking up on this reference in his catalogue essay for the 1977 Whitney retrospective, novelist Michael Crichton quoted part of the Stuckey letter (which had been titled *Johns: Yet Waving?*) in his notes, appending a stunning disclosure evidently conveyed to him by the artist: "As a boy Johns was shown a statue of Sergeant Jasper by his father, who told him that the figure was [indeed!] the namesake of them both."[27] Paraphrasing Crichton, *Newsweek* in its cover story on the exhibition said Johns's "parents . . . named him after 'Sergeant Jasper'—a Revolutionary War hero."[28] Overnight, an idle speculation by an art historian linking Johns with an eighteenth-century soldier was confirmed by the artist, deposited in the public record of a catalogue, and disseminated through a major print medium to people at large. The story was dropped after that, then repeated increasingly during the 1980s, though never critically connected with *Flag*. In 1984, linking the war hero rather grandly with a new proposed background for the artist, Barbara Rose said, "Johns [was] . . . named after a hero of the Revolutionary War" and was "a descendant of an antebellum Southern plantation family."[29] In his catalogue that same year for Johns's retrospective of drawings, again at the Whitney, David Shapiro repeated the namesake story uniting the artist with the sergeant, adding this striking comment, "Johns, with his shattered family history," followed by the non sequitur, ". . . remembers a statue of that hero pointed out by his father."[30]

These various references to Johns's father never led to disclosures of his father's first name. I hunted in vain through the literature on Johns trying to find it. A sketchy profile consisting of a dozen or so facts was published in 1964 and thereafter accompanied Johns in his artistic progress until the present. It was told and retold with variations, sometimes inaccurately, and with slight elaborations such as Rose's "antebellum Southern plantation family" complement. This 1964 sketch was written by John Cage, Johns's friend, mentor, admirer, and occasional colleague since 1954; it was culled from a conversation he had with the artist on a visit to his house on Edisto Island in South Carolina. In his account of Johns's childhood, Cage outlined its essentially peripatetic nature, which could explain Shapiro's attribution of a "shattered family history." The only proper name in Cage's account was Johns's Aunt Gladys with whom he lived for six years, bracketed by time spent with his mother, stepfather, and three half-siblings. His father wasn't mentioned at all. Cage reported,

His earliest memories concern living with his grandparents in Allendale, South Carolina. Later, in the same town, he lived with an aunt and uncle who had twins, a brother and sister. Then he went back to live with his grandparents. After the third grade in school he went to Columbia, which seemed like a big city, to live with his mother and stepfather. A year later, school finished, he went to a community on a lake called The Corner to stay with his Aunt Gladys. He thought it was for the summer but he stayed there for six years studying with his aunt who taught all the grades in one room, a school called Climax. The following year he finished high school living in Sumter with his mother and stepfather, two half-sisters and his half-brother.[31]

The reason for all this itinerancy was omitted—his parents' separation circa 1930. On my first trip to South Carolina in 1988 the first thing I looked for was his father's name. Jasper was an obvious guess for his father, whose "namesake," like his own (as he claimed) was Sergeant William Jasper. This was confirmed at the vital records building in Columbia—South Carolina's quiet, low-lying capital of wide, empty avenues built along the Congaree River. Founded in 1790, named after Christopher Columbus, the city was burned down by Sherman and his troops in 1865; it still flies a controversial Confederate flag from the state house. The city is the home of the University of South Carolina, which Johns attended for three semesters in the late 1940s.

His father was indeed Jasper Johns, according to his death certificate, which cites his date of death as March 9, 1957. Seventy-two miles south of Columbia, the additional name of William is incised on his father's tombstone in the Swallow Savannah Cemetery, on the southern outskirts of the once-flourishing farming community of Allendale. "William Jasper Johns" resonates quite closely with Sergeant William Jasper and suggests that Johns's own first name, going by the namesake story, was also William. In 1990 Johns added something to the story when an interviewer from *Interview* magazine asked him if the American flag in his paintings was a "stand-in" for himself. After giving the interviewer a hard time, apparently irritated by the inexactness of the question, Johns succumbed to what he thought must have been behind its clumsiness and recounted the namesake tale, amplifying it slightly: "The only thing I can think is that in Savannah, Georgia, in a park, there is a statue of Sergeant William Jasper. Once I was walking through this park with my father, and he said that we were both named for him. Whether that is in fact true or not, I don't know. Sergeant Jasper lost his life raising the American flag over a fort. But according to this story, the flag could just as well be a stand-in for my father as for me."[32]

The statue Johns said he saw in Savannah with his father is New York sculptor Alexander Doyle's 1888 bronze in Madison Square, a park laid out in 1839 and named for the fourth U.S. president. Doyle's fifteen-and-a-half-foot-tall bronze monument depicts the heroic sergeant bearing the colors of the Second Regiment of South Carolina Continentals during an unsuccessful attack of American and French forces against the British defenses on October 9, 1779, in the siege of Savannah. Sergeant Jasper was mortally wounded while attempting to plant the flag on the parapets of Spring Hill redoubt a few hundred yards from the site of the statue. Striding forward on his pedestal, head uplifted, the sergeant holds the staff of the flag in his upraised left hand, while his right hand, holding a saber, is pressed tight against the bullet wound in his side; his bullet-ridden hat lies at his feet. Bas-relief panels on the north, west, and east sides of the pedestal represent the three episodes in Jasper's career for which he is renowned, including his dying moments after the fatal attack, which shows him being held by two comrades as he lay wounded, while groups of American and French soldiers looked on mournfully. He had already distinguished himself at the battle of Fort Moultrie in Charleston harbor, or Sullivan's Island, as it was first known, on June 28, 1776. In this first decisive American victory of the war, he recovered the flag after it had been shot away and had fallen outside the fort. The other heroic episode depicted on the pedestal was his daring rescue of a group of Patriot prisoners near Savannah sometime after the British captured the city in December 1778.

Johns's uncertainty over his father's assertion that they were both named after this hero of the Revolutionary War—saying he didn't know whether it "is in fact true or not"—perhaps reflects on the questionable credibility his father might have had for him. Johns Sr. had abdicated his role as a father. A binge alcoholic and the survivor, around the age of thirty-six, of a serious auto accident that dramatically altered his appearance, he never supported his son and had great difficulty supporting himself. Since the sergeant was not a Johns, clearly he was not an ancestral sort of namesake. Johns may have wondered if his father made the story up that day in Savannah, since he had never heard it before.

There is every likelihood that Johns's grandfather had the war hero in mind when he named his second son, born July 22, 1900, William Jasper. William Isaac Johns (called W.I.), the artist's grandfather, must surely have been schooled in "the brave daring of the hero who kept our flag visible" (as Stuckey put it). Born 1869, he had three uncles who fought in the Civil War, two of whom died in it. The sites of Sergeant Jasper's heroism during the 1770s were not further than seventy miles from the Johns family seat in Bamberg and Colleton counties, and the town of Allendale where W.I. Johns had settled by the turn of the century. When residents of communities in Hampton and Beaufort counties decided in 1910 to move for the creation of a separate county, they chose to name it Jasper, after the valiant soldier. In 1919, when W.I. Johns helped found Allendale County, the recently formed county of Jasper was separated from it to the south only by that of Hampton. Along with William, the name Jasper already existed in the Johns family. Since W.I. was founding a family (his son William Jasper being the last of four) while acquiring very large tracts of farmland in the 1890s and showing signs of becoming a town father, his ambition for the Johnses, who had been relatively modest farmers, could have led him to name one of his sons after a man who had emerged from obscurity to bring honor to his country.

In any case, the artist's claim through his father gives his *Flag* a plangency it never had before 1977—a rumble of distant booms and patriotic exploits befitting the startling emblazonment that appeared out of the blue on the walls of Leo Castelli's new gallery in 1958, affixed there by an artist who had been as obscure as his namesake was before the Revolutionary War. Very little is known about the Sergeant. He was born about 1750, presumably in the vicinity of Georgetown, South Carolina, as he was living there July 7, 1775, when he enlisted in the infantry. He may have been a skilled artisan or carpenter by trade, and apparently he could neither read nor write. He married one Elizabeth Marlow, with whom he had two children. Their son died without issue, and their daughter had children who died young.[33]

After Jasper's first heroic deed at Fort Moultrie, rescuing the fallen colors through a shower of British gunfire, Governor Rutledge presented him with his own sword "as a reward for . . . bravery and an excitement to farther deeds of valour" and offered him a commission. The Sergeant is reported to have said, "Were I made an officer, my comrades would be constantly blushing for my ignorance, and I should be unhappy feeling my own inferiority. I have no ambition for higher rank than that of a Sergeant."[34]

We know that Jasper Johns was thrilled by his overnight success in 1958. (Catherine Rembert, a teacher he had at USC with whom he remained close, remembered seeing him in New York at the moment of his triumph, the Museum of Modern Art having just bought three of his paintings out of the show for its permanent collection. She said she had a dinner date with Johns, and when he arrived he picked her up and danced her about the room.)[35] And we know he was ambitious. But he sometimes expressed a modesty and self-depreciation in the vein of his namesake. He could, and still can, project a sense of awe and respect for the immortals of his medium, and of himself—autodidact and latecomer—almost as an interloper.

Johns deliberately destroyed all the work he did before *Flag* that he had in his possession. There is extant early work, but clearly he meant to stake his career on *Flag,* from which the rest of his "commonplace" images followed. While we might assume a nationalistic gloss for an image of perfect fidelity to the prescribed components of the American flag, lavishly worked (involving a painstaking process using encaustics[36]), and presented as flag qua flag, there is no indication whatever that the artist was patriotically motivated in those governmentally hysterical, patriotic, paranoid, McCarthyesque and anti-Communist times when *Flag* was painted. The involuntary origins of *Flag* in a dream already signifies something more personal and unconscious than the knowing reflexes required for national pride. Following the lead of Johns's later myth-making, linking himself with Sergeant William Jasper, a hero so thoroughly identified with the emblem of paternal *communitas* and a relation configured through Johns's father, one might see *Flag* as invested with ancestral longings, both for his roots in the South and for family redemption, growing out of a displaced, unfavorable childhood.

The flag raised at Fort Moultrie by Sergeant Jasper on June 28, 1776, three years before his death at Savannah, was of course not the American flag as we know it today. Sergeant Jasper's flag, designed by Colonel William Moultrie, consisted of a blue field bearing a white crescent in the upper right corner and the word "Liberty" on it. Subsequently the General Assembly of South Carolina adopted this image as the state flag, adding a silver palmetto tree upright in the center of the blue ground, a reminder of the palmetto logs used in the construction of Fort Moultrie.

This flag flies now in Columbia from the state house dome along with the American and Confederate flags.

Uprooted from a very conservative state, a state proud of its heritage as the leader in 1860 of the great secession of eleven states, as the site of the first shot of the Civil War in 1861, and as guardian of the courtesies inherent in the Old South, Johns had not been a permanent resident in Yankeeland more than two years when he painted the symbol of American unity. Taken up as an icon of youthful optimism, coinciding with the victorious emergence of American art, and the onrushing moment of national celebration in the Kennedy years, *Flag* had a boring textual profile until Johns (via Stuckey) put it in the hands of a provincial namesake, providing a reading for the dream. "The more we learn about [*Flag*]," Barbara Rose has said, "the more it seems it has something to do with [Johns's] own personal history."[37]

Perhaps the most stunning piece of this history is the discovery of Johns by his dealer Leo Castelli at almost the precise moment of his father's death in 1957, and the first appearance of *Flag* within that year. The timing of a father's death and a son's success can be one of the bejeweled features in the myths of patrimony.

III.

My gallery really began with the Johns show in 1958. . . .
That show is the basic fact of my career.
—LEO CASTELLI

When fathers have plans, children have destinies.
—JEAN-PAUL SARTRE

William Jasper Johns died March 9, 1957, age fifty-six, in Charleston, South Carolina, where he had been living for two years. He died intestate, of "natural causes," leaving his only child and son a personal estate valued at one hundred dollars.[38] The following day, March 10, a group show of twenty-three artists opened at the Jewish Museum in New York, including Jasper Johns with *Green Target* (1955), his first serious exposure in a legitimate space.[39] Seeing *Green Target*—worked up like *Flag* into a rich texture with encaustics, using both brush and collage materials—Leo Castelli found it "a very singular painting, quite unlike anything I'd seen before."[40] He said he was "riveted by the picture's spare geometry and sensuous surface, and after he finished looking, he read the wall label. He had never heard of the artist before, but he liked the sound of his name—Jasper Johns."[41] He was struck by the assonance, it lodged in his mind.[42] Leo Steinberg recalls *Green Target* being shown "as if the organizers were embarrassed by it . . . hung in a shadowed rear wall."[43]

Castelli, then fifty years old, born and raised in Trieste, trained as a lawyer but with a career in banking and insurance and some sporadic experience in art dealing, had arrived in New York in 1941, a refugee from Nazi-occupied Europe. Just one month before the Jewish Museum show, on February 7, he had opened his first gallery on the fourth floor of his townhouse on East Seventy-seventh Street. On March 11, one day after Castelli saw *Green Target* at the museum, Johns was in Allendale, South Carolina, for his father's funeral. A relative remembered him getting there late, which suggests that he had attended the opening in New York the day before.[44]

Two months later, Johns's *Flag* was shown for the first time, in a group exhibition of ten artists at Castelli's new gallery. With the show spanning May 6–25, Johns's twenty-seventh birthday, May 15, occurred in the middle of it. Then on January 20, 1958, Castelli gave Johns his first one-man exhibition, *Flag* once again showcased. From the moment of their meeting, their fates were entwined, their rise as artist and dealer as interrelated as a family business, like the corporate enterprise of, say, a father and a son.

Castelli has said that a few days after seeing *Green Target* at the
Jewish Museum,

> As luck would have it . . . I went to [Robert] Rauschenberg's stu-
> dio [on Pearl Street in lower Manhattan] to see paintings for a show
> I wanted to do of his work. Rauschenberg said . . . we wanted to
> have a drink perhaps while we are looking at his paintings, he had
> to get ice cubes and he didn't have an icebox but Jasper Johns on
> the floor below had one. So either he was going to ask him to bring
> the ice cubes back or . . . somebody would go down and get them.

Having heard the name, Castelli exclaimed,

> Jasper Johns? The man whose green painting is in the Jewish Mu-
> seum? . . . I said well you'll excuse me but I really would like to in-
> terrupt our session here and go down and see what he's doing. Be-
> cause I really couldn't concentrate without finding out. So good guy
> that Rauschenberg was, he said fine, let's go. And we went down.
> And then I was confronted with that miraculous array of unprece-
> dented images—flags, red, white and blue, white . . . all white . . .
> large ones . . . smaller ones; targets . . . with . . . faces . . . parts of
> the human body . . . numbers . . . alphabets. Just an incredible sight
> . . . something one could not imagine . . . new . . . and . . . out of
> the blue. So then I was tremendously impressed. Never in my life
> had I been so impressed . . . about the work of a painter. Seeing it
> all for the first time, all at one fell swoop like that.[45]

Castelli was looking at a complete body of work, the result of
more than three years of sustained effort. He has likened the experience to "seeing the treasures of Tutankhamen."[46] And he offered him a show on the spot.

Another version of their meeting has Rauschenberg going
down one flight for the ice cubes and telling Johns that Castelli
was upstairs wanting to be introduced, with Johns being surprised
and, "having a refined sense of the appropriate," knowing that
Castelli had come to see Rauschenberg's art, suggesting "that the

art dealer call him later." But Castelli, as we know, persisted. Johns remembers "liking" his future dealer, "thinking him sophisticated, direct and not condescending."[47] Looking back in 1978, Johns said, "Leo and I were very lucky to encounter one another when we did. . . . I had lost most of my interest in showing when he appeared."[48] It seems he had not been trying.

> All the other New York galleries that I know existed then had an attitude toward work into which my work could not comfortably have fitted. . . . I don't think any of those dealers would have shown my work, but if they had I think it would have been treated in a very different way. The only dealer I wanted to show my work was Betty Parsons [with whom Rauschenberg had had his first show in 1951]; I felt her artists were not of one kind. But that didn't work. So the fact that Leo appeared was interesting and a marvelous coincidence from my point of view; the fact that my work existed was a marvelous thing for him. Instead of putting him in competition with other galleries with the same kind of interests, it made a very clear difference between what he was doing and what other people were doing. That kind of clarity brings a sharpness to the situation. It demands either that the new work be deliberately ostracized or paid attention to.[49]

Integral to the story of Johns's portentous meeting with Castelli in 1957 is the shift it equally augured for his relationship with Rauschenberg, a man who had a father story with striking parallels to Johns's own and with whom he had been intimate since 1954. By then Johns had lived in New York for two years, impoverished and solitary, trying to go to college, dropping out, working at the Marlboro bookstore on Fifty-seventh Street, painting at night in his twenty-five-dollar-a-month walkup cold-water room on East Eighty-third Street. When the two men met, Rauschenberg, four years older, was an entrenched art-world denizen, with a controversial reputation, two one-man shows behind him, and another immediately before him. Through

Rauschenberg's example, Johns would learn the ropes of the trade: having a loft, dealers, shows, and a cadre of supporters; knowing the people who made up this world. Most importantly, he would acquire the confidence to devote his full time to painting, and Rauschenberg would help him do it by making him a partner in his window-decorating business at Bonwit Teller, the perfect kind of freelance work for rent or pocket money.

In March 1957, at the moment Johns's father died and Leo Castelli was launching a gallery, Rauschenberg clearly was ready for a new dealer and his fourth one-man show. And Castelli just as clearly favored his younger confrere, the unknown Johns. Castelli, described as "flawless, elegant, impeccably groomed," a "fastidious visitor from uptown, was disturbed . . . by the 'dishevelment' of Rauschenberg's new work and irritated by his wife's [Ileana Sonnabend] positive reaction to it." He thought "Bob had gone too far." He found Johns's paintings "had all the structure and organization" that Rauschenberg's work "not only lacked but exulted in the lack of."[50] But Rauschenberg was not to be denied by Castelli, who gave him a show in March of 1958. Called a *succès de scandale,* it hardly matched Johns's sensational debut three months earlier, when he stepped out of the shadow of his friend and mentor in a big way. By 1961 the two men had parted painfully, thereafter to "pursue their careers as rivals," the way Castelli has put it.[51] Rauschenberg's first big popular, critical, and financial success came with his 1963 Jewish Museum retrospective and his Venice Biennale victory one year later when he won the golden lion. Like Johns before him, his ascendancy was linked with the death of his father in October 1963.

Both fathers died in their fifties, and both had been Cronus son-eating types, disapproving and unloving, playing parts in family complexes that made their survivors and only sons contrary, or recusant. Their failures as fathers gave rise to conquests by their sons elsewhere, in worlds unimaginably different from

those of their origins. If Johns's *Flag* belied, however unknow-
ingly, the distance he had achieved from his father and paternal
roots, Rauschenberg similarly embraced the very history he had
seemingly escaped, once his father was dying. In 1963, the year
of his father's death, Rauschenberg painted *Barge,* an oil and
silkscreen work of enormous proportions (6½ by 32 feet) and exuberant artistic frontiersmanship. It depicts an allegory of life in
America involving the progress of a somewhat ennobled immigrant family, described in print within the picture. The images
featured in the painting include the recumbent Velázquez
Rokeby Venus (printed a number of times by Rauschenberg in
his silkscreen series), a highway cloverleaf, an army truck, a satel-
lite package known as a Venus probe, a space capsule handled by
four astronauts or technicians, a fireman in action, a football
game, a man swimming, a building construction site, and a pho-
tographer's umbrella.

Rauschenberg's Americana fervor erupted at this time in his
repeated images of the national bald eagle, of the astronauts and
their gear, and of John F. Kennedy—represented by a hugely
blown up silkscreen of a well-known photograph showing the
president speaking, his right hand extended and pointing at us,
like Uncle Sam in the ubiquitous World War I recruitment
poster. Rauschenberg began exploiting this image immediately
following JFK's assassination in November 1963, one month
after the death of his father. A silkscreen painting called *Archive*
of 1963 advertises a patriotic display of American flags—a photo
of armed forces bearing them on parade down a city or town
street, silkscreened in a large rectangle at the bottom center of
the painting.[52] Besides capturing the new optimistic spirit in
America ushered in by the Kennedy era, Rauschenberg had very
personal reasons for his ascendancy just then. The death of an op-
pressive parent can be tremendously liberating, especially for a
son whose patrimony may amount to nothing more, or less, than

the spirit of the fatherland, an inheritance often instinctively understood by ambitious, deprived sons. Various paternal deliverers can put in a helpful appearance while a personage as important as a father is dying. Rauschenberg already had Castelli; the big transference he made was to America's chief executive and commander of the armed forces, whose death put him somehow on an equal footing with the artist's obscure father.[53]

Johns's rise, similarly so related to his father's impending and actual death, was not reflected, like Rauschenberg's, in towery, soaring, supernal or transcendent work. In 1962 Rauschenberg opened up the skies and flew into them along with his beloved heroes the astronauts, leaving all his closed, tight, densely packed, rectangularly collaged images of his 1950s combines behind. In the silkscreens his images float free; they're absolutely aerated. They even look liberated within the familiar boxes and rectangles that often enclose them. Johns, the cool, detached, thinking artist, the classical Ingres to Rauschenberg's romantic Delacroix, as Castelli has compared them,[54] had built up a body of images in the mid- to late 1950s embalmed in encaustic or caught in controlled high-density crayon-and-pencil hen tracks and scribbles. Without Flag, his signature work, so fraught with associations of the American dream, one wonders whether Castelli, himself an enthusiastic transplant, and the art community, ready to celebrate its victory over Paris, would have given him the great career send-off they did. But with Johns, dynamic coincidental forces of destiny seem to have been powering his progress. Such forces lie in their predetermination, the thrust of an irresistible course of events.

"When fathers have plans, children have destinies," said Jean-Paul Sartre. The kind of "plan" imprinted on Johns was by default rather than by intent or design. This had the effect of throwing him out of his family locus, ultimately toward a role in the wider world. Fathers who groom sons for their place in family history generally are present and persuasive. Johns's father abdicated his role of father when his wife deserted him, circa 1931, when Johns was one. Johns's mother was unable to take her son with her when she departed Allendale. He was left, in one stroke, both motherless and fatherless. His father, who had been deserted himself by a mother who died in 1906, lived vagrantly in and around the town of Allendale, inconsistently or minimally employed (at the time of his death in Charleston he was identified as a clerk in the civil service) and plagued by alcoholism.

Taken in by his father's father, W.I., Johns was raised in the same household his father had known, with W.I.'s second wife, Montez, whom he married in 1911, and assorted black servants. Johns Sr.'s older sister Eunice and older brother Wilson R. also lived in Allendale, raising families there when the future artist was a ward of his grandfather. Gladys (b. 1893), the eldest child of W.I.'s four by his first wife, was raising a family further north in Lexington County, on the western end of Lake Murray. Both Eunice and Gladys were teachers, while Wilson R. was a farmer. At some point Johns went to live with his uncle, W.R. as he was called, presumably to have the benefit of proximate playmates close in age, W.R.'s twins Bill and Betty, who were one year older—an experiment that lasted a year or less. Life with his grandfather and step-grandmother Montez resumed until he was nine, in 1939, when his grandfather died, at which time Johns left Allendale, moving north to stay a while with his mother, stepfather, and three half siblings. After that, he spent six years on Lake Murray with his Aunt Gladys, who had four sons, attending her one-room school and then the Batesburg-Leesville High School. In his senior year he moved to Sumter to live once again with his mother's family, graduating from Edmunds High School in 1947.

Johns has always said he wanted to be an artist from early childhood, and that all he understood about such a profession was that to do it would mean going to another part of the world. In a 1990 interview he went so far as to say that "to some degree this suggested a discontented relationship with my childhood, a wish to be somewhere else."[55]

By the age of nine he was launched on his trajectory toward "somewhere else" when circumstances caused his departure from the paternal seat in Allendale. Johns would be freed from a cultural backwater and the embarrassment of a father's failure. With a certain occlusion in the male line, as well as a dispossession of land and loss of opportunity in a once-thriving South Carolina farming area, the disgorgement of a son into the wider world could be the key to a family renascence, unrecognizable perhaps in its new incarnation but carrying that all-important index of continuity, the family name.[56]

IV.

The flag must . . . be said to be a private dream-image with enormous psychic weight. It is an extraordinary instance of the restorative powers of art that the son could create a portrait of lost time with this image that seems to be testing the real.

—DAVID SHAPIRO

For Phaethon, as for Michelangelo, the existence of the ideal loving father remained problematic and uncertain; he set off across the world in search of proof, until finally (like Jupiter in the house of Saturn) when he "had come beneath the roof of his sire whose fatherhood had been questioned, straightway he turned him to his father's face, but halted some little space away; for he could not bear the radiance at a nearer view . . . filled with terror at the strange new sights."

—JAMES SASLOW, OVID

Juxtaposing Johns's 1954–55 *Flag* with his 1982 *Perilous Night*, in the spirit of his own collocations and displacements, it's possible to imagine a fallen standard-bearer in the Grünewald soldier painted more than a quarter century after *Flag*, and five years after Johns laid claim to Sergeant William Jasper as a namesake. The title itself is said to be taken from the "Star-Spangled Banner," though Johns's direct reference is to a John Cage composition—*The Perilous Night* of 1943–44—that Cage said derived from an Irish folktale he remembered in a volume of myths collected by Joseph Campbell concerning a "perilous bed."[57] The phrase in the national anthem from which the title supposedly comes is actually "perilous fight," though some people think it's "night," and sing it that way. The event that gave rise to the "Star-Spangled Banner," the poem written by Francis Scott Key, was of course a "perilous fight"—the bombardment during the War of 1812 by the British fleet of Fort McHenry in Baltimore's harbor in September 1814. Writing about Johns's *Perilous Night* in 1984, John Ashbery noted the "title taken from the Star Spangled Banner."[58] The outcome of the "fight," in any case, and the event celebrated in the poem turned song, is the surviving flag, left standing after a brutal engagement. While a fallen soldier with a sword is the event glorified in Johns's 1982 *Perilous Night,* the title reminds us of a flag that endured. Title and image together bring Johns's (and his father's) namesake, Sergeant William Jasper, into focus—a man who saved another flag thirty-eight years before Francis Scott Key wrote what would become the American anthem; in another harbor (Charleston), under another barrage of British gunfire.

A sword figures prominently in the legend of Sergeant Jasper, as it does in Grünewald's portrayal of his fallen foreground soldier—a linear geometric item, a "pointer," which can serve to orient the viewer in identifying Johns's tracings of the figure, which besides being submerged may be flopped or turned in different pictures. Following Sergeant Jasper's first act of bravery, raising the flag at Fort Moultrie in Charleston, the president of the Carolina provincial government, John Rutledge, presented his own sword to Jasper for his heroism. This occurred July 4, 1776, the day a group of "founding fathers" in Philadelphia signed the Declaration of Independence. When fatally wounded in 1779 at Savannah, Jasper is said to have pointed to his sword and uttered the words, "That sword was presented to me by Governor Rutledge for my services in the defense of Fort Moultrie. Git it to my father and tell him I have worn it with honor. If he should weep, say to him his son died in the hope of a better life."[59] Johns may not know these stories, but he would have seen the sword as represented by Alexander Doyle in his bronze statue of the sergeant in Savannah, sticking up vertically from Jasper's right hand, which he also presses to the wound in his side.[60] In the bas-relief panel beneath the bronze depicting the fatally wounded recumbent hero attended by his two comrades, a bit of his sword protrudes from under Jasper's left arm, lying on the ground alongside his thigh.

Grünewald's soldier is only wounded by a vision—the sight of the rising, brilliantly illuminated Christ, which has caused him to fall, turn violently away, and shield himself with his upraised left arm. While Johns's selection of the image has roots in personal experiences dating from 1976, the year he first saw the Altarpiece, his mythological account of himself and his father, which emerged at that time, appears convincingly invested in the image, whether consciously or not.[61] Perilous Night is Johns's first dramatic figurative work. Against the backdrop of his whole crosshatch oeuvre since Scent of 1973–74—a body of work that evolved into skeined striped embryos for hatching human forms—Perilous Night of 1982 is a triumph of that maturation process. Of course Perilous Night is one picture for viewers who can identify the soldiers; it is another, more mysterious picture for those who can't. Even after recognizing the soldiers, the painting is mysterious due to its narrative syncopes or elisions. Overtly missing is the rest of Grünewald's Resurrection panel from which Johns lifted the soldiers. Having relocated the figures in his own context—a dark ambience abraded by a handkerchief "nailed" to a section of painted wood-grain siding, a page from a John Cage music score, a "nailed" picture representing one of his own crosshatches, and three hanging hand casts—Johns's picture stands on its own. At the same time his omission, once perceived, compounds the picture's meaning.

"There is something lonely and ghostly about *Perilous Night,* something ineffable and hard to trace," wrote one critic in 1984.[61] In 1988 Mark Rosenthal filled in some gaps, while making the only extended remarks on the work up to that time. Finding it impossible to leave out Grünewald's Christian scene, he even related the "discolorations" of Johns's three hand casts to the "arm wounds" of the fallen Christ in the predella under the Crucifixion scene. Noting Johns's "wounded arms hanging as if hunks of meat and a handkerchief used in mourning," he freely associates to the Grünewald, calling *Perilous Night* a "still-life composition [that] documents appearances following a death." Providing a final touch to his Grünewald attributions, Rosenthal sees the inclusion by the artist of "John C." under the page from the composer's music score as "perhaps adding a clue in the direction of Christendom."[62]

In 1984 one critic familiar with the Grünewald made an astonishing link between the soldiers in *Perilous Night* and the omitted Grünewald Resurrection scene above them, visualizing how the sword of the foreground soldier, in the large tracing consuming the left panel, being both flopped and turned, would "intersect with the risen Christ precisely at the wound in his side."[63]

Johns's hanging casts, his "hunks of meat," can be further referenced to Christ "as a model amputee"[64] in Grünewald's Crucifixion panel. The savior's extended right arm was routinely cut off from his body any time the panels were opened, a symbolic reminder of the affliction the Altarpiece was created to address.

Christ as amputee resonates with mythic and pagan precursors, such as Adonis or Attis or the great Egyptian corn-god Osiris, who was buried alive, then rent to pieces by a jealous brother. After his scattered limbs were found and reconstituted by his sister-wife Isis, his death and resurrection were celebrated every year during the vernal equinox, in the same season as that of many other resurrection gods of the temperate zones, including the later Christ.

The dispersion of parts and pieces in individual works and throughout his oeuvre is Johns's most abiding trope. His stray components, including parts of bodies painted or cast and strewn through canvases and also such "whole" images as his *Flag,* are constantly dismantled, shuffled, reorganized, and recontextual-ized, challenging his audience to gather and connect them up, or awaiting his own analytic resolves. The whole human figures introduced with *Perilous Night* would become pawns in the same collage tactics. But by submerging these figures he keeps them, and us, in the dark. They're the missing pieces in various collage puzzles. We can connect up their accessories perhaps, but not to much avail when the figure around which they collect is absent. In *Perilous Night,* no resurrection was intended. This, I believe, would come with the *Seasons* five years later, in 1987.

Engulfed in a sea of mottled black and grey-greenish paint, Johns's tracings of the Grünewald foreground soldier and the sec-ondary figure falling over his midsection in the large left panel of *Perilous Night* are expressive of the chthonic character of men just delivered a *coup de grâce* by an entombed "criminal" they had been guarding who is suddenly miraculously rising in a great lu-minous circle to eternal life. "His countenance was like lightning, and his raiment white as snow: and for fear of him the keepers did shake, and became as dead *men.*"[65] Mere mortals *"men"*, their denial, as they fall away stunned and unbelieving, is part of the picture Mark Rosenthal has described as a "still-life composition [that] documents appearances following a death." So Johns's omitted Resurrection scene supports his narrative: two men overcome, "wounded" by a vision too much to bear, objects of the artist's compassion and lament. His condolences are almost melodramatically connoted by the three hanging arm casts in the right panel of the painting, fingertips of the two to the right nearly touching the top of the small inset version of the traced soldiers, the fingers of the leftmost cast aimed at the handkerchief "nailed" to the wood paling below, a slight yet vivid red drip, a sort of arrow, reinforcing the direction.

Depriving his viewers of ready access to the soldiers, over whom all the fuss is made, Johns makes "reconstitution" here difficult or impossible. This is quite apart from aesthetic postmodernist considerations he faced in deciding to render musty old Renaissance personages, breaking completely with his nonfigurative past, reaching an appreciable compromise through subterfuge and disguise. But concealment here can be said to strengthen his theme of the lack of recognition on the part of his protagonists. Work is required to see what the picture is about, to get into it, to share the feelings of the artist and his projected actors. Integrating things has been hard for him, why should it be easy for us, he might wonder.

Johns was fifty-two when he painted *Perilous Night*. In February 1987 when the *Seasons* were first shown, he was fifty-six, the age his father was when he died. Beginning in the late 1970s, with several series of works—*Usuyuki, Cicada, Dancers on a Plane, Between the Clock and the Bed, Tantric Detail*—Johns showed an increasing absorption in transience and mortality. The theme is picked up grandly once embodied by the Grünewald soldiers and the St. Anthony victim, who are in important ways interchangeable—both of course concealed, both consuming the left sides of two-panel paintings, and both accompanied by some of the same supporting icons, like the double image young wife and old crone, the skull and crossbones, the bathroom fixtures, and furniture. Asked why he would "be moved to confront his own mortality with such directness and urgency," being "in good health" after all, Johns said, "I suppose I've become increasingly aware of the way things can be cut off."[66] He mentioned the loss of friends, but it seems unlikely that what was probably the most meaningful loss in his life, that of the father whose name and namesake he shared and who had been so absent from his life from the very start, was far from his mind as he approached the age his father had been at his death in 1957.

Just as his father's death was attended by the beginnings of Johns's spectacular rise, the thirtieth anniversary of his father's death in 1987, when he himself was fifty-six, was the occasion of another amazing ascension. Kicking off a celebration marking the thirtieth anniversary of the inauguration of his gallery on January 31, 1957, Castelli opened two exhibitions on January 31, 1987: *The Seasons* in his West Broadway gallery, and a retrospective of the major artists he had represented through the years including Johns, Rauschenberg, Jim Rosenquist, Roy Lichtenstein, and Frank Stella, in his Greene Street establishment in Soho. *The Seasons,* Johns's most ambitious work since *Untitled* 1972, and before that, *According to What* of 1964, all preceded by the *Flag,* show a powerful, perhaps urgent, drive toward integration. Here his pieces and parts are made to be read as a "collection," unified by its owner, the artist's reliably present self-portrait as a shadow appearing through the changing seasons. And here Johns has at last revealed a figure, serendipitously timed to the anniversary festivities arranged by the dealer-father who had replaced his real one in 1957 and who had raised Johns's *Flag* over newly claimed art territory, making good his destiny as family standard-bearer. The fallen hero, a fatally wounded eighteenth-century sergeant and a failed father, traumatized by life, who might have said on his deathbed, "If he [his son] should weep, say to him his [father] died in the hope of a better life"—these two converge in the image of a raised figure, be-shadowed though it is, flag by his side (in *Summer*), practically in hand, as heroic in its way as the Savannah statue.

"And behold, I send the promise of my Father upon you," said Christ at the Resurrection.[67] The dark vision of *Perilous Night* is redeemed by the risen artist of the *Seasons*. For a sign of what his effort must have cost him, note the "stigmata" in the palm of each hand in the four paintings. Turning fifty-seven in May of the year *The Seasons* opened, Johns survived his father's age at death. His inheritance then perhaps seemed secure, the redemption of a Southern father binding. And the art world none the wiser—a critical condition of triumph. The two interlocking components in the progress of America's wealthiest artist—a powerful dead father and a helpless driven son—are the very sorts of circumstances the art world conspires to help its practitioners forget and transcend. The commodity is art, not the life story that propelled it. The code of biographical irrelevance in art has been as well exploited by Johns as by any other card-carrying member in good standing.

Following Castelli's anniversary exhibitions, the art establishment on both sides of the Atlantic feted America's favorite son in several important venues. At the 1988 Venice Biennale it was hoped that Johns might bring home the golden lion—a prize it could be said Johns had awaited for twenty-four years, ever since 1964 when it was won by his former partner turned competitor, Robert Rauschenberg. Mark Rosenthal, curator of contemporary art at the Philadelphia Museum, was designated to put together the Johns show for Venice, *Work since 1974*. Then he brought the show to Philadelphia in October, a month after it closed in Venice.

In the fall of 1989 an opening at the Anthony d'Offay Gallery in London of paintings by Johns along with framed scores by John

Cage and dance videos by Merce Cunningham was the occasion for various lectures, performances, luncheons, and dinners. One year later Johns was celebrated in London again, this time with new drawings at the d'Offay gallery and a retrospective of drawings at the Hayward, an exhibit that had opened at the National Gallery in Washington on May 15, the day of Johns's sixtieth birthday. Both in London and in Washington, then later in New York when the show traveled to the Whitney, the obligatory expensive black-tie dinners, with trustees, lenders, and assorted friends, were socially crowning events.

PAINTINGS AND
DRAWINGS

Mathias Grünewald, Isenheim Altarpiece, c. 1515, Unterlinden Museum, Colmar, France: middle state, left to right, Annunciation, Angelic Concert, Nativity, Resurrection; below, Lamentation.

Mathias Grünewald, Isenheim
Altarpiece, c. 1515, Unterlinden
Museum, Colmar, France: open
state, *left to right*, Meeting of St.
Anthony with St. Paul, St. Augus-
tine, St. Anthony, St. Jerome,
Temptation of St. Anthony; *below*,
Christ and the Twelve Apostles.

ABOVE: *Grünewald, fallen Roman
soldier, detail from* Resurrection
panel, Isenheim Altarpiece.
OPPOSITE: *Grünewald,* Resurrection *panel, Isenheim Altarpiece.*

Pablo Picasso, Straw Hat With Blue Leaf, *1936, oil on canvas, Musée Picasso, Paris. © 1996 Estate of Pablo Picasso/Artists Rights Society (ARS), New York.*

LEFT: *Marcel Duchamp, L.H.O.O.Q.,
1919. Rectified Readymade: pencil on a reproduction. Private collection.* © *1996 Artists
Rights Society (ARS), New York/ADAGP,
Paris.*

BELOW: *Marcel Duchamp,* Self-Portrait in
Profile, *1958. Torn paper. Collection of
Mr. and Mrs. Julian Levy.* © *1996 Artists
Rights Society (ARS), New York/ADAGP,
Paris.*

Marcel, Duchamp, Tu m'...,
1918, oil and pencil on canvas, with
bottle brush, three safety pins, and
bolt. Yale University Art Gallery,
gift from the estate of Katherine S.
Dreier. © 1996 Artists Rights Society (ARS), New York/ADAGP,
Paris.

INTERLUDE:

THE PUBLIC IS NOT INVITED

I.

The public plays no part whatsoever in the process [of the
discoveries of artists and their acceptance]. All the glories of
Modern Art after the first World War have not occurred because
it was "finally understood" or "finally appreciated" but rather
because a few fashionable people [le monde, the culturati]
discovered their own uses for it.
—TOM WOLFE

Jasper Johns's presence seemed to inspire half the New York art
world to make a pilgrimage to Venice to honor him.
—MICHAEL BRENSON

The Venice Biennale, the oldest and most prestigious of international contemporary art exhibitions, with over forty countries
participating, was started in 1895. In 1972, amid student protests
that art was becoming too commercial, the Biennale jettisoned
its prize system and turned itself into a noncompetitive sympo-

sium. The prizes were restored in 1986, when sculptor Isamu Noguchi represented the United States. Before Johns won the golden lion in 1988, the last American to be awarded the prize was Robert Rauschenberg in 1964. Prior to Rauschenberg's victory, only two Americans, James Whistler in 1895 and Mark Tobey in 1958, had been so honored. Since World War II, the grand prize for painting had gone almost without exception to School of Paris artists with long-established reputations: Braque in 1948, Matisse in 1950, Dufy in 1952, Ernst in 1954, Jacques Villon in 1956. Rauschenberg's triumph was an acknowledgment of the spectacular rise of postwar American art, led by the New York School, which had made New York the new capital of the international art world. Mark Rosenthal said, "Venice is a tremendously important show in Europe. It is so important for Europeans that they have always been shocked that Americans did not take it seriously. The Johns show is showing the world that we want to take it seriously. We are sending to my mind one of the greatest artists produced in America and showing a body of work that has not been seen in Europe."[1]

Americans certainly took the show seriously in 1964 when they performed cartwheels in Venice to make sure their man would win it. The jury was ready to disqualify the small retrospective of Rauschenberg's work—twenty-two paintings and assemblages, organized by Alan Solomon—because it had been installed in the U.S. consulate, not in the American pavilion on Biennale grounds, due to dissatisfactions with the building. Finally Solomon came to an understanding with the Biennale jury, agreeing to move three Rauschenbergs from the consulate to the pavilion, and the award was made.[2] With an increasingly inflated market during the 1980s and the prize reinstated, the United States got serious again for the 1988 Biennale, when clearly it was thought that Johns was a good prospect to take the prize.

Early in 1988, just in time for the Biennale, it was announced that the U.S. government planned to establish a new funding agency to assist American artists invited to perform and exhibit outside the country. The Fund for United States Artists at International Festivals and Exhibitions was a partnership between the National Endowment for the Arts, the United States Information Agency, and the Rockefeller Foundation. A contribution of two hundred thousand dollars was made to the Philadelphia Museum for the Johns show of thirty-three paintings in Venice. The museum had to raise another hundred thousand dollars or more.[3]

At the Biennale, I became one of the 250 to 300 people, at least double the number originally invited, who were ferried to Torcello by three large speedboats and about twenty water taxis for an evening of gawking at a famous mosaic in the Cathedral of Santa Maria Assunta and a late dinner at a restaurant close to the cathedral called the Locanda Cipriani. Additional art crowds had been contributing to the congested tourist-mad streets and vaporettos of Venice, come to see Johns take Europe by storm. "Jasper Johns's presence seemed to inspire half the New York art world to make a pilgrimage to Venice to honor him," wrote Michael Brenson in the New York Times.[4] Mark Rosenthal and Anne d'Harnoncourt, director of the Philadelphia Museum, were working on the restaurant seating on the speedboat going over to Torcello, trying to accommodate the huge number of extra guests, including a German party of ten led by one Princess Thun und Tuxis that crashed the party. The princess also crashed my incipient encounter with Johns before dinner. I had just bumped into him, we were having eye contact, and I was about to smile and open my mouth to say something when his attention was diverted by a small blond woman being introduced to him as princess somebody or other. Later, the princess plunked herself down next to Johns at his table.

At least a thousand people jammed the premises of the Peggy

Guggenheim Collection on June twenty-third for a party thrown by the United States embassy, and hosted by the American ambassador to Italy. I spotted Johns, who was staying at the Gritti Palace, one of the big, smart, old hotels on the canal, being discharged from his water taxi onto the Guggenheim's broad stone terrace. Later I saw him speeding away again, after meeting more princesses no doubt, standing up by the helm like a figurehead and roaring off in the direction of the Doges' Palace to claim, one could imagine, the spoils of the city.

The artist left Venice before knowing the grand prize was his. He would hear the news over the radio while riding in a taxi hundreds of miles away, in Basel, Switzerland. Rosenthal said there had been a "hullaballo" over the award. It was thought that "giving the prize to an acknowledged master . . . one of the most celebrated artists alive . . . was too safe a choice for an exhibition that is supposed to highlight new art."[5] But the Johns exhibition was "new art" to Europeans, who knew him essentially by the early flags and targets that established his reputation in the 1950s. *Work since 1974* was surprisingly European, compared to Johns's paintings before then. Americans were honoring him, Michael Brenson noted, just "at the point where his work implicitly challenges the orientation that made him an American hero." He had gone "deep into European art and culture, developing the kind of large themes, such as the cycles of life or the ages of man that Pop Art was supposed to have helped to excise from American art." In Brenson's estimation, it's "the blend of European and American art that has enabled Johns to evolve to a degree that no other Pop artist has . . . the greatest American artist since Jackson Pollock."[6]

He had certainly evolved into the richest American artist. The Biennale took him to a new level. The grand prize at the show is held to be tremendously important in the marketing of an artist.

It is said that nothing could have given Rauschenberg's career a faster boost than winning it in 1964. Five months after the 1988 Biennale, Johns's *White Flag* (1955) sold at Christie's for more than seven million dollars, becoming the costliest painting by a living artist. One day later his *False Start* (1959) was sold at Sotheby's for seventeen million dollars, setting an auction record for all contemporary art. What did Johns think of the prize at Venice? Asked by Rosenthal if he cared whether he would win or not he looked pensive before replying, "Well, it's better to win than not win"—punctuating his conclusion with one of his uproarious laughs.[7]

As I prepared to board an Alitalia flight for London, I encountered Johns in line for a flight to Brussels. He said he'd only seen me from afar at the Biennale. He looked glum and lifeless, withdrawn and vulnerable. Was this his mode for being in transit? Or possibly the result of having been drained, crushed, by the social demands at the pavilion and the parties? Or was it the anxious suspension of leaving without knowing if he won the grand prize or not? His round face, as one writer described, "can lock up like a banker's. The eyes can gleam . . . but even then the mouth droops dourly, and imparts few secrets."[8] Now there was no gleam in his eyes. I told him his show looked great. Had he participated in installing it? I knew he had, but he didn't answer me anyway. Another superfluous question to which I also knew the answer, about whether his canvases came rolled or stretched (they arrived stretched), was left unaddressed as well. But when I went afield and mentioned rocking on the sidewalks (either from the aftermotion of the vaporettos or because all of Venice is a ship afloat), he agreed impassively, saying flatly he had that sensation too.

How lucky to be alive at the same time he [Jasper Johns] is.
— J O H N   C A G E

In October 1989 I went to London to attend an opening at the Anthony d'Offay Gallery commemorating the long friendship and historic collaboration between Johns, John Cage, and Merce Cunningham. Johns was artistic adviser to the Cunningham Dance Company from 1967 to 1978. Cage and Cunningham had been artistic collaborators since 1943. Johns was represented at the d'Offay by paintings from the 1970s and 1980s relevant to his involvement with the composer and choreographer, including the ravishing large ink on plastic *Perilous Night* of 1982, a companion to the monumental encaustic on canvas *Perilous Night* of the same year. The big ink drawing in the show makes Cage's name, title page, and score sheet from his composition *The Perilous Night* much more obvious. Included also were three oils and one drawing all titled *Dancers on a Plane*. One of the oils, dated 1980–81, a gift to Cunningham, displays the choreographer's name in stenciled letters along the bottom of the canvas, alternating with the letters of the painting's title. Cunningham was represented in the exhibition with a roomful of dance videos. Another room was devoted to a selection of Cage's framed scores. A large sit-down place-name dinner was staged at the Victoria and Albert Museum to celebrate the gallery opening. And the following night Cunningham's company opened a two-week season at the Saddlers Welles Theater.

Another opportunity for an inconsequential exchange with Jasper presented itself at a luncheon that took place in a small room adjoining the d'Offay gallery. This occurred because we both wanted to sit at the table with Teeny Duchamp, a mutual friend, who had arrived with her daughter Jackie Matisse. Born Alexina Sattler in 1906 in Ohio, she was first married to Henri

Matisse's son Pierre, with whom she had her three children, and then to Marcel Duchamp, whose widow she became. Teeny, as she was known to friends, was the doyenne of these survivor gatherings of the old avant-garde, whose god was Duchamp. When she appeared just inside the doorway of the luncheon room leaning on her cane, I urged her into a chair at the round table closest to her and then sat down to her right, in all probability taking the seat John Cage, who had been hovering nearby, wanted or should have had.

Since Duchamp's death in 1968, Cage had filled in for him, visiting Teeny frequently in France, playing chess with her using the set she and Marcel had used, enjoying her support at his concerts abroad as well as in New York on her stopovers. The moment Teeny and I sat down, Jasper took up a position on her left and John Cage flanked me on my right. Jackie and the English critic and curator David Sylvester completed the table. We paired off in the obvious way, once Jasper and Teeny claimed each other. I was left with Cage, Jackie with Sylvester. Cage and I had both lectured on Jasper a year before at the Philadelphia Museum on the occasion of Jasper's *Work since 1974* opening there. Our lectures had been as much alike as a Buddhist chant and a cartographer's guide. Cage's lecture—which he was about to deliver again after lunch—was a very long poem of sorts, which he had made by submitting a number of Jasper's artistic pronouncements to random reorganization by computer, resulting in a complex construction of repeated fragments of Jasper's statements. Because of the fragmentation, *other* statements were produced, a method joining the composer as cocreator with the author. He had used this method over the years, famously uniting himself with such dead heroes as James Joyce and Henry Thoreau. My own "cartographer's guide" in Philadelphia, no less an exercise in its way than Cage's in claiming the artist, who had not been present, was a recounting of my effort, illustrated with slides, to identify the Grünewald St. Anthony victim.

Cage seemed happy in London, in company with Teeny and her daughter and the man of whom he once said, "How lucky to be alive the same time he is"[9] and whose painting he once described as being "applied so sensually that there is the danger of falling in love."[10] He and Jasper had known each other since 1954, when they were introduced by Rauschenberg. Cage was nostalgic for the old days when he and Merce saw a great deal of the two younger artists. In 1988 Jasper told an interviewer, "There was a period in my life where . . . Merce, John and Bob Rauschenberg and I were very close. And we all were together very often. . . . As time has gone on, we're not close in the way that we were and everybody has obligations to areas of society that don't overlap with the other people. It's very odd what's happened. So that I'm not sure that I know what the proper connections are between what we're all doing now."[11]

Cage once made a special trip to Baltimore to spend an afternoon looking at Jasper's big encaustic *Perilous Night,* owned by longtime Johns collectors Robert and Jane Meyerhoff. Earlier that year of 1989, while having dinner at the loft he shared with Cunningham on Eighteenth Street in Manhattan, Cage told me he wished Jasper would give him a *Perilous Night.* I said I myself would die to have the ink-on-plastic *Perilous Night* (the one in the London show). On a later occasion I proposed being instrumental in obtaining one for him. I was aware that Jasper had made a special *Perilous Night* drawing for a woman he barely knew, who was noted for playing Cage's and other alternative music.[12] Cage exclaimed, "Really?" I said, "Yes, very indirectly."

"You mean you could say something in passing . . . it's strange John doesn't have a *Perilous Night,* like that?"

"Yes, but I thought also of dropping it in an article."

"Oh no," he concluded, "then people would know I didn't have one."[13]

Another time he told me he thought of Merce's *Dancers on a Plane* as his too. Someone had called, wanting to borrow the painting, and Cage said no and didn't tell Merce!

Our lunch in London went swimmingly, so far as I was concerned, as long as I was paired off with Cage, confabbing in the art-world style—you amuse me, I'll amuse you—about nothing. I had just been in Florence engorging Renaissance masterworks. He had just been at Arcosanti in Arizona, one of five "minds" invited there to speak on various panels.[14] He commented that he had never seen the culture of Florence, he only went there to perform. I said, "Well, you're a mind, not a man of culture," making us laugh foolishly. When the six of us at the table looked up, sensing that the moment for a group exchange was at hand, I asked Jasper if it had been a while since he'd been in England, making just the wrong kind of small talk. "Yes, some time," he replied coldly. How did he like it? "It's a nice place to be with friends," he enjoined, gesticulating expansively with open arms to right and left toward his lunch partners Teeny and David Sylvester. A gentlemanly gesture, making Jackie smile appreciatively.

I tried the insider thing. John had different food from the rest of us, a macrobiotic soup and salad. I joked, "He has to be different." Jasper corrected me, in all seriousness, *"Is* different." Toward the end, in one more round of the group dance, Jasper became suddenly flushed and very animated, turned on by my remarks about art restoration. I had been saying I hated the restorations I saw in Florence. He described a Cézanne restoration—he had just been to a Cézanne show in Basel—where a picture had been cut into three parts and "restored" by being put back together. I said *that* was all right. He began laughing, "Oh, you approve of this kind" (gesturing with his hands touching side by side), "but not this" (one hand on top of the other). I said yes, you might say that. His face had lit up, a lantern switched on inside his normal death mask, very pleased it seemed with the opportunity to make this creative distinction with his hands and perhaps to convey an implied sexual innuendo.

Roused in turn, apparently by this exchange, Sylvester put the topping on our puffcake ensemble, launching into florid vapors over a Masaccio fresco in Florence in which restoration had revealed "the most wonderful cock." I muttered that I would make sure not to look for it or something like that and Sylvester persisted ardently, in some kind of ecstasy. I had to imagine a woman at the table going ballistic over a restoration revealing "the most wonderful cunt." She'd be dead before the words left her mouth.

III.

The Queen would be totally unamused by Johns's paintings.
Prince Charles, on the other hand, would understand.
— RICHARD GENOCHIO

One year later, November 1990, there I was in London again for another opening at the d'Offay gallery, but this time also a very big opening at the Hayward Gallery of the Johns drawing retrospective that had first opened at the National Gallery in Washington, D.C. Now more practiced in the art of alienated behavior required for meeting artists of long personal acquaintance, even friendship, in public settings where the object is lionization, I made no move at the d'Offay, as I had before, to advance on my quarry, or to provoke a mutual greeting. I stole glances in his direction and kept a steady disinterested look.

Then when he swept by within feet of me to talk to some princess or collector or someone, I reached over and deposited a pin in his jacket pocket. It was an image of the Mona Lisa designed in puzzle pieces I had just bought at the Musée d'Orsay in Paris. As he looked down at his trespassed pocket, then up at me, I brandished a rueful, one might even say heroic, smile.

At the Hayward that evening for the retrospective drawing show hung by David Sylvester, I was studying the gorgeous series of large ink-on-plastic drawings, all featuring the Grünewald St. Anthony victim upside down on the lefthand panels, still of course identifiable only to a privileged few. Turning around, I happened to glance upward at the people on the second-tier ramp and caught Jasper gazing down at me—a squinty-eyed dragon-faced Chinese man in an old spy movie staking me out, I thought fleetingly. With eye contact, we executed a perfect stand-off—no recognition on either side.

I had begun to suspect Jasper was the coolest guy in the world, that he had a highly evolved sophisticated plan for meeting people in public, or even in private. I imagined he had the details all figured out beforehand, knowing just how close or distant he intended to get, what he would say or not say, when to let go and laugh, when to withdraw and look forbidding, and so on. It couldn't be exactly a spontaneous life. The evidence all around in fact indicates a life led at one end of the spectrum of control—both controlled and controlling to an immoderate degree. His chief strategy for such exsanguinating restraint would lie in his enormous passivity. He would always be lurking in wait, never make an initial move. He needs to size things up, calculate his position, then strike, or remain coiled, ever the great observer.

In his "Sketchbook Notes" of the 1960s Johns describes the "Spy" who "must be ready to 'move,' must be aware of his entrances and exits . . . must remember and must remember himself and his remembering." He "designs himself to be overlooked." His other character is the "Watchman," who "falls 'into' the trap of looking."[15] That was what I was doing while he "spied" on me from the second-tier ramp. When I looked up and caught his gaze and he didn't alter his stance to perform any recognition or humanize our positions, having "[designed] himself to be overlooked," any countermove had to be mine. As an old friend of Johns's dating from the 1950s has put it, "When you're with Jasper the ball is always in *your* court."

At the sit-down dinner afterward at Simpson's restaurant, to which a couple of hundred guests had been bussed, I tried to pay no attention to the artist, sitting in easy eyesight a table away. I had been assigned to an all-Texaco table. A man at my table asked, "Whose wife are you?" Texaco was the sponsor of the exhibition and the underwriter of the dinner. The man on my left, one Richard Genochio, claimed responsibility for the Texaco sponsorship, costing, he said, between twenty and thirty thousand pounds. Ford Motor Company, which paid for the Washington, D.C., show at the National Gallery, came in to pay touring costs. Genochio said he saw Johns's works in a catalogue and the "wit, humor, color, design and style" in it made him think this was something Texaco would like to be involved with. Texaco, he said, is not a newcomer to the sponsorship of the arts, but the Johns drawing show represented their first major sponsorship in the visual arts. As a subsidiary of U.S. Texaco, they would like to bring to Great Britain works of art "which reflect the American creative spirit at its best." He said he had not heard of Jasper Johns before this, and being shown the works was a revelation—"a great American artist who could talk directly in a lively style to all sorts of people." He was "far more interested in his artistic merit than in his market value." He had heard this evening of some "amazing figures." But "Texaco would be as interested in sponsoring an unknown who had very little market value provided he had something to say which was relevant to people we are also trying to address." Genochio became expansive: "I draw, I have always been interested in art."

He wanted to tell me about The Inner Life of an Oil Executive. "Ninety-nine percent of the human race is boring. . . . I find things outside myself interesting . . . challenging. . . . If I'm left to myself I get very bored. What I like most of all is running businesses. . . . I'm sort of a zombie . . . I have no inner life. . . . I paint social commentary: basketball players, vacant-looking people or politicians. I paint when I feel like it. I could be just as good as [Johns] but I'm not. I don't have the application." He was happy to honor someone who did. He thought the artist "would naturally regard this sort of environment as some kind of joke. . . . He puts these scrawls on pieces of paper and all these well-fed gentlemen come to lionize him. . . . He's thinking this whole thing is a farce." He noted that the artist wasn't wearing a tie. Genochio said he wouldn't dream of going to a thing like this without a tie. A man being honored at such a dinner without a tie must be extremely special. He took the high-minded view of the artist's role in society: "Artists interpret for people things they can't readily understand. Artists are filters, they have binoculars, they show us things and once we see them we know them to be true." Otherwise, I thought, why would Texaco be paying for all this?

I also thought it would be nice for the artist to have the queen see his show. Her profile is featured, after all, in a number of his works of the 1980s including the *Seasons,* many of them on view at the Hayward. Facing the profile of her consort, Prince Philip, she belongs, with him, to part of the trick double image of his Rubins cups. Of both Irish and English ancestry, Johns's ultimate "somewhere else" could be Britain, should he be welcomed "home" by the royal couple who appear to symbolize for him some ideal parentage. Profile likenesses of the couple were formed in the negative space of a porcelain vase manufactured in Germany in 1977 for the silver jubilee of the queen. This was the first three-dimensional example of the Rubins cup optical phenomenon he had seen.[16] Only knowledge of Johns's previous interest in and use of such cups or of the coronation vase would reliably make viewers look here for the "hidden" profiles.

One drawing in the show however, *A Souvenir for Andrew Monk* (1987), makes the royal couple singularly visible. They appear in high relief in the space with a life-size tracing of Andrew Monk, the same child traced by Johns for *Spring,* but here with his head turned in profile to align with the queen and prince. In this *Souvenir* Johns has the boy take the place he occupies in *Spring.* Appearing off to the right of the child's head, drawn larger than usual on a sheet of paper "nailed" to the picture, the profiles here, more fully defined and standing out in white, are meant evidently to be seen as prominently as the vase whose negative space they inhabit. The substitution of boy for man (the two figures already identified in *Spring*), his "wall" adorned by pin-up paragon (unknowable) parents, makes sense for an artist who grew up not intimate with any, or not being raised by the pair he knew was his.

Mr. Genochio, my Simpson's restaurant table companion, assured me the queen would be totally unamused by Johns's paintings. Prince Charles on the other hand would understand. Another Texaco man explained, "He likes things that are genuine, and this is a very genuine and painterly exhibition."

THE DIOSCURI

I.

Is there a worse shame to carry than to be failed
as a man or woman?
—SUSAN GRIFFIN

If Johns's *Perilous Night* documents appearances following a death, its corollary subject is a pair of men, the fallen soldiers taken from Grünewald's Resurrection panel, who carry the emotion suggested by the title and receive "ministrations" from amputated limbs—the forearm-and-hand casts hanging from the top edge of the canvas. The casts were made from the arm of a friend's son, done at three-year intervals, thus increasing in size as he grew.[1] The smallest arm, hanging in a dark space of its own to the left of the other two, points downward at the "nailed" handkerchief. Johns claims the middle-sized arm as his, in the sense that it hangs over a crosshatch "picture" representing his work. The largest arm, to the far right, he identifies with John Cage, by placing it to cross and partially obscure the score sheet from Cage's *The Perilous Night*—the fingertips practically touching the letters "John C" as well as the top edge of the "picture" inset of the Grünewald soldier tracings.[2] The forefinger of Cage's hand is also contiguous with the top part of a vertical inwardly slanting shadow cast from the attached stick that runs the length of the right edge of the painting and marvelously echoes in shape and length the sword of the foreground soldier tracings.

The "camouflage" pattern of the cast arms—resulting from colored materials applied to the inside of the arm molds—which "sign" two traced figures literally camouflaged by paint treatment, can communicate a sense of something hidden there. The concealed Grünewald victim similarly conveys the clue that something is being concealed by such a design. No casual viewer will pick out the soldiers in *Perilous Night,* but once they're perceived, the ostensible subject of the painting appears to be two (male) artists at work. The instruments of work (arms and hands), the examples of work (painting and score sheet), and the names of the workers (John C. and J. Johns) are the identifiable icons and words in the painting, apart from the handkerchief "nailed" to the wood siding. The theme of artists at work is made clear in the ink-on-plastic companion piece to *Perilous Night* with the same title, by the tiny "logo" of three stick figures in the lower right margin, all apparently holding brushes.

But why are the artists, the composer and painter, embedded in a work so gloomy, tenebrous, full of foreboding? Associated with "a sense of something terrible occurring," as Mark Rosenthal reads the whole left side of the diptych, a "mysterious Baroque darkness [in which] the image [of soldiers] is virtually unfathomable." Rosenthal sees the right side of the painting portraying the aftermath of whatever has happened on the left, which he feels "the viewer sorely wants to learn the nature of . . . for this is the only available source for what has resulted on the right half."[3] Of course there's an "available source" on the right, with the soldiers repeated in cameo, but Johns has laid them out in dramatic outsized exposition on the left, like a movie sequence showing a close-up of stunned, terrified protagonists, who then recede in a subsequent frame as they are surrounded by grieving or compassionate relatives. On the right side of his diptych Johns makes his case for identification: two artists, their arms, instruments of work, severed from their bodies—a drastic dematerialization, as if their work is all that is worth mentioning about them, or that they don't exist otherwise; their works touching, flush along one side, as close as the two soldiers literally under their fingertips. The hands of the artist and composer reach down for the Grünewald, the past, to a time of unbridled self-expression, which Johns has seized and amplified, yet submerged in a state more mysterious than the graves of unknown soldiers. By extracting the pair from Grünewald's Resurrection scene, Johns shifts the meaning of the relationship of the two soldiers. Where one is seen as simply falling over the other in Grünewald's picture, the same one can now be understood in Johns's appropriation as gently attending the plight of the other. Out of context they become sympathetic cronies. Here are the missing bodies (still missing so far as the general viewing public is concerned): Johns and Cage—two artist soldiers, two men in common struggle, overcome by emotion.

Struggle and emotion—hardly conditions generally associated with John Cage, one of the great transcendent artists of the late twentieth century. But there was a time when Cage made work invested with feeling. To understand Johns's *Perilous Night* is to know its source in Cage's *The Perilous Night,* a 1943–44 suite of six pieces written for prepared piano. By 1940 Cage had transformed the grand piano into an instrument calling for a performer to bypass the keys and utilize the strings directly, reaching inside to manipulate various objects that act as mutes, inserted beforehand between the strings. *The Perilous Night* specifies a piano heavily muted with materials ranging from standard bolts, nuts, and weather stripping to bamboo slivers.[4] Described as "one of his most personal and expressive statements,"[5] the piece was said by Cage to be concerned with "the loneliness and terror that comes to one when love becomes unhappy."[6]

Cage was referring to a personal crisis in his life. He had been married to Xenia Andreevna Kashevaroff, the Alaskan daughter of a Russian Orthodox priest, since 1935, when he was twenty-three. In 1942 the couple moved from the West Coast to New York City, where their relationship disintegrated over Cage's interest in Merce Cunningham. He had known Cunningham since 1938 when they met in Seattle at the Cornish School, where Cage had been a composer-accompanist for modern dance classes and Cunningham a nineteen-year-old student. A year later Cunningham moved to New York, having been invited by Martha Graham to join her company. In 1942, the year Cage moved to New York, he wrote a prescient piece called *Credo in Us* to accompany a dance by Cunningham, which marked the beginning of their lifelong collaboration. In the meantime Cage was still married and living with Xenia; in 1943 he and Xenia, along with Cunningham, performed at the Museum of Modern Art in a much-publicized concert that included the first performance of *Amores*. In this suite of four pieces, reported Calvin Tomkins, Cage "had tried to express his belief that even in wartime, beauty remains in intimate situations between individuals," presumably a reference to Xenia, but perhaps also to Cunningham.[7] *The Perilous Night,* a sequel, "tells a story of the dangers of the erotic life and describes the misery of 'something that was together that is split apart.' "[8] Cage was evidently thinking of a bed, which he transposed to "night," since he said he got his title from an Irish folktale concerning a perilous bed that rested on a floor of polished jasper.[9] He has referred to that time "as a particularly dark period in my life."[10] This is the period, reflected in *The Perilous Night,* that Johns recaptured and updated in his 1982 painting after the Cage title, reinstating a moment as expressive in its way as the Grünewald he also exhumed, doubling his sources.

After composing *The Perilous Night* Cage wrote *Four Walls,* which he said "deals with the disturbed mind."[11] He was disturbed just then by more than his dissolving marriage. One critic, writing that the last movement of *The Perilous Night* sounded like "a woodpecker in a church belfry," prompted the composer to say, "I had poured a great deal of emotion into the piece, and obviously I wasn't communicating this at all. Or else, I thought, if I *were* communicating, then all artists must be speaking a different language, thus speaking only for themselves."[12]

More than the obtuseness of a critic that gave him the feeling he must be "speaking a different language," the emotion he poured into his piece over the love that went wrong was complicated by his new relationship with a man. By his marriage to a woman in 1935 he had insulated himself from homosexual alliances, which had been a source of increasing distress to him in his late teens and early twenties. Revealing this side of his life for the first time during 1992, his eightieth and last year, Cage told Thomas Hines that by the age of twenty, when he was living in Los Angeles with Don Sample and having affairs with other men on the side, he "began to have doubts about his sexually chaotic life" and to "conclude, in fact, that 'the whole thing was impossible.' " Hines says Cage "was still with Don when his relationship with Xenia began," an overlap curiously echoed a decade later when he was still with Xenia as his relationship with Cunningham was beginning. Cage said, "I was very open [with Xenia] . . . I didn't conceal anything so that even though the marriage didn't work any better than it did, there wasn't anyone to blame. She was aware of my past." Hines thought that "as a bisexual married man, Cage may have drawn comfort from the example of his mentor, the composer Henry Cowell, who lived with the same complex dualities."[13]

A most curious friend of Cage and Don Sample in Los Angeles, before Cage married Xenia, was Harry Hay, born—like Cage—in 1912 and destined to become the founder of the Mattachine Society, which gave rise to the modern organized gay movement. The separate courses of Cage and Hay read like diametrically opposed solutions to the same problem. Yet Hay, like Cage, also tried marriage, a normal accommodation at that time and even now to the unspeakable social crime of being gay—a resolve frequently facilitated by one or more visits to a psychiatrist. A doctor consulted by the French writer and homosexual André Gide told him, "Get married. Get married without fear. And you will realize very quickly that everything else doesn't exist, except in your imagination."[14] In the late 1930s, Hay was persuaded by a Jungian therapist, whom he saw once, to stop "discounting heterosexual relationships" and to look for a "boyish girl." He married in 1938. A year earlier, he had had a telling final, surely painful, encounter with Cage, when Cage brought his wife home to his parents' house in Los Angeles and Hay paid a social call. "John would not let me in and would not say why. He spoke to me at the back porch. It was very awkward, and I finally left. I could only guess I looked too—obvious."[15]

Cage also saw a Jungian therapist once, but it was in 1945, at the juncture where his marriage was ending and he was taking up with a man again. He told David Revill, "I was disturbed . . . some friends advised me to see an analyst,"[16] without revealing the nature of his disturbance. Telling the story in 1949 or 1950, (printed later in his first book, *Silence*) with even more reason then not to say what was bothering him, he also dissembled over the outcome of his visit, turning it into an amusement. "I was never psychoanalyzed. I'll tell you how it happened. . . . When I went to the analyst for a kind of preliminary meeting, he said, 'I'll be able to fix you so that you'll write much more music than you do now.' I said, 'Good heavens! I already write too much, it seems to me.' That promise of his put me off."[17] Evidently the analyst assumed that his client's emotional interest in men was blocking his ability to create. Cage, of course, went on writing "too much" music and separated from Xenia to boot. That same year, 1945, Cunningham left Martha Graham's company and began touring with Cage. By 1950, when Harry Hay founded the Mattachine Society (his marriage—described by him as "living in an exile world"—ending one year later), Cage was well on his way to engineering a cover-up, surely never imagined or articulated by himself as such, for his new unmentionable life.

Where Harry Hay went political, having previously been a card-carrying Communist, Cage took up religion, which he wedded to his art. He felt saved apparently by his introduction to Indian music and to the ideas and tradition behind it. Following his failed visit to the Jungian analyst, he says, "And then in the nick of time, Gita Sarabhai came from India."[18] Through Sarabhai he learned that "the purpose of music is to sober and quiet the mind, thus making it susceptible to divine influences."[19] Already inclined to the impersonal and ascetic in his music, and recently disappointed by a critic's dismissal of The Perilous Night as sounding like "a woodpecker in a church belfry," Cage moved unerringly in the late 1940s toward a new kind of composition through which he could give up "communication" and promote his disappearance.

Besides Sarabhai, Cage was deeply influenced by his studies with Zen master Daisetz T. Suzuki at Columbia University. He felt that the teachings of Suzuki "catapulted him into conceptual and emotional adulthood." Eastern thought "performed for me the function that psychoanalysis might have performed."[20] His youthful passions and conflicts had caused him much angst. Through his new teachings he learned he could ignore the self or leave it behind and develop a philosophy of transcendence and the coded acceptance of difference. His "code" became the elaborate scaffolding of the "chance operation," after he discovered in 1951 that he could apply the methods of the *I Ching,* or Chinese Book of Changes—charts and the tossing of coins to determine outcomes—to organize sounds. Cage's idea was to remove so far as possible his ego, his likes and dislikes, and to let procedures take over every eventuality: the kinds of sounds, tempos, timbres, durations, and so on. Sounds, now redefined as noises, needed no interference on the part of the composer to make them "better," to harmonize and unify them into (higher) entities that obscure their individual natures, their *differences.* Through Cage, the great nature-versus-culture argument central to the Dada movement of the teens and early 1920s was revitalized.

Culture is exclusive, Cage noted. In art or culture, beauty must be constructed and nurtured; in nature, beauty is manifest. Cage said, let's pay attention to nature, to what's around us, acknowledge all the sounds and everything, make it all part of our experience. "Pitch," he observed, "is separated from noise. Sounds are no longer just sounds, but are letters—A,B,C,D,E,F,G," and "if a sound is unfortunate enough not to have a letter . . . it is tossed out of the system on the grounds: it's noise or unmusical."[21] Besides chance operations, Cage's other strategy for "opening the doors of music to the sounds that happen to be in the environment"[22] was the use or practice of silence, which had noticeably punctuated his compositions for some time. His signature work became *4′ 33″,* composed in 1952, which called for a performer to come on stage and to sit at a piano for the specified time of four minutes and thirty-three seconds without engaging in any other activity.

Silence, chance, and finally the politics of anarchy (embraced by Cage also in the fifties) are three powerful responses to aesthetic and governmental practices that are exclusive, prejudicial, hierarchical, denying difference. The traditional artist "takes himself seriously, wishes to be considered great, and he thereby diminishes his love and increases his fear and concern about what people will think."[23] Silence is a form of passive resistance. As a schoolboy Cage discovered "silence in antipathy as a positive thing." He found school interesting but terrifying because he was different. "As a child I was precocious and the other children . . . considered me a sissy, and they made fun of me at every opportunity, so much so that . . . if I read one of my papers I had written they would simply respond by laughing. . . . People would lie in wait for me and beat me up and I never would defend myself because I had gone to Sunday school and they had said to turn the other cheek, which I took seriously."[24]

"Cage's silence . . . opens inevitably onto difference and polyvocality, admitting the discourse of Others" writes Caroline Jones, the only commentator thus far whom I have seen make a case for Cage's inventions as a "homosexual aesthetic"—a muted but potent version of such overt epiphanies or rebellions as Allen Ginsberg's *Howl* of 1956, "with its exuberant homoeroticism and its savage outcry at the repression of Otherness in America."[25] Cage was a role model for that very repression, having sworn himself to silence (the name of his first book!) on the subject of his difference. "My feelings belong, as it were, to me, and I should not impose them on others . . . leaving them where they can function without hurting other people." Sounding much like an exponent of a "don't ask, don't tell" policy, he said, "I try to keep this fact of being myself *for myself,* that is . . . I do not disturb your center, you do not disturb mine."[26] Silence as a key facet of his music can be construed as an exemplary cover, a "speech act" from the closet, the expression of a homosexual who is "empowered to speak, but unable to say"—the contradiction, as Thomas Yingling writes in his book on Hart Crane, within which "gay [artists] have historically hidden, erased, universalized or otherwise invalidated not only their homosexual desire but also the shape (or mis-shape) their lives have taken as a result of the social taboos against it."[27]

Keeping a part of himself—his dedication to a relationship with one man, his most basic preference after all—in reserve, as a kind of privileged difference, Cage railed against the world through theories and practices metonymically signifying his repression by the state: the passive resistance of silence; the fragmentation resulting from chance operations; the belief in the abolition of government through anarchy. But he railed in a religiously calm way, methodically directed, puritanically work-habituated, unshakably optimistic, certain that, as he said, "what is heroic is to accept the situation in which one finds oneself."

Jasper Johns honors Cage's cover-up in his *Perilous Night,* and includes his own, by making the human deputies or representatives of himself and the composer—the two Grünewald soldiers—invisible to the general public. With at least part of the privileged sector, the art world, aware of the identity of the figures, this division between an ignorant public and an art cognoscenti precisely reproduces the partition in knowledge that exists over the hidden sexual identities of members of other professions. The world at large is not aware that one person or another in any particular profession is homosexual unless they come out. Within any profession, the much used phrase "but everyone knows" is understood to mean that nothing (more) need be said about it. What everyone knows about in this compartmentalized sense matters as much as it does in families where members of the stigmatized persuasion are or have been protected if they remain silent and hidden. In Johns's big *Perilous Night* oil, the overt signs of Cage's presence are minimized, crowded into an upper right slot against the edge of the painting, the blurred sheet of music mostly obscured by the hanging forearm-hand cast, his name shortened to "John C," who could be anybody, the title of his work under his name cut off and not easily readable—*"The Perilou."*

In his big ink-on-plastic *Perilous Night* drawing, the sumptuous black and purple masterwork, Johns brings his old friend, mentor, and admirer into the open. Now the single dropped forearm and hand, no longer the cast of another but an imprint of Johns's own, featured alongside the Cage score sheet and title page (his name and title fully printed out) on the right side of the diptych, make an intended identity of the two men with the (invisible) soldier tracings consuming the left side clearer. Here it's just the two of them—no accessories or extras—writ large, and we can read Johns's arm as his and as representative of his work through reference to the big *Perilous Night* oil, where the middle arm cast is laid down over a "picture" of his crosshatch work. The ink-on-plastic work is oceanic and dark in feeling, loose or licentious through the medium of running ink, creating great accidents including the "secondary image" (for example, a blotted face appears unmistakably within the Cage title sheet). Emotions suggested by the title are fully blazoned forth.

"Emotion," Cage said repeatedly, "is something to be suppressed, something that removes one from art." "Love," he explains, "makes us blind to seeing and hearing." He was "entirely opposed to the emotions."[28] His emotions of course were what he demoted and discarded as time went on after the disappointment of his marriage, the critical reception of *The Perilous Night,* and his new, necessarily secret, love for a man. His denial of the latter for his art is emphatic in a statement he made to Thomas Hines in 1992. Hines said Cage "acknowledged the growing contemporary interest in 'gay composers,' such as Franz Schubert, a reassessment, he averred, 'which takes the relationship between art and sex seriously. I do not. Once I am doing something 'serious' I don't think about sex." The equation of gayness and sex that Cage expresses here reveals his pre–Stonewall understanding of gay identity: limited only to sex.

Sex per se is hardly what Johns seems to have had in mind by exhuming a title by the composer so explicitly connected with his emotional past, predating the inventions and aesthetic by which we know him. Or even by tracing and painting two (armored) men in an intimate, one could say compromised, choreography. Yet in another painting featuring the two soldiers, an untitled painting of 1984, Johns did sexualize them. A pointed piece of hardware in Grünewald's picture, attached to a sword or pike between the soldiers, sticks straight up from the groin area of the foreground figure. Johns further phallicized this item in his tracing for *Untitled* 1984, enlarging the tip such that it can be read easily as the soldier's erect member. But here he has obscured the helmet of the second warrior falling over him by the "taped" picture of an image he made in the 1970s—the lithograph *Face* from *Casts from Untitled* 1973–74. It is a very murky rendition of an originally murky image and no one would know this is a face without being able to read the mirrored and flopped stenciled letters "FACE" in the image's lower right corner.[29] If Johns has compounded the difficulty of imagining the secondary soldier— his helmeted head replaced by an obscure image of a face— poised to give his companion head, he has also inserted himself, by way of an old work known to be his, into a sexualized scene.

But if he had fellatio in mind two years earlier when he painted *Perilous Night,* he didn't try to concretize it by tracing Grünewald's spiked tool. Taken literally, the soldiers in *Perilous Night* are shown simply in a compassionate entente, which we can link with a traumatic moment in the history of a homosexual composer when decisions were made dividing him from his authentic feelings.

Johns could identify with such a history, his own version of it transpiring a decade after Cage's agon, devolution, and denouement, when he knew Cage as a close friend and supporter and Cage's influence over the course of art was beginning to be so extraordinary.

II.

I'm not frightened of the affection that Jasper and I had, both personally and as working artists. I don't see any sin or conflict in those days when each of us was the most important person in the other's life.
—ROBERT RAUSCHENBERG

It was the effigy of the Individual Ego that Cage burned in his meteoric rise to avant-garde heaven.
—CAROLINE JONES

Johns's defense is withdrawal, a remarkable degree of public silence.
—ROBERT HUGHES

In 1954 Johns had lived in New York for two years. He had been in New York earlier, in 1949, after attending the University of South Carolina in Columbia for three semesters, working then as a messenger boy and shipping clerk, enrolling in a commercial art school that he attended for two semesters before leaving the city when drafted into the U.S. army. He was stationed at Fort Jackson, South Carolina (just outside Columbia), for one year, then posted in Sendai, Japan, for his last six months of service. In Japan he made posters that advertised movies and told soldiers how not to get VD. He also painted a Jewish chapel.[30] Back in New York in 1952, he tried school again, registering in the Bronx division of Hunter College on the GI bill, this time quitting after a single day. "The first day," he said, "I had a class in Beowulf, then a French class in which I couldn't understand a word and then an art class in which a handsome redhaired lady in a hat told me I drew a 'marvelous line.' Near home I passed out in the street. I was rescued and stayed in bed for a week and that ended my career in higher education."[31]

He moved to East Eighth Street and Avenue C, painting in his spare time while working as a clerk in the Marlboro Book Store on Fifty-seventh Street. One winter evening in 1954 Johns was introduced to Robert Rauschenberg on a street corner by Suzi Gablik, a young artist and fledgling critic, one of the few people he knew in New York.[32] Through Rauschenberg, Johns was introduced to a world of artists and composers, including Cage, Cunningham, Richard Lippold, Lou Harrison, Morton Feldman, Paul Taylor, and Cy Twombly. It would also include Rachel Rosenthal, who would play a kind of Xenia role to Johns during Rauschenberg's courtship of him. Rosenthal was a student of dance, drama, and painting who had become part of the social group around Cunningham, Cage, and Rauschenberg. She and her parents, French-Jewish refugees from World War II, had settled in New York in 1941.

She remembers Rauschenberg collecting Johns every evening after he finished work at the bookstore. Then at a party at artist Sari Diene's studio on Fifty-seventh Street near Sixth Avenue early in 1954, Johns, whom she knew only a little but enough to know he was gay, "kind of threw himself on me and started to kiss me with great passion."[33]

It was the beginning of a brief affair. Her understanding was that he "was trying to avoid a relationship with Bob, not that he wasn't attracted to Bob, but probably because of the stigma, and the fact that in those days it was a real problem." For her part, she fell "hopelessly in love" with him, as she once told Calvin Tomkins.[34] Johns was twenty-four at the time, quiet and withdrawn, and immensely attractive to both Rachel and Rauschenberg. Rauschenberg told Tomkins, "I have photos of him then that would break your heart. Jasper was soft, beautiful, lean, and

poetic. He looked almost ill."[35] Rachel describes him in hyper-
boles: "so beautiful, you have no idea. . . . He had almost silver
hair, golden silver, very very light hair . . . closely cut, like a brush
crewcut. He had these immense blue eyes, and his face was very
very pale, and he had the complexion of moonstone, almost like
light coming out of his face. He was just astonishing . . . very
thin . . . just a gorgeous young man, just a beautiful young man,
and I thought maybe, maybe [despite his being gay], who
knows."

Rachel was a young woman of means, brought up, she said,
"in an atmosphere of tremendous luxury." Her father, an im-
porter of pearls and precious stones in France between the wars,
lost everything when he left, but was able to rebuild his fortune
in America.[36] She bought a lot of Rauschenberg's work, which
especially enthralled her. She got her parents to help Johns out
(her father gave him one of his winter overcoats, her mother
bought a couple of his little paintings) and she acquired things
herself. He had made a painting in the shape of a cross and placed
it inside a box covered with glass—one of the works that Rachel
loved and that he destroyed in 1954. She told him if he made a
Jewish star of David, she would buy it. Johns made one, she
bought it, and it became one of his few pre-*Flag* pieces that survived.[37] Another that survived, evidently only for the reason that
he gave it to Rachel or she bought it (she can't remember which),
was *Untitled* 1954, a collage of printed matter in a box, with a
cast of Rachel's face under the shelf upon which the bottom edge
of the collage rests.[38] More than twice as tall as Rachel's cast face,
the collage in the top part of the box makes it roughly resemble
one of those ancient Egyptian high headdresses, an image Johns
conceivably had in mind.

Rachel found the "torture" of having her face cast in Johns's
tiny room on East Eighty-third Street—lying on his bed waiting for the plaster to set, bits of the plaster stuck in her eyes—an

"erotic experience." What changed things, and ended their affair, was a move they both made to lofts on Pearl Street. Rauschenberg had been urging Johns to get a loft to help him think of himself more seriously as an artist. Johns teamed up with Rachel, who had been living at her parents' Central Park South duplex, to look for something. They both found a "perfect," condemned building on Pearl Street in lower Manhattan, where she took the top floor and Johns the floor below. Around the corner on Fulton Street was Rauschenberg's fifteen-dollar-a-month walk-up loft, which had no running water. Johns's Pearl Street loft had pressed tin ceilings so low they could be touched, old floorboards with gaping half-inch spaces between them through which the floor below was visible, a bed on a platform, a refrigerator, hot plate, shower, and toilet. Rachel installed a hot water heater and bathtub in her place, which everyone used.

When they moved in, Rachel made the mistake of telling Jasper she was in love with him, and *that* ended their relationship. This had the effect of throwing Johns and Rauschenberg more decidedly together. Rachel then "grieved and mourned" and was "totally depressed" for months. She had someone to commiserate with in Cy Twombly, who had been intimate with Rauschenberg since 1951 and was now, having lost Rauschenberg to Johns, a dumpee like Rachel. When Rachel's father died in the summer of 1955, she found an excuse to leave, moving to California, where her mother lived after her father's death. Rauschenberg then took over her Pearl Street loft. It was here, less than two years later, in March 1957, that he turned into a fateful medium of Johns's discovery by Castelli.

Rauschenberg's role in making an intimate and professional partner out of Johns in a triangle of two men and a woman— the woman acting as sacrificial catalyst for the forbidden union of two men—was played out several years earlier by Cy

Twombly for Rauschenberg when Rauschenberg was stuck in a relationship to a woman he had loved and married. He had met Sue Weil, another artist, in 1948 in Paris, where they had both gone to study at the Académie Julian. He was twenty-two, Sue, eighteen. That summer they went to Black Mountain College in North Carolina, the experimental college in the foothills of the Appalachians that hosted a number of well-known innovative artists during its brief existence from 1933 to 1956. Cage and Cunningham had been there in April, appearing in a kind of residency along with Willem and Elaine de Kooning, Richard Lippold, and Buckminster Fuller. In June 1950 Rauschenberg married Weil. A year later, in July 1951, Christopher Rauschenberg was born. A month after that the couple went to Black Mountain with the baby, this time accompanied by Cy Twombly, whom they had both met while studying at the Art Students League in New York. Nineteen fifty-one was a big year for Rauschenberg. He had a son; he had his first gallery show in New York with Betty Parsons; he was included in an exhibition of Abstract Expressionists on East Ninth Street organized by Jack Tworkov and Leo Castelli; he met John Cage, who introduced himself after seeing the Parsons show; and he fell in love with Cy Twombly. Twombly offered escape from the marriage, which, with the baby, had become strained and difficult. He wasn't solvent enough to support a family, he said he was too immature for the responsibility, and he chafed at the conformity of marriage. By June of 1952 the marriage had collapsed and Rauschenberg returned to Black Mountain with Twombly alone.[39] His wife, left holding the baby, experienced the double devastation of losing both enough time to do art and a very stimulating creative partner rich in enthusiasm and ideas. A decade earlier, Merce Cunningham had enacted the Twombly role for John Cage in the dissolution of Cage's marriage, just as

Rauschenberg performed that function for Johns in 1954. Twombly in the end also played a kind of (spurned) girl's part along with Rachel.

The fabulous foursome of Cage, Cunningham, Johns, and Rauschenberg, as they would come to be seen, was consolidated during the mid- to late 1950s in a tightknit group of mutual artistic support: two couples unencumbered by commitments to women and children, working out an aesthetic of personal denial, of emptiness, of opening up to "multiplicities" from both nature and culture. Abrogation of choice or diminution of personal preference functioned as ideology as well as methodology. By the mid-1950s the aesthetic of Cage and Cunningham was set for the duration of their careers. Under Cage's guidance, Cunningham introduced chance operations to dance making, constructing a choreographic area filled with "incidents." This created a kind of all-over look, with no dancer or movement or point in space meant to be more interesting or important than any other, such as had never before been seen in either ballet or modern dance. Just as Cage's notion was to admit all sounds into composition, Cunningham got the "idea that first of all any kind of movement could be dancing."[40] With such limitless possibilities, especially as leveraged by aleatory methods, movement became its own end, meant to signify nothing beyond itself. Deadpan delivery was obviously the appropriate presentation for this new kind of abstract dance. The only emotion ever evinced by Cunningham dancers is the irrepressible pleasure elicited by moving through certain exuberant passages.

Cunningham has described one of his early narrative, affective dances, made the same time as Cage's *The Perilous Night*. *Root of an Unfocus* (1944), with music by Cage, was one of his first solos. He said, " 'Unfocus' here refers to a disturbance in the mind, an imbalance, it's a photographic term which signifies a blur, an unclarity. . . . I was still concerned with expression. It was about fear. The dance was in three parts. The first part gave the impression of someone realizing there's something unknown. The second part shows the dancer struggling with this but it's futile because there's nothing there. In the third part he is defeated by it. The ending was a series of falls and crawling off the stage."[41]

During 1944, when *Root of an Unfocus* was made, Cunningham was part of a fraught triangle along with Cage and Cage's wife Xenia. In the dance, Cunningham is "defeated" by "something *un*known"—an absence that vibrates to that historically unspeakable condition articulated by Lord Alfred Douglas in 1894 as "the love that dare not speak its name." But "defeat," as expressed in "a series of falls and crawling off stage," was not to be brooked for very long by either Cunningham or Cage, both essentially cheerful characters with a zest for both art and life. "Guilt, shame, conscience," Cage noted when alluding to "the things we know about Freud," brought about "the inability eventually to act at all,"[42] and were not, it could be added, feelings he and his partner were predisposed to suffer from.

Johns and Rauschenberg were not so fortunate either in background or temperament, and as artists they were directly engaged in discursive counterpoint with the reigning masculinist Abstract Expressionist aesthetic. Like Cage and Cunningham, Rauschenberg emerged from an intact "nuclear" family, but his father—a lineman for a Gulf States power company in Port Arthur, Texas, and the son of a German immigrant father and a Cherokee mother—wanted him to be other than he was and heaped physical and emotional abuse on him. The fathers of Cage and Cunningham were, by contrast, if not overtly supportive of their sons' interests, quite laissez-faire. Cage admitted that his father disliked a "decidedly nonmasculine 'secret vice' " he had as a child—a favorite hobby of an interest in paper dolls—and tried to discourage him from it. Perhaps that was his father's only lapse. A man "always delighted with whatever situation was at hand," as Cage has described him, optimistic and good humored, he was always on easy terms with his son.[43] Cunningham has said his father "loved very different people" and he didn't care "what profession you followed as long as you really worked at it."[44]

Curiously, or not, all four men were college dropouts. Cage was clearly their senior member, spiritual guide, and intellectual polestar. Of the two younger men, Rauschenberg, by virtue of his age, experience, reputation, and a garrulous outgoing personality, set the tone and led the way. By the time he met the unshown Johns, Rauschenberg had exhibited among other things two series of monumental "empty" paintings—one black, one white—with surfaces of "uninflected neutrality." They were much admired by Cage, who saw them as " 'landing strips' for dust motes, light and shadow" and said they inspired him to write his 1952 silent piece *4′ 33″*.[45] For the black series Rauschenberg laid his paint down on textured relief forms subtly built up on canvas with newspaper, a type of "ground" that Johns would adopt (among other Rauschenberg ways of doing things) beginning with the 1954–55 *Flag*.

While Rauschenberg's painting, especially starting with his postwhite and postblack red works of 1954, often incorporated the painterly gestures, drips, and spatters of the Abstract Expressionists, and he was friendly with and admiring of the artists, he "immediately perceived in this new art an exciting frontier from which to depart."[46] His inclination was to resist every movement, including his own. The great variety of media, materials, and techniques he embraced during the early 1950s, and has continued to employ throughout his career, show a restless, reactive, inventive, and autonomous personality. A special resistance to

Abstract Expressionism was manifest in his famed roguish erasure of a Willem de Kooning drawing. He proposed to de Kooning that de Kooning give him one of his drawings for the purpose of turning it into his own work of art by erasing it. De Kooning agreed, choosing a work he thought would be especially difficult to erase. "After one month and forty erasers spent rubbing out the thick crayon, grease pencil, ink and pencil markings, Rauschenberg produced *Erased de Kooning Drawing,* 1953."[47]

Rauschenberg joined with Cage that same year in a collaboration called *Automobile Tire Print.*[48] After inking the front left tire of Cage's Model A Ford, he directed the composer to drive his car down Fulton Street across twenty sheets of paper assembled end-to-end (a 264-inch roll), leaving the imprint of a single inked tire tread.[49] The Dada, or antiart, display of the de Kooning venture and the Cage collaboration, along with works using such urban detritus or found objects as earth, rocks, fabric, newspaper, rope, wood, nails, and the like, violated the prevailing Abstract Expressionist aesthetic of pure painting (painting as hallowed for itself and as self-discovery) and also other modes of the day, figurative work and hard geometric abstraction. Rauschenberg was a controversial dissident, a meagerly successful artist until his breakthrough in 1963, with the silkscreen series, the year his father died. With this series, the cultural emblems he had been importing into his work for years now took on the look of a national identity. Proud to be an American during the Kennedy years, his images, taken as a whole, fairly scream for flag and country. The "secrets-in-view" (that is, known to "everyone who knows") in Rauschenberg's earlier, densely collaged Combines, made during the years he was with Johns (1954–61), became more deeply coded in the silkscreens. Older images in the Combines include a faded photo of Johns; the full-length photograph of a dandy in a white suit in *Untitled 1955;* and pictures of Judy Garland (beloved by gay men). The even earlier famed series of photographs, *Cy and Roman Steps* (1952), show Twombly descending steps in Rome and bring his crotch into enlarged and "framed" focus.

In keeping with Cage's programmatic egolessness, Rauschenberg frequently disavowed self-involvement in the choices and meanings of his presentations, though hardly in Cage's transcendent Zen style. "I don't want my personality to come out through the pieces. That's why I keep the TV on all the time. . . . And I keep the windows open. I want my paintings to be reflections of life." "When I go to work I have to feel invisible to get away from the inferiority that is attached to Bob." "It's *your* mind that makes [the work] add up to something."[51] "Listen, in the 50s, I already had a problem, it's been documented many times. I said if my work doesn't look more like what's going on outside my window, you know, then I shouldn't be doing it."[52] "I don't think about me that much. I have enough problems just getting through a day."[53] His self-disparagements, rare in writings by or about either Cage or Cunningham, are echoed in Johns's much quoted statement, "In my early work I tried to hide my personality, my psychological state, my emotions. This was partly to do with my feelings about myself and partly to do with feelings about painting at the time."[54]

With their varied pop or public images, from flags and targets and beer cans to coke bottles, eagles, and presidents, Johns and Rauschenberg universalized their subjects, taking cover under icons of the national consensus or of common usage. All problems of personal preference—the basis of difference—could seemingly be nullified. In another arena, Cunningham would accept the conventions of heterosexual partnering so central to dance history, forms that he inflicted on his medium as a *preference*. He would override his contract with chance operations, through which supposedly every manner of movement would find its outlet, and no importance would attach to one kind of movement over another. In partnering, with women cast in traditionally weak and dependent relations to the men (for example, by habitual lifts and supports), Cunningham made a significant exception. Preference in this case was perhaps deemed a social necessity, if not an obeisance to "nature," as prescribed as the way the knees bend. It certainly suggested Cunningham's interest in artistic survival over the long haul. Cage had no such dilemma in his more abstract medium; he happily appealed to the experience of Everyman in his call for awareness of the noises that surround us. Of the four men, the suppression of self seemed most difficult for Rauschenberg, whose work was often irrepressibly autobiographical, and heroic in its size and bids for attention. (Not surprisingly, he fell out with Cage and Cunningham in 1964 while on a world tour with the dance company as lighting, set, and costume designer, when he upstaged the company by winning the Venice Biennale and then found it impossible to keep a low profile.)

Johns, the youngest, most quiet and most reticent, ironically would deal with the closet status common to all four in a manner most intrinsic to the actual issues of identity and of secrecy that constitute the fulcrum of the closet. Neither Johns nor his three friends consciously created a homosexual aesthetic. But their closet status was reflected in the aesthetic they fashioned. Denial of self in Johns's work would become a heuristic enterprise. To his transcendent embrace of the world, manifest in *Flag* and its descendants, in the targets, numbers, alphabets, he would begin to add, by 1956, work of puzzling, subtle, internal contradictions.

What is precious for Johns is whatever doubt he can elicit as to the identity of the thing he creates.

—MAX KOZLOFF

The critic wants at all costs to return this orphan [the child-painting] to its proper owner, as in the return of the law after the commission of a crime.

—JEFF PERRONE

I'm interested in things which suggest the world rather than suggest the personality.

—JASPER JOHNS

Canvas, 1956, and *Book, Drawer,* and *Newspaper* of 1957, all in encaustic grisaille, show a common object that hides or destroys its function and contents. The gift of a book that you can't open is the contradictory essence of *Book*. The open book that constitutes *Book* provides the surface for encaustic gray paint, supplanting canvas and stretcher; though it's in a boxed frame, it also frames itself, both representing its subject and existing as the subject represented. But whereas the first *Flag* reveals its contents—stars and stripes in the prescribed format and national colors—*Book* is like later flags that practically obliterate the flag's design (as in *Flag*, 1957, a pencil on paper drawing, dense and dark with overlaid scribbles), suggesting they could be "any flag," a further universalization of *Flag. Book,* not any particular book but a generic representation, was chosen, Johns once said, because it had the shape he wanted, not because it had any personal significance for him.[55] Opened at the middle, its exposed "pages" are unreadable, impossible to turn. Leo Steinberg called it "a paralyzed book." Roberta Bernstein said, "It provokes our curiosity," becoming an "enigmatic object," and compared it to the hidden canvas of *Canvas* and the permanently closed drawer of *Drawer*. For *Canvas,* the artist placed a small canvas backward, its stretcher visible, against a larger one, and painted both the "receiving" canvas and the attached inner and inverted canvas-*cum*-stretcher with the same grey encaustic.

Drawer, so named for its drawer with two real protruding knobs set into a square field, is likewise painted all over, drawer and "field" in this way appearing synonymous. *Canvas* and *Drawer,* like *Book* and *Newspaper,* frustrate the desire to know their contents, forcing attention to the works as self-sufficient art objects. The "contents" are what you see. The works are confrontational and oxymoronic, presenting objects that hold things that are obliterated, or that the artist would like to have us think of in a new way, as meaningless apart from how they operate in his work. "A drawer," Bernstein wrote, "is a container which holds objects and Johns is identifying its function with that of a painting."[56] The drawer of *Drawer,* being tangibly real, with no "ground," devoid of specificity or contents and having no sense of personal possession by the artist, has no existence apart from the object it helps to form. The painting exclusively references itself. Johns cast a net to incorporate the real image of a drawer, then held it fast in an object demonstrating the concept that a painting can be about nothing but itself.

Book is similarly configured. As Bernstein deconstructed it:

> Although the book's expected function has been ironically altered, it still suggests the idea of reading, now in the context of a work of art. Reading a book or a painting basically involves receiving and interpreting visual information. In a book, we read letters, words and sentences in a linear sequence. In a painting, we "read" the syntax of pictorial elements (brushstrokes, colors, shapes) in a different way . . . depending on the structure or composition the artist devises. By using the book as a subject, Johns is calling attention to the process of visual perception. He specifically contrasts the idea of linear reading with non-linear looking, as he does in his *Alphabets, Numbers* and related works.[57]

Canvas, with its centered "picture" of a canvas, turned to show its innards or backside and painted the same as the canvas surrounding it, poses a "figure" that is defined by its absence and even more directly makes the statement that the painting is only about itself. Early on, Johns made it clear that his subject was painting, or painting about painting, and he would spell it out or elucidate it through retroversions and torques with recognizable images. Though his methods have changed since that time, his ideas and goals remain the same, as he showed in his 1990s objection to the curiosity about the sources of his Grünewald figures: "I thought it was of no particular interest that an [image] was once one thing or another or something else."[58] For those of us interested in what things once were, the Grünewalds provide greater incentives and pay-offs than drawers, newspapers, books, or canvases. *Canvas,* however, can resonate as an "image" standing in for the artist. Leo Steinberg found "a perpetual sense of waiting [in the] canvas face-to-the-wall that waits to be turned."[59] If the critic's job is to turn it around, the image revealed might be what Jonathan Katz saw as a "self portrait."[60] Like Johns himself, *Canvas* had a figurative past, as functional canvas; now it is an abstraction. As an artist, he can magically obliterate both his own and his medium's histories. In life as in art, Johns negotiates his own absence.

For Johns himself between 1954 and 1958, or any time later, there was perhaps no sense whatever of "a perpetual waiting . . . [for something] to be turned." *Flag, Target with Plaster Casts* (1955), *White Flag* (1955), *Green Target* (1955), *Gray Alphabets* (1956), *Gray Numbers* (1958), *Canvas, Book, Drawer,* and *Newspaper* all show great composure. Images are centered, paint is evenly distributed, and a thematic consistency runs strongly through the work, absorbing apparent differences in signs or subject. About his early years, Johns has only said he was hiding. He had "feelings about [him]self" that caused him "to hide . . . [his] psychological state," a concealment of self directly reflected in his work, with its simultaneous exposure and burial or consumption, its translation of common objects into autonomous systems. Secretiveness is a general feature of the human condition. Considered by itself, Johns's early work with prosaic entities bears no evidence of any particular kind of hiding. It universalizes hiding, illustrating the strict separation of private (hidden) and public (open) spheres endemic to civilized life.

Johns's work was an art-for-art's-sake critic's dream. Nothing outside the work should discompose its value for itself. "That the intimate life of the artist was somehow to be identified with the essential content of his art would not have occurred to us," wrote one such critic (in 1980), for whom "such a view," when Johns was young in the 1940s and 1950s, "would have seemed bizarre." He was "struck by the emphasis . . . critics [were giving] to Picasso's private life and by their implications that only biography would yield the true meaning of his work."[61] Of course by 1980 Picasso was dead.

English art historians Fred Orton and Charles Harrison noted in 1984 that it was "hard to resist the impression that a conspiracy of silence has served to limit interpretation of [Johns's] work."[62] In an article outing Johns to some extent, their theme is the nearly exclusive critical attention to formalist values in Johns's work at the expense of a consideration of his subjects.

> [While] Johns's strategy as a Modernist has been to assert the decorative potential of surface, and to establish surface in terms of reflexive relations which go back either to his own art or to the art of others, he has been able to admit . . . and to develop . . . the representation or expression of vivid subject matter [which] has been generally overlooked, or at the least played down . . . because of the . . . plausibility of the kinds of Modernist surface he has been able . . . to produce.[63]

In this and in a later article by Orton alone, the "extra-work" information introduced, both personal and social, is largely about homosexual themes, particularly in relation to Johns's use of the Frank O'Hara title for his 1961 painting *In Memory of My Feelings—Frank O'Hara* (see chap. 4, IV). At stake are issues of identity, the condition of being oneself and not necessarily another or even not anybody at all (face turned to the canvas/wall, don't look at me, look at the work). The subject is posed by Johns all through a pictorial rhetoric of interrogation and problematics using everyday articles, long before he hung his queries on the human figure.

Shifting ground in 1959, Johns's pictures, now mainly in oils rather than encaustics, fairly explode with primary colors and a loose brushstroke resembling the Abstract Expressionist style. The first of the group, *False Start,* was so named, Johns has said, after a horse-racing print he saw in that famed hangout of artists during the 1950s, the Cedar bar. With its "colors . . . set loose and appear[ing] to be celebrating their liberated condition"[64] (prompting the thought that in 1959 Johns had recently become a celebrated young artist, no longer in the shadow of his older peer), its field is studded with stenciled words: the names of the colors that appear in the painting—red, yellow, blue, white, orange, and gray. The color-name words, posited every which way in stencils resembling packing crate labels, are anything but situated on their corresponding color areas. Moreover, most of the words are not themselves represented by the colors they spell out. Orange letters may be white, yellow letters blue, white ones red, blue ones orange and so on. And parts of a number of the words disappear within or behind the painted terrain or off the edge of the canvas, adding to the primary play of ambiguities or contradictions—names of colors stenciled in colors different from their names, and mismatched on the spiky, blotchy, spastically painted field. Another oddity is the singular appearance of the word "green" (in gray letters), a color not in the field. As labels the words will surely lead us astray. Things are not necessarily what they seem, Johns was apparently saying, a sense conveyed by the title, *False Start*. Bought from Leo Castelli in 1960 for $3,150 by taxi mogul Robert Scull, sold to Schlumberger oil heir François de Menil in 1981, this was the painting that made market history in December 1988 when it was acquired at auction by media tycoon Si Newhouse for $17.1 million, setting a record for contemporary art.

Johns painted *Jubilee* after *False Start*, and organized it schematically the same way, but painted it all in black, white, and gray, with tinges of red showing through, like traces of its flamboyantly colored predecessor. Of *False Start* Johns said the interplay of labels and colors "retains the objectness of the painting—I had a need to maintain that quality in the work."[65] *False Start* and its successors, including besides *Jubilee*, *Out the Window*, and *0 Through 9* (a play on superimposed numbers), also from 1959, have been called "Abstract Expressionism in drag" and a "misfiring of emotional authenticity,"[66] a "studied mimicry."[67] This reading is enhanced by the observation that *"False Start* does not seem to *use* color; it is *about* color, a suspicion confirmed by the presence of *Jubilee*, its negative in somber black and white."[68] Johns was at pains to purge subjectivity from his work—that animation of a canvas through personal claim on it—"the action and reactions of the artist as a process generat[ing] the painting's form," as Harold Rosenberg defined the hallmark of Abstract-Expressionist artists.[69] Johns's opposition was intellectual and explicative. That riot of color in *False Start* is an ironic display. The free-for-all look, not (supposed to be) the "real" thing, is another kind of calculated misidentification.

Identity itself was, and remains, his subject. Later, Johns would call attention to real objects attached to his canvases with arrows and words, like the word "cup" appearing in black handwriting over the object, and an arrow pointing from word to cup in the 1962 painting *Zone*—as if addressing fools. In fact, a painting he made the same year, *Fool's House,* with a real broom hanging vertically from a hook, also a real towel, real stretcher, and real cup, all identified in a sort of moronic redundancy by handwritten and drawn names and arrows, was a title he said came from a comment by a friend who saw the labels and remarked, "Any fool knows it's a broom."[70] Two years earlier Johns had begun tilting at critics for their inability, as evidently it appeared to him, to see, or to know what he was doing.

Hilton Kramer has been Johns's only insistent detractor. His hostile campaign stands out in a field that has been exceptionally sympathetic to the artist through the years. In 1959 in *Arts* magazine, one year after Johns's triumphant debut at the Castelli gallery, in covering a group show of collage and construction called *Beyond Painting* at the Alan Gallery in New York, Kramer said the work of Johns and Rauschenberg (both in the show), "speaks directly to current taste, and touches art only on the periphery and by virtue of a breakdown in standards." Rauschenberg was singled out as a "very deft designer with a sensitive eye for the chic detail." Alluding with knowledge aforewriting to the window display work that Rauschenberg and Johns did for Tiffany and Bonwit Teller to make money in the mid-1950s (under the name Matson Jones), Kramer excoriated Rauschenberg, seeing "no difference between his work and the decorative displays which often grace the windows of Bonwit Teller and Bloomingdale's. . . . Fundamentally, he shares the window decorator's aesthetic: to tickle the eye, to arrest attention for a momentary dazzle." He compared both Johns and Rauschenberg unfavorably to the Dadaists, with whom he thought they had a lot in common, saying that while "Dada sought to repudiate and criticize bourgeois values . . . Johns, like Rauschenberg, *aims to*

please and confirm the decadent periphery of bourgeois taste" (my emphasis).[71]

Just how veiled this unprecedented homophobic attack by innuendo appeared to the art community at the time would be hard
to know. Johns himself seemed to understand what Kramer was
really saying when he fired off his first and only letter-to-the-
editor, which appeared in the March issue of *Arts,* one month
after the Kramer broadside. He noted "a kind of rottenness [that
runs] through the entire article—Mr. Kramer's presumed insight
into . . . aims ('to please')." And he called special attention to
Kramer's "funny and vicious" phrase, " 'like *Narcissus* [my em-
phasis] at the pool, they see only the gutter.' " Ostensibly he
meant to take Kramer to task for his "critical pretensions"—not
seeing works as "valid [in] themselves," but rather "historically
and aesthetically, as a sort of substitute painting."[72]

A lot more than likely, Johns had Kramer in mind when he
made his sculp-metal piece that year called *The Critic Smiles*—a
lifesize toothbrush with four bristles or "teeth," laid out on a sar-
cophagal plinth. Speaking of the piece, Johns said, "I had the idea
that in society the approval of the critic was a kind of cleansing
police action. When the critic smiles it's a lopsided smile with
hidden meaning. And of course a smile involves baring the teeth.
The critic is keeping a certain order, which is why it is like a police function. The handle has the word 'copper' on it, which I
associate with police."[73]

While Johns undoubtedly had only art in mind himself, consciously at least, this interesting annotation might be read by any
politically aware gay man of the 1990s, in the context of the
Kramer charge and the Johns counterattack, as a commentary on
the power of straight society, and the vulnerability of the (gay)
artist. "Keeping a certain order . . . like a police function"—to
maintain proper gender differentiations and the illusion, cer-

tainly the necessity, of universal heterosexuality. The "handle" with the word 'copper' on it—the club or gun or "tool," genitals that "work," of the cops.

In his second sculp-metal piece to challenge critics, *The Critic Sees* of 1961, Johns played on his identity theme:

> I was hanging a show of sculpture and drawings, and a critic came in and started asking me what things were. He paid no attention to what I said. He said what do you call these? And I said sculpture. He said why do you call them sculpture when they're just casts. I said they weren't casts, that some had been made from scratch, and others had been casts that were broken and reworked. He said yes, they're casts, not sculpture. It went on like that.[74]

Johns's frustration was similar to his letter-to-the-editor response to Kramer's article.

In *The Critic Sees,* Johns fashioned a pun on the functions of looking and speaking, placing a cast human mouth within each round frame of a pair of men's glasses raised slightly from a surface of his sculp-metal rectangular brick. One mouth is opened slightly wider, showing more teeth and more black cavern or interior. It's a surreal piece in the Magritte tradition. Since they're mouths, it's clear they can't see, and since the mouths are where the eyes are supposed to be, they can't speak either; they are just "mouthing" things. Johns made his critic blind and dumb. The critic deserved it apparently, not having been able to get the identity of anything straight. For eyes and mouth, substitute ass and elbow; the critic couldn't tell the difference so far as Johns apparently was concerned.

In 1979 a critic took an interesting swipe at *The Critic Sees,* attempting to explain Johns's antagonism in terms of framing. He saw Johns as objecting to the "frame around sight" made by critics, in fact to any kind of frame, including the frames around glasses. He noted Johns's dislike of glasses, causing him to see only the frames. And he had Johns framing critics with his glasses in *The Critic Sees*—a kind of tit for tat. Johns himself is *"not guilty of framing."* Instead, he "problematizes the frame . . . by disframing, dismantling its authority and neutrality." But what for? For this critic, "the frame functions conventionally as quotation marks, as a marking separating the painting from the world, as a quotation from it. And the disappearance of this marking makes a Johns painting a quotation without quotation marks, *a stolen image absenting its source, to which it cannot be readily returned"* (my emphasis). The "source" is Johns's "nomadic biography"—his original "homelessness" in which "home" and "origin" failed to coincide (the "proper father" replaced by grandfather, uncle, stepfather). Here the "framing critic" is a more complex "policeman" than Johns imagined—engaged in "returning the child-painting to his home . . . in a policing action which returns [work] . . . deliberately given without familial ties." "The critic wants at all costs to return this orphan to its proper owner, as in the return of the law after the commission of a crime."[75]

But critics of Johns generally were and remain content, often thrilled, to leave Johns's paintings as unframed as he made them, "returning" them only to themselves. They have warmed to "pictures familiar as . . . objects," not having "subject matter," but rather existing as "so many abstract forms, upon which social usage has conferred meaning, but which now, displaced into their new context, cease to function socially."[76]

Hilton Kramer's policing action was an effort to "return" Johns (and his friend Rauschenberg) to their homosexual origins, evidently with the hostile purpose of discrediting the two artists, whom he saw as upstarts, usurping the hard-won place of the Abstract Expressionists. By 1978 Johns, rich and celebrated, confronted by an interviewer with that despicable line of Kramer's in the 1959 *Arts* article—"Johns, like Rauschenberg, aims to please and confirm the decadent periphery of bourgeois taste"—

could loftily reply, "I have no interest in that remark. Most of what Kramer says means nothing to me. I don't want to criticize Kramer."[77] Kramer himself never gave up. As recently as 1989, interviewed for a film about the artist, he said, "Johns's career has been a long downhill course from a point that was never very high to begin with."[78] In a passionate article he also wrote in 1989, he denounced a show of Johns's map pictures—paintings and prints based on maps of the United States that Johns produced between 1960 and 1971. Kramer, no longer couching his attack in homophobic innuendo, cried for the loss of "prestige" suffered by the "New York School at the very moment of its greatest success" when Johns came along and made a "studied mimicry" of the entire Abstract-Expressionist style with his "brushy surfaces . . . turning the whole pictorial enterprise into a Duchampian jest." One can feel real pathos in Kramer's retrospective view: "You had to have been around in those days— the days of Mr. Johns's early exhibitions at Leo Castelli's—to understand the depth of the bitterness that these paintings and their quick success caused so many members of the Abstract Expressionist movement to feel. For some, this development looked like the beginning of the end of an era."[79] Many Abstract Expressionist painters felt the same way. Mark Rothko, after looking around at the targets and flags at Johns's first one-man show, commented, "We worked for years to get rid of all that."[80] Another abstract artist remarked sadly, sometime after the opening, "I might as well give up."[81]

By 1963, when Pop art—which Johns in some ways prefigured—was established, another view had taken hold. In the mid-1950s "when Johns did . . . the large *Green Target,* the situation in New York was something like that in Florence in 1520 when all the problems posed by High Renaissance painting had been solved, but lip service was still being paid to the outworn vocabulary."[82] Another Johns apologist saw his loose brush work—

that "studied mimicry"—in positive terms: "Through this belligerent transfer of heroic individualized paint strokes into the trite configurations of common signs, Johns without doubt uncovers a source of freedom."[83] By the time of his retrospective at the Jewish Museum in 1964, a heroic account of his accomplishment was not uncommon. "Johns almost singlehandedly deflected the course of Abstract Expressionism six years ago."[84] A cap to this bottle of the past was screwed on in 1977, on the occasion of Johns's next important retrospective, at the Whitney Museum. "Myth sweetens history," said *Newsweek* in its cover story on the artist.

> The story of Johns's first show in New York is sometimes told as a variation of the Biblical story of David and Goliath. As the curtain rises on the late fifties, the lords of Abstract Expressionism rule New York. Their canvases, mirrors to the soul, are full of Sturm and Drang. Perhaps they have ruled too long and successfully. . . . Enter Jasper Johns. At a new gallery called Castelli, this shy David displays a beautifully painted picture of an American flag. A mere flag? . . . but the picture bristles with an irony so astringent, a presence so cool, that the action paintings of Abstract Expressionists seem, by contrast, gassy with rhetoric.[85]

Two writers in the late 1970s, Calvin Tomkins and Moira Roth, contrasted the aesthetics and styles of the parvenus Johns and Rauschenberg with the so-called New York School. Tomkins, in his journalistic treatment of that axial moment in American art when a new kind of figuration (descended from Dada and Duchamp) upstaged the reigning abstract modality, dealt directly with the sexuality of the protagonists. "The leading artists of Pollock's and de Kooning's generation have been almost without exception aggressively male, hard-drinking, and heterosexual. Quite a few of the sixties artists were either bisexual or homosexual." Making a most debatable point, Tomkins saw them as "not a bit uptight about it," possibly because of the luster their immense success gave them and the favorable effects of long experience in dissimulation. Johns and Rauschenberg could "pass." Andy Warhol on the other hand, arriving in the early 1960s, and included along with Johns, Rauschenberg, Cage, and Cunningham by Tomkins in his band of homosexuals, was more obviously gay. Tomkins defined the threat of this group in terms of publicity. "Everyone knew that homosexuals had been prominent in the arts since at least the fifth century B.C. The real irritant was publicity." As if to say no one minded if homosexuals were active on the scene, so long as they kept a low profile and allowed the dominant group to remain so. It was the attention and money lavished on the newcomers—on Johns at least—that had aroused the "policeman" in Hilton Kramer on behalf of the Ab-Ex heterosexual community. Tomkins reported "talk of a 'homintern,' a network of homosexual artists, dealers, and museum curators in league to promote the work of certain favorites at the expense of 'straight' talents." He added that it had even been suggested "that there was such a thing as homosexual art, and that its characteristics—narcissism, camp humor, and decorative intent—were visible on all sides."[86]

Moira Roth tied Cage, Cunningham, Johns, and Rauschenberg together, with Duchamp as their distant guiding star, under a common aesthetic and ideology that she called the "Aesthetic of Indifference." Her thesis was that the "neutrality, passivity, irony and often negation" of these artists was a response to the anti-Communist hysteria generated by Joseph McCarthy and his henchmen after the war. She outed the four men in a way similar to Tomkins and compared the "homosexuality and bisexuality permissible and even common among the new aesthetic group" to the *"machismo* attitudes proudly displayed by the Abstract Expressionists."[87] But she made no connection between the

sexual orientation of her Indifferent group and the extreme ho-
mophobia that existed in conjunction with that era's anti-
Communist hysteria. Curiously, she omitted mention of that dark
substratum of government policy altogether. Without it, her case
for the *special* "indifference" of her four men in those repressive,
paranoid times is not very strong.

In the 1950s homosexuals were considered enemies of the
state, as in Nazi Germany; it was as un-American to be gay as to
be Communist. Investigations and purges of homosexuals in
government bore out a certain fusion of the two persuasions in
the minds of inquisitors. "Leaders of the anti-Communist right
such as McCarthy explicitly aligned homosexuality with Com-
munism, declaring both to be moral failures capable of seducing
and enervating the body politic."[88] McCarthy specifically identified a "homosexual menace" to national security, making it an
issue throughout the 1950s.[89] "Perverts Called Government
Peril" read a headline in the *New York Times* on April 19, 1950.
Press and government alike agreed that "homosexuals *by their nature* were unfit and unreliable public servants." A Defense Department regulation requiring the dismissal of gay men and les-
bians was officially promulgated in 1949.[90] A Senate report of that
time resonates with statements in the 1990s by military brass opposing lifting the ban on homosexuals, asserting that homosexuality is incompatible with military service. The report said,
"Those who engage in overt acts of perversion lack the emotional stability of normal persons. . . . The indulgence in acts of
sex perversion . . . weakens the moral fiber of the individual."
Such people, the report implied, would be more interested in seducing fellow employees than in performing their job.[91] Johns
and Rauschenberg, both servicemen in the late 1940s and early
1950s, had obviously been at risk. As artists, in a world in which,
as Tomkins said, "everyone knew that homosexuals had [always]

been prominent" they had protection, but of course only by their (tacit) guarantee of silence and concealment.

Moira Roth described certain acute differences between her Indifferent group and the Abstract Expressionists. Interviewed by Roth, George Segal, a young artist at the time, remembered the typical Abstract Expressionist as having a "heavy-set appearance with drooping moustache and corduroy jacket." " 'If you had an education, you had to hide it and sound like a New York cab driver.' " Duchamp and Cage, when he first encountered them, "struck him as models for a new 'slender, cerebral, philosophical, iconoclastic type,' physically and intellectually very different from the Abstract-Expressionist one. For Segal and others, the new artist had a dandylike elegance of body build and a manner which delighted in cool and elegant plays of the mind."[92] Of course as Johns and Rauschenberg reached an age comparable to that of most Abstract-Expressionist artists in the 1950s, just as prone to drink and excellent food, they would look pretty "heavy-set" themselves, if never to be seen in drooping moustaches or corduroy jackets.

Roth's "dandy"—a hackneyed code word for gay men— rumbles through the literature on Johns. When Johns's Whitney retrospective made it to London in 1978, Bryan Robertson said, "Johns's attitude to art has been invigorated from his earliest beginnings with the spirit of the dandy, if you'll accept . . . my idea of a dandy in art as a highly self-conscious man."[93] Robertson's equation of "dandy" with the "self-conscious man" had a degree of sophistication relevant to recent deconstructions of the homosexual worldview. Johns has been nothing if not excessively conscious of himself as an object of observation to others, a natural inclination for those who have come of age as outsiders, sexually and emotionally, to their natal culture. Another, yet related equation involving the dandy concept was made in 1964 by Andrew Forge, the author five years later of the first major work on Rauschenberg.[94] "Where painting had proceeded from a standpoint of a highly charged personal expression, an explosive signature [in Abstract Expressionism], [Johns's] paintings proceeded from a dandyish and stoical anonymity." Forge's equation of "dandyish" with "stoical anonymity" could seem advanced if, as seems unlikely, he was thinking of the essential removal of self from work that being homosexual at that time demanded. As Johns explicator Fred Orton has put it, "In Johns's generation of the 1950s . . . we should expect a tendency to the private . . . exchange of meanings and a matching cultivation of public irony; a withdrawal from prevailing forms of self identification in social behavior, including those which structure sexual relationships."[95] Strangely echoing Forge's thought, a 1972 description by Robert Hughes had Johns sporting "the mask of cool, of a dandy who shuts up and puts up." Here though, the word "dandy" was linked oxymoronically with a classic heterosexual image. "Jasper Johns's face . . . resembles that of William S. Hart, the silent gunslinger of the silent Westerns. The narrow, crinkled eyes stare flatly, with an expression of ironic watchfulness, across the V of a gun sight . . . the mask of cool, of a dandy."[96] We can imagine the artist as "gunslinger" perhaps— pulling out brushes, aiming and firing them at targets, "cool" and removed. Western gunslingers aren't normally called dandies.

Moira Roth thought Johns "more than any other artist" had "incorporated in his early art the Cold War and the McCarthy era preoccupations and moods." Noting that he was "17 when the CIA was created in 1947; 18 when Hiss was accused of perjury; 20 when McCarthy rose to power; 21 when the Rosenbergs were put on trial . . . and 24 when McCarthy's power collapsed," she saw in his work the "dense concentration of metaphors dealing with spying, conspiracy, secrecy and concealment, misleading information, coded messages and clues" that were the "very subjects of newspaper headlines of the period, reiterated on the radio and shown on television." Her chief exhibit for his "indifference" was *Flag*. She saw him as having taken the American flag, beginning in 1954, a year of "hysterical patriotism," and "[reducing] it from a potentially emotional symbol to a passive, flat, neutral object."[97] It seemed most unlikely to her that it was "merely inspired by a dream." The dream puts the flag in quite a "neutral" space indeed, but Roth preferred having Johns *consciously* select a hot image that he *knowingly* neutralized. The assessment itself of Johns's *Flag* as "passive . . . neutral" seems wide of the mark. It looked very enterprising to critics and other artists when they saw it. Johns in any case has described himself as "politically stupid." His personality and background were simply remarkably in tune with those times. He had something to hide, he was well hidden, and he had a precocious talent for developing strategies in his work that simultaneously amused, attracted, and threw people off. With such attributes he could have been a consummate counterintelligence officer for the CIA.

By 1961 the normal Johnsian mode was disrupted and threatened. Following his break-up with Rauschenberg, overrun at that point evidently by feelings of loss and abandonment, as well as by excruciating questions regarding his identity, Johns removed himself for major parts of the next few years from New York and painted some intimate pictures representing both his location and his inner state. Still a closed, secretive, and self-censorious person, he developed an ingenious strategy for his new expressive work, becoming a kind of ventriloquist, "throwing" his voice, impounding others to speak for him.

IV.

What of Hart Crane

— F R A N K   O ' H A R A

I had the sense of arriving at a point where there was
no place to stand.

— J A S P E R   J O H N S

Using the title as an image enabled Johns to allude to his own
feelings without making a direct autobiographical statement.

— R O B E R T A   B E R N S T E I N

His [Jasper Johns's] reserve about himself . . . masks
a profound vulnerability.

— A L A N   S O L O M O N

Johns has said that going to Edisto changed his life. It was part
of his growing rift with Rauschenberg. Viola Farber, a dancer in
the Cunningham company then, remembers how "exquisitely
awful to each other" Bob and Jasper were on a trip south by car
that she made with them both during the summer of 1961.[98] That
year he bought property on Edisto Island close to the beach.
Linked by causeway to the coast of South Carolina, Edisto is forty
miles southwest down the coast from Charleston, the city where
Johns's father had been living when he died four years earlier.
It's approximately eighty miles southeast of Allendale, the low-
country town where Johns was raised until he was nine. Retir-
ing to Edisto he was going "home," an ideal retreat for any warrior after a major contest, which was perhaps the essence of what
his relationship in New York had become (and the way his success felt within the embattled art scene).

Now the work Johns had been doing since 1959, when his
stroke became more expressionistic, got much brushier and more
gestural, forming a broad atmosphere, no longer so carefully
modulated for surface attention alone, but rather to support or
create "background" for incidents and figures of clear emotional

content. Descriptive of his new life to come, with major vacations from the center of art, was an encaustic and canvas collage work called *Disappearance I* (1960), its title referring to the disappearance of the sides of a canvas upon being folded when collaged to the surface of a canvas, forming a square within a square.

In his forward and backward movements during his "disappearance" Johns literally identified his "step." The image of the foot—imprints, tracings, casts, drawings—figured prominently in his new work. *Edisto,* a simple drawing, shows a footprint inside a traced shoe form; the one other image on the paper, a tracing of a seashell, and *Edisto* as title indicate the foot's presence on a beach. *By the Sea* of 1961, the title of an exuberant encaustic and collage work on canvas, also conveyed location. But *By the Sea* belongs to a series of color-name pictures dating from 1959, beginning with *False Start* and *Out the Window.* The latter, with its organization in three horizontal panels, the stenciled word "red" centered in the top panel, "yellow" in the middle, and "blue" at the bottom, is the direct progenitor of *By the Sea,* which has an additional fourth panel at the bottom with the word "yellow" repeated on it.

Johns first "signaled through the flames" in 1962. With four works that refer to the poetry of Hart Crane, he broke out of his emotional closet. In two of them, *Land's End* and *Diver,* he appears to be crying for help. Communing with Crane, the dead homosexual poet, Johns evidently found solace and fellowship. He had already communed with the living homosexual poet Frank O'Hara in a 1961 painting called *In Memory of My Feelings—Frank O'Hara,* its title and mood presaging the later more explicit and figurative expressive dramas inspired by Crane. With other titles of 1961—*Liar, No, Good Time Charley, Water Freezes,* and the un-Johnsian *Painting Bitten by a Man* (in which someone, maybe the artist, literally attacked the canvas, taking a bite out of a thick layer of grey encaustic)—Johns also evoked a new emotional range, including refusal, denial, suspicions of character, sarcasm, accusation, coldness, bitterness, rage, and frustration. *In Memory of My Feelings—Frank O'Hara* encompasses them all and more, including nostalgia as well. According to O'Hara's biographer, he began his long autobiographical poem *In Memory of My Feelings* on what he believed to be his thirtieth birthday. Johns's painting appropriating O'Hara's title is from his own thirty-first year.

O'Hara had been writing reviews for *Art News* as well as performing curatorial duties at the Museum of Modern Art since 1955. A very popular figure with both poets and artists, he became a key player at MoMA as director Alfred Barr increasingly favored exhibitions of contemporary American artists, many of whom were O'Hara's friends. O'Hara was perhaps the first reviewer to affirm Rauschenberg's stature as a major artist. Covering a show by Rauschenberg at the Egan Gallery in the January 1955 issue of *Art News,* he spoke of "ecstatic work" by a "serious lyrical talent."[99] That same month he picked out Cy Twombly for praise in his first one-man show at the Stable, and two years later, on behalf of the museum, placed a Twombly work in the fourth International Art Exhibition in Japan. Hardly slighting Johns when he came along a year after that with his first show at Castelli's, O'Hara recommended to Alfred Barr the purchase for MoMA of Johns's large *White Flag* (1955).[100]

O'Hara was a power in a world that Johns was just beginning to seriously impact. They shared the company of a number of other artists, poets, spouses, and friends—Johns usually appearing with Rauschenberg—at sprawling beach and other parties of the late 1950s, and early 1960s, in the Hamptons on Long Island. The regulars included Larry Rivers, Kenneth Koch, Willem and Elaine de Kooning, Bill Berkson, Jane Freilicher, Jane Wilson, Maxine Groffsky, John Myers, Paul Brach, and Miriam Shapiro. On one particular weekend in 1959, finding himself on the train to the Hamptons with Johns, O'Hara drew him out about his painting. Johns has commented, "There was this weird thing of Frank's interest in and understanding of other artists that seemed to put no obligation on his own work. . . . I had no sense that he needed anything from me about his work but that his interest in me was about my work."[101] In his double life as poet and critic-curator, O'Hara deferred to his artist friends, putting himself on hold as he enthusiastically serviced art and artists ("Sometimes I think I'm 'in love' with painting," he said[102]), while reserving as vehicle for self his very autobiographical poetry.

Appending O'Hara's name to *In Memory of My Feelings* is a marquee gesture; it gives something back to the poet while adopting him like a ventriloquist to say something Johns couldn't say himself. "Using the title as an image enabled Johns to allude to his own feelings without making a direct autobiographical statement."[103] In a largely all-over paint field of agitated, mostly vertically overlaid darkish blue-green-grey, black, and white strokes, there are three "incidents," not counting two metal hinges down the center binding the two panels of the work. The upper left grey rectangular form makes the work reminiscent in a ghostly way of the flag paintings. A fork and spoon hang backward from a wire attached to the canvas by a screw eye. The words "DEAD MAN" appear in the lower right of the canvas. Though large, the words are nearly obscured by paint and are invisible to the casual viewer without prior knowledge of them. Reproductions of the painting don't reveal the image at all. When I learned the words were there, I found it spooky, considering O'Hara's sudden death in 1966 after being run over by a beach taxi on Fire Island. "DEAD MAN" can be read as both the "signature" of the artist and an allusion to O'Hara. (In 1956, when he wrote the poem, O'Hara was mourning the death of two close friends and of Jackson Pollock.) The words appear above and spaced between the stenciled letters "O'HARA" (the last word of the title) along the bottom of the canvas and the artist's actual signature and date, "J. Johns '61."

Johns's use of projection—expressing feelings or wishes that are unacceptable to oneself, too shameful, disturbing, or dangerous, and engaging a well-known figure for the job—is powerful stuff. Years later, in 1983, Johns actually titled a work *Ventriloquist*. His "dummy" in that painting is apparently a whale, the partially submerged tracing of an image of Melville's Moby Dick taken from an engraving by Barry Moser, its mouth gaping open on the left panel of the canvas, as if speaking at a collection of art work in the right panel. The "ventriloquist," the artist himself, can be imagined on the right side of the diptych, invisibly stretching out toward us, feet facing his painting, in the bathtub indicated by the meticulous rendering of its fixtures, next to the top part of a laundry basket in the bottom right of the canvas. He is regarding tokens of his career and success—flags ("taped" to wall), renderings of his Barnett Newman litho and Rubins cup. The whale, specter of a voice from another world, representing the unconscious, the mysterious origins of things, looms up in his imagination on the left. An interesting detail in Johns's *Ventriloquist* of 1983 are the two painted hinges down the center— a "souvenir" from the two *real* hinges of his 1961 *In Memory of My Feelings—Frank O'Hara*.

In the early O'Hara projection, the "dummy" poet seems oddly more primary, in the sense that it's a "voice" preceding the trappings of success at a time when the painter could have felt insecure about his survival as an artist, or at least as a very successful one, given the seeming shambles of his personal life. It was O'Hara's *human* nature that Johns wanted, the fearless homosexual poet, one who would have been incomprehensibly open to Walt Whitman and Hart Crane before him. O'Hara's poem carried not only unacceptable feelings, all surrounding

death or the lament for lost lives and loves, but personal transcendence as well in his bid for resurrection of the self as artist,
identified at the end of the poem as "the serpent." ("And I have
lost what is always and everywhere / present, the scene of my
selves, the occasion of these rules, which I myself and singly must
now kill / and save the serpent in their midst.") The artist could
wish through the poet, in a poem whose "central theme [is] the
fragmentation and reintegration of the inner self—a self that
threatens continually to dissipate under the assault of outer
forces."[104] The exchange, unilaterally designed, is instructive: a
mute artist "steals" feelings from an articulate poet and in return
offers status—acting as de factor publisher, broadcasting the title
of a poem not yet in print, along with the name of its author.
The homage, to an acclaimed and accomplished poet whose in-
come derived solely from his services to artists, came from an artist
who appreciated poets and was precociously solvent. The practice established in his O'Hara "collaboration" became service-
able later on in similar exercises involving Picasso, Edvard
Munch, Céline, and Pollock, not to mention his appropriation
of Cage's emotionally charged title *The Perilous Night*.

Johns had other changes to ring on O'Hara. The year before
the *Memory* work he made a drawing that was a plan for a sculpture featuring a rubber cast of the poet's foot. The sculpture was
completed in 1970, four years after O'Hara's death. A cast of
O'Hara's foot is affixed to the inner side of a lid, which is hinged
to the top of a small wooden case with three drawers full of sand:
when the top is closed, it makes an imprint in the top layer of
sand. Opened again, both cast and footprint are visible. O'Hara
referred to the drawing in 1963 in a letter-poem to the artist.
"Dear Jap, when I think of you in South Carolina I think of my
foot in the sand." By then, Johns was no longer trekking to the
sands of Long Island. Both the 1961 drawing and the 1970 sculpture were titled *Memory Piece (Frank O'Hara)*. Johns recalls the

plan, "I cast his foot and did a drawing [in Johns's New York studio on Front Street] for the piece"; the problem of executing it, "At the time I had a house in South Carolina. I needed a carpenter but could never find anyone to do it"; and its completion, "I think it was done after his death. But I gave Frank the drawing for it."[105]

In his letter-poem O'Hara also said, "I miss my drawing which I think you are still looking at." Presumably Johns got it back and was keeping it for a time with a view to executing the sculpture. Johns was quick to seize the poet again in 1965 when, for a special issue on the relationship of poetry to painting for *Art in America,* twenty-two painters were asked to choose a contemporary poem to inspire a work in black and white in the medium of their choice. Three New York painters had to make a second selection because Johns chose O'Hara first.[106] Johns's choice, O'Hara's *The Clouds Go Soft* (1963), gave rise to his most poignant O'Hara collaboration, *Skin with O'Hara Poem* (1963–65). His last communion with the poet was a coup of sorts. The Museum of Modern Art's 1967 deluxe memorial volume of thirty O'Hara poems illustrated by artists, which includes a drawing by Johns titled *In Memory of My Feelings,* is itself titled *In Memory of My Feelings.*

Skin with O'Hara Poem matched O'Hara's autobiographical passion more directly, although the muted externalized *The Clouds Go Soft* is an atypical poem for O'Hara. Marjorie Perloff calls it O'Hara's dejection ode—"a meditative lyric, whose . . . subdued tone . . . sets it apart from most of the poet's work." Johns's image closely resembles the "self-portrait" of *Study for Skin I* (1962), also subdued, yet fraught with feeling, for which he coated his head and hands with baby oil and pressed them up against sheets of drafting paper and then dusted the image slightly with powdered graphite. The face in *Skin with O'Hara Poem* is fractured and blurred, and thus more abstract than the face in

Study for Skin I, where the image can easily be read as a mute or silenced child, whose outspread hands are imprinted on either side of the face pressed up against the artistic plane from behind as if appealing for release or limning a resigned, helpless entrapment. Johns had the O'Hara poem typeset to the right, above the figure's spread-fingered left hand. The poet of movement and self- transformation here describes "only the external landscape" as capable of change, "and even then, the movement is, in Wallace Stevens's phrase, 'downward to darkness.' "[107]

Johns probably liked the poem for its descriptions of clouds that "disperse / sink into the sea," and sand that "inevitably seeks the eye." But a clue to Johns's inner state, the feelings of the figure "pressed up against the artistic plane from behind," lies in O'Hara's lines of despair and surrender:

> *at 16 your weight 144 pounds and at 36*
> *the shirts change, endless procession*
> *but they are all neck 14 sleeve 33*
> *and holes appear and are filled*
> *the same holes anonymous filler*
> *no more conversion, no more conversation*
> *the sand inevitably seeks the eye.*

The holes in this context, suggests Perloff, "are not armholes but graves." And "struggle, this particular poem tells us, is simply not worth it."[108] The Johns figure, in "helpless, resigned entrapment," perhaps is *not* expressing "an appeal for release."

Speaking of his *Study for Skin I,* a critic wrote, "Nowhere in Johns's work has there been a more poignant effect of imprisonment, of the artist himself striving to break free from the physical limits of a work of art in which he has willfully impregnated his image."[109] Snared in his medium, the artist outmaneuvers himself, capturing vital images in paint where they can't get out, creating a solipsist world where it is difficult or impossible to produce the witnesses, the "others" who complete the work by see-ing it, who can help reify or cathect the story the images tell. But the others can as easily damn, not implausibly murder, the frag-ile subject once exposed—either way dangerously threatening to render the very practice of art futile or invalid, leaving the artist without his most reliable defense.

Trapped in paint or hidden behind others, Johns's secret self, or identity, was an opportunity for great invention. With an aver-sion to making anything up or to claiming responsibility for his own states or feelings, he became a master of appropriation. It was Johns's genius in melding contradictory traditions—the Duchampian readymade (read theft) and the Abstract-Expressionist dedication to the painterly gesture—that brought him to the forefront of modernism. Clement Greenberg, the leading Abstract Expressionist critic of the day, said, "Johns brings de Kooning's influence to a head by suspending it clearly . . . be-tween abstraction and representation."[110] The abstract painters hated the seeming abnegation of self—the unique individual self being the very thing they sought through their own work—that they saw in Johns's theft of images, not to mention feelings, from the culture or others. Johns precociously signaled "the death of the author," making him a postmodernist before his time.

His work evoked a self that couldn't be revealed or spoken of, that seemed still embryonic. Herein lay its power. The "pres-ence" of an actor can be attributed to withheld emotions, thoughts, and desires. The need to hide the personal self is al-ready an expression of the self. Through ventriloquism, Johns "threw" his inner voice onto canvas and paper. With *Land's End, Diver,* and *Periscope (Hart Crane)* of 1962 and 1963, his "voice" was the suicidal figure of Hart Crane, echoing the "DEAD MAN" in his O'Hara work, *In Memory of My Feelings,* but bring-ing this figure out to the forefront of the canvas, illustrating Crane's last reported earthly gesture.

*[Johns] failed to indicate a single position from which to view the
changes his representations undergo . . . to express himself, to
mark the "position" of his person. . . . He seeks to escape all
proprietary authorship.*

— R I C H A R D   S H I F F

*As fill'd with friendship, love complete,
the Elder Brother found,
The Younger melts in fondness in his arms.*

— W A L T   W H I T M A N

*The union with Whitman Crane describes in "Cape Hatteras,"
and the legitimacy this grants to acts of male homosexuality,
must be seen . . . as a singularly brave attempt in the canon of
modern American literature.*

— T H O M A S   Y I N G L I N G

Harold Hart Crane jumped overboard from the *Orizaba,* a Mexican ship bound from Vera Cruz to New York on April 27, 1932, when 275 miles north of Havana. He was thirty-three years old. A report on the suicide from the master of the *Orizaba* said, "Mr. Crane was seen to come on deck clad in his pajamas covered by an overcoat. He walked rapidly aft, threw the coat on the deck, climbed up on the rail, and jumped over the side. Life preservers were thrown at once, the ship was manoeuvred and a boat put over the side, but no trace of Mr. Crane was found. He had been seen once after his body struck the water and apparently he made no effort to reach the life preservers thrown him."[111]

In Philip Horton's *Hart Crane: The Life of an American Poet,* a copy of which Johns owned, according to Roberta Bernstein, he would have read this description: "Heedless of the curious glances that followed his progress along the deck, Crane walked quickly to the stern of the ship, and scarcely pausing to slip his coat from his shoulders, vaulted over the rail into the boiling wake. The alarm was general and immediate. There was a clangor of bells as the ship's engine ground into reverse; life preservers were thrown overboard; a lifeboat was lowered. *Some claim they saw an arm raised from above the water"* (italics added).[112]

Johns has said *Land's End* was given its title "because I had the sense of arriving at a point where there was no place to stand."[113] He told Bernstein he had no specific location in mind. The title, she pointed out, could indicate any location where land meets ocean. Johns illustrates the act of Crane's suicide in *Diver,* and the poet's arm seen above the water the moment before he disappeared in *Land's End.* The arm in the painting was created by ·repeated, superimposed handprints and a strip of scraped paint. The arm's backdrop of three horizontal color-name spaces (red, yellow, blue) in *Land's End* derives from Johns's 1959 *Out the Window* and 1961 *By the Sea.* There is of course no "perspective." The arm can be viewed naturalistically, reaching from the deep, or surrealistically, lying flat on the bed of "sea" as seen from above. Ground (sea) and figure (arm) are not hierarchically related. Nonetheless the arm is what we notice—a human body part gesturing dramatically in an otherwise abstract painting. We can read desperation in its reach upward directly through the "e" of "YELLOW"—a placement highlighting "yell." An arrow pointing downward, housed in a rectangular area of grey paint, gives a narrative thrust to the arm's direction: vanishment from sight, dispersion to the sea, death of the victim to whom it belongs.

By this time Johns's fugitive methods of creating meaning through displacement—transposing motifs, objects, and ideas, from one context to another—were already well developed. Working on accreting one new subject at a time, he slowly stored up images like assets to be drawn on yet transformed by their new appearance or context. And since so many of these images were "found," in the work and lives of other artists, a tremendous sense is conveyed of the artist as a disembodied presence, partially visible in pieces, like puzzle parts crying for retrieval and integration. Johns's strategy of displacement and dispersive relocation has roots in his biography—severed early from parents and home, located and relocated like a refugee with various relatives during childhood, later a Southerner in Yankeeland; an artist sundered from a middle-class paternal heritage; further removed, not only from society at large but from the heterosexual conventions, often exaggerated, of the art tradition in which he sought asylum. Johns required *other* biographies through which he could exteriorize his sealed inner life.

With Hart Crane, who died when Johns was just two years old, he had much in common, not least the condition of "conforming . . . overwhelmingly [to the] heterosexual conventions and expectations" of his medium, if lofty ambitions were to be fulfilled.[114] Crane's parents were married in 1898. He was born a year later, and raised in three locations in Ohio: Garrettsville, Warren, and Cleveland. His father, C. A. Crane, was a successful candy manufacturer, the man who invented "the candies with the hole"—the Lifesaver (which, as life preserver, was thrown in vain to his son when he leaped from the *Orizaba*). Crane's early misfortune was to be the only child of parents who made him a party to their dire personal conflicts, particularly over sex. His identification with his mother, who found relief for her own frustrated ambitions by living through him, wasn't Oedipally promising. Crane dropped the "Harold" as a young man, adopting his middle name and his mother's maiden name, Hart, to please her. "She had given the world a poet. The least he could do would be to give the world her name." After his death she tended his estate and made sure his work was published. When Crane was fifteen he attempted suicide twice, by slashing his wrists with a razor and by swallowing all his mother's Veronal sleeping powders.[115] His parents divorced when he was eighteen. Having acceded for years to his mother's demands for love, sympathy, and attention, in short for the whole of her emotional welfare, at length when he was twenty-nine he swore off her and would never see her again. According to John Unterecker, his later biographer, Crane's life from then till his suicide was a "series of flights" from her, "each flight—prompted always by terror that she might persuade him to return—[leading] to an orgy of drunken escape and complex moves from place to place . . . swearing friends to secrecy, [as] he attempted to cover his trail."[116] Crane's father remarried twice and died of a coronary at fifty-six, in 1931, nine and a half months before his son's death by drowning.

By contrast with Crane, Johns was set free from the parental disturbance as an infant. What for Hart Crane became a heavy, unbearable responsibility, was for Johns a void. If the complex in Crane's case was possession, in Johns's it had to be abandonment. O'Hara, like Crane, incidentally, was overidentified with a problematic mother. With both poets, Johns must have sensed enough content to fill his own void, putting himself up for adoption in a way. His relationship with Rauschenberg had been a type of adoption, by an older brother figure who had, like Crane and O'Hara, grown up "too much" with family. In 1962, the date of his first Crane-inspired paintings, Johns was thirty-two, the same age as Crane at death. A "failure of love," identified by O'Hara with death the year he composed *In Memory of My Feelings,* was common ground for the two poets and the artist.[117] Perhaps for Rauschenberg too, if his transfer drawings illustrating the thirty-three cantos of Dante's *Inferno* in 1959, two years before he and Johns separated (one year after Johns's triumphant debut at Castelli's), can be considered to signify intimations of mortality consigned to a "failure of love."

Such failures have had different meanings for homosexuals and straights. Homosexual love itself, in the society of Crane in the 1910s and 1920s, of Johns, Rauschenberg, and O'Hara in the

1940s and 1950s, was judged a failure before any instance of it failed. Crane's conflicts over his sexual orientation apparently played a leading part in his trajectory toward suicide. Over a span of just a few months, four years before his death, Crane both came out to his mother and made his final break with her. After his death, his mother wrote "of his emotional perversion of which he calmly told me. . . . It was a great shock to me but he never knew it, and it took me a long time to get my mind adjusted to such a condition."[118] Crane told a friend that his mother "grew visibly upset, rushed from the room," and for days afterward seemed to him "cold and contemptuous."[119]

In their talk "he described the years he had suffered from the sense of his difference from other men and the corrosive consciousness of guilt; he told also of his vain efforts to cure himself by attempting normal relationships." His mother, feeling "she wanted to be alone after experiencing such a profound shock," made a "sudden decision to spend the night at a hotel in town rather than with Hart, as she had originally planned." Crane "interpreted her sudden change of plans as one more in the crippling series of attacks that, he decided, she had for years been making on his personality."[120] Nonetheless, soon after, he softened, as usual, and was persuaded to move into her Hollywood apartment where she was caring for her dying mother. When she suffered a "nervous collapse" he became sole companion and nurse to his grandmother and to his mother as well.

It was from this situation that he rocketed himself out of his mother's life forever, the precipitating factor his "nights out," when he "devoted most of his comparatively rare 'free' time to the pursuit of sailors and the patronage of bootleggers." His mother "accused [him] of callous indifference each time he spent an evening out . . . [and he] became convinced that [she] kept him busy waiting on her so that he would have no opportunity to visit waterfront bars." "Each move on his part toward an evening's freedom found her 'collapse' worsening." There was finally a big scene; Crane stormed out and bought a one-way ticket to New York.[121]

When Crane's grandmother died a few months later, his mother attempted to blackmail him by withholding her signature from an inheritance left to him by his grandfather, telling the bank that "she would not sign until her son joined her in California." When she gave in and signed, she urged Crane's father "to use his influence at the bank to prevent [Crane] from collecting any money. They would not turn over money . . . to a drunkard." This was the final straw for him. When he got the money, Crane used it up in flight from her to Europe. He wrote to friends, "My mother has made it impossible for me to live in my own country."[122]

The epithet "drunkard" coming from his mother had an implied prefix of "homosexual," though not to Crane's father. On a visit to his father in Ohio in 1929, hearing that his mother had appeared nearby, he promptly left and begged his father to have "nothing to do with her." He feared she might carry out her implicit threat and reveal to his father "the history of homosexuality and drunkenness that had been confessed to her in California."[123]

Crane grew closer to his father after the break with his mother. C. A. Crane, like the fathers of Johns and Rauschenberg, was dismayed by his son's failure to turn into a regular boy. Crane's early interest in dolls and his mother's clothes evolved into a love of poetry, painting, and music; instead of "playing baseball with the neighborhood boys, [he retreated] to his room to read or go on solitary walks."[124]

In the end, having lived to see his son's magnum opus, *The Bridge,* published and accorded due attention by the literary establishment, Crane's father was proud of his accomplishments and pleased to contribute to his financial survival. Crane too was "proud" that his father "had at last found a reason to take pride in him." In sober moments "he acknowledged that C.A. had done more than many fathers would do to support and encourage a 'literary' son." Their initial differences turned out to be misleading, as do so many family appearances.[125] But for Crane the positive identification with his father came too late, or the sense of it was too fragile to withstand his father's untimely death at fifty-six. His slide toward suicide, adumbrated by alcoholic blackouts, became very pronounced after his father died.

Crane's belated identification with his father was attended by a last ditch, token affair with a woman, whom he said he planned to marry. Peggy Cowley, wife of the poet and critic Malcolm Cowley, was on board the *Orizaba* with him when he jumped to his death. She told the master of the ship, for his postsuicide report, that "she had expected to marry Mr. Crane when she obtained her divorce [from Cowley]."[126] In her account of Crane's last days, Peggy said that the day they boarded the *Orizaba* in Vera Cruz, when introduced to a number of the officers, whom Crane already knew, she "noticed some raised eyebrows among the uniformed men when Hart informed them of our marriage in the near future."[127] From previous voyages, Crane's reputation for trouble and sailors was well established. Reports of such excesses on this last trip and the tragic outcome of the trip indicate the likelihood that at this moment the conflict between his "abnormality" (as a close friend of Crane's and student of psychology later defined it to his mother[128]) and his socially prescribed straight identity, the most powerful link with his father after all, had reached its zenith.

The executors of his conflict—his "intended" and the sailors, representing his true object of desire—were together with him on board this last journey. Crane got involved in a wild escapade with an unidentified member of the ship's personnel. In one version it was a cabin boy; in another, one of the sailors; in still another, several men. He was beaten and robbed, also "jailed." At the end of his tear the purser had locked him in his room. In the morning he confessed to Peggy, "I'm not going to make it, dear. I'm utterly disgraced." It seems unlikely he had never felt "disgraced" before, but here he had created a spectacle of himself—parading his "abnormality"—in front of a shipful of men who knew he was on board with a woman he said he planned to marry. Minutes later, at noon, having already been drinking "copiously" from a bottle of whisky, he went up on deck and "vaulted over the rail" of the ship's stern "into the boiling wake."[129]

In his classic, now quaint, introduction to the first *Collected Poems of Hart Crane,* published in 1933, Waldo Frank noted that in his final six lyrics of *The Bridge,* called "Voyages," "Crane is using the symbol of the Sea as a principle of unity and release from the contradictions of personal existence . . . [denoting] a return to a 'beginning' before the life of reason . . . and a unity won by the refusal of human consciousness." Then, eliding the distinction between literature and life, he added, "Crane knew the Sea—the source of life, first Mother—as death to man; and that to woo it was death."[130] Crane and Jasper Johns shared the sea, their sexual orientation, and their roles as creators; they were both only sons and self-educated white middle-class males. From an early age, Crane enjoyed seashore visits to a family house on the Isle of Pines, just south of Cuba. Crane the poet showed talent as a child at drawing and painting. Later, painters were among his closest friends; he evolved aesthetic theories in discussions with them.

Johns the painter was a poet manqué; he wrote poems in his youth and has always befriended poets, and of course he ventriloquized them in his work. The poet's ending in the sea must have given him great pause. His own jumping-off point, *Land's End,* shows a hand reaching for help in the midst of a sea of paint, or a painted sea, a "boiling wake" of feeling–paint–surf. Its companion work, *Periscope (Hart Crane)* (1963), is the same size (67 by 48 inches), with identical elements—the arm-hand, the half ("device") circle, three horizontal bands labeled "RED," "YEL-LOW," and "BLUE" from top to bottom, and the downward pointing arrow. But *Periscope* shows a relative calm and control. The arm-hand, withdrawn from this painting's less agitated "open surf," is enclosed within the half circle of scraped paint, suggesting it had been used as the scraping device and thus returned, as it were, to its symbolic function as the hand that makes the work. The letters of the words within their areas are clearer, not so broken up or smudged. Besides its role as executor of the artist's bidding, the arm also functions, presumably, as the "periscope" of the title, a scanning instrument, now regarding the seascape from within its womb–body–submarine or circle, indicating distance and contemplation. The arm here points rather than reaches and is separated by a clear boundary from the vagaries of atmospheric conditions, from the world beyond the circle.

"Periscope" is a word in Crane's poem "Cape Hatteras," from *The Bridge*. Cape Hatteras, in North Carolina, is 250 miles from Edisto Island. The word appears in a stanza that reflects on time past:

> The captured fume of space foams in our ears—
> What whisperings of far watches on the main
> Relapsing into silence, while time clears
> Our lenses, lifts a focus, resurrects
> A periscope to glimpse what joys or pain
> Our eyes can share or answer—then deflects
> Us, shunting to a labyrinth submersed
> Where each sees only his dim past reversed . . .[131]

The "joys or pain" of the past have become "dim" and "reversed" when viewed from a "labyrinth submersed." With proximity to the ocean, and the voice of a poet who could describe his feelings for him (make the self real, or know the truth of his emotional states through a mirroring other), Johns could perhaps let the break with Rauschenberg better recede to the abstractions of memory, as *Periscope* suggests.

In his brilliant contemporary study of Crane, *Hart Crane and the Homosexual Text,* Thomas Yingling remarks that "the intended message of 'Cape Hatteras' seems to be that literature transcends history."[132] This is borne out by the feeling Johns conveys in *Periscope* that art (also) will surpass what Waldo Frank called "the contradictions of personal existence"—an indirect reference by Frank, a Crane family friend as well as critic, to the problem from which Crane was incapable, ultimately, of finding release except in death.

In "Cutty Sark," the poem just preceding "Cape Hatteras" in *The Bridge,* the old sailor narrator has Crane's pretranscendent profile. "He is alcoholic and quite unable to make narrative sense in telling the story of his life, an effect that suggests not only his drunkenness but the fragmentation that has made that drunkenness seem necessary. *It is evidence of the inability to authorize one's own life*" (italics added).[133] Johns depicts such a person in *Land's End,* "speaking across the body," as Freud characterized a subject unable to reconstitute his or her history. The arm in *Land's End* is the "speaking" member, the "sea" of paint the body. It's a disembodied voice, representing the failure of literature to save the poet. Johns himself went on "speaking across the body" in his work, in which fragments of things, disconnected signs, and parts of organisms littering canvases are evidence and emissaries of an unrecognized totality. But Johns apparently had an advantage in his muteness and his immense withdrawal—signs of an original abandonment. He started already dead, in a sense. Crane, who had had to "Shoulder the curse of sundered parentage,"[134] unable to "authorize [his] own life" or even to obtain the kind of foothold in poetry that Johns had in art, was fated to live it up, make a lot of noise, to jump in, to abandon himself.

In quoting just one word from "Cape Hatteras," omitting some 1,670 others, the question of what Johns left out must be interesting. Crane himself made an important omission in the epigraph to "Cape Hatteras." "The seas all crossed, / weathered the capes, the voyage done,"[135] from Walt Whitman's *Passage to India,* was one line short of the following: "As fill'd with friendship, love complete, the Elder Brother found, / The Younger melts in fondness in his arms."[136] (This could play as epigraph to Johns's submerged tracings of the two Grünewald soldiers from the 1980s.) Crane's homage to Whitman in "Cape Hatteras" was an affirmation of his homosexuality, however indirect or buried in oblique allusions. Yingling says that "the union with Whitman Crane describes in 'Cape Hatteras,' and the legitimacy this grants to acts of male homosexuality, must be seen . . . as a singularly brave attempt in the canon of modern American literature."[137] Johns's homage to Crane in his *Periscope (Hart Crane)* partakes of their mutual heritage in Whitman, the "authorizing precursor," according to Yingling, of *The Bridge.* Crane's last lines in "Cape Hatteras" have him personally stretching back across time to walk hand in hand with the poet who called himself the "tenderest lover" of men:

> *Recorders ages hence, yes, they shall hear*
> *In their own veins uncancelled thy sure tread*
> *And read thee by the aureole 'round thy head*
> *Of pasture-shine,* Panis Angelicus!
>
> > > > *yes, Walt,*
> *Afoot again, and onward without halt,—*
> *Not soon, nor suddenly,—no, never to let go*
> > *My hand*
> > > *in yours,*
> > > > *Walt Whitman—*
> > > > > *so—*[138]

Crane speaks also of Whitman in the poem, "As thou . . . O, up-ward from the dead," bringing "a pact, new bound, / Of living brotherhood!"[139]

For Whitman, Crane, and Johns, "brothers" can be the "ten-derest lovers"—that panic-inducing extreme at one end of the spectrum of patriarchy's homo*social* fraternal alliances. In myth, the Dioscuri—the twins Castor and Pollux, sons of Jupiter and Leda the Swan—are prototypes of the avenging and inseparable brothers. When Castor was slain, Pollux was inconsolable and wanted to give his own life as ransom to him. Jupiter consented to having the brothers enjoy life alternately, passing one day under the earth and the next in the heavenly abodes. In another form of the story, Jupiter rewarded the attachment of the broth-ers by placing them among the stars as Gemini, the Twins. As the result of an incident during an Argonaut expedition, the brothers became patron deities of seamen and voyagers. Crane's hymn to Walt Whitman in "Cape Hatteras" has inscribed within it another invocation: to the Wright brothers, whose experi-ments off the coast of North Carolina at Kitty Hawk—on the barrier-beach complex of islands called the Outer Banks that in-cludes Cape Hatteras—gave the world its first engine-powered flight.

> *Stars scribble on our eyes the frosty sagas,*
> *The gleaming cantos of unvanquished space . . .*
> *O sinewy silver biplane, nudging the wind's withers!*
> *There, from Kill Devils Hill at Kitty Hawk*
> *Two brothers in their twinship left the dune;*
> *Warping the gale, the Wright windwrestlers veered*
> *Capeward . . .[140]*

In "Cape Hatteras" Crane both soars with the brothers and crashes with them, seeing the destruction inherent in the inven-tion and use of machines.

>   *. . . down whizzing*
> *Zodiacs, dashed*
>   *(now nearing fast the Cape!)*
>   *down gravitation's*
>   *vortex into crashed*
> *. . . dispersion . . . into mashed and shapeless debris . . .*
> *By Hatteras bunched the beached heap of high bravery!*

The Wrights of course often crashed while conducting their experiments. But the symbolism of the brothers' exercises in flight reaches to deeper levels, both personal and mythological. Yingling finds Crane using the brothers to express "the ecstatic flight and crash of homosexuality." "Freud reminds us that flying is symbolic of phallic power, and the Wright brothers are not only historical figures of invention in the text; they represent as well a metonymic displacement of that other brotherhood of homosexuality the text traces. The plane that crashes is not a so subtle phallic image of the pitch and tragedy of Crane's life as a homosexual."[141]

Johns's dramatic arm in *Land's End*, representative of the arm of Crane, is a vestige, the last Icarian surviving mark, the male member if you will, of the "plane that crashes," that "failure of love" called homosexuality. Johns recorded something that was and largely remains of little or no consequence to the world. Just as W. H. Auden projected the Icarian tragedy in that famous passage in "Musée des Beaux Arts":

> *In Brueghel's Icarus, for instance: how everything turns away*
> *Quite leisurely from the disaster; the ploughman may*
> *Have heard the splash, the forsaken cry,*
> *But for him it was not an important failure; the sun shone*
> *As it had to on the white legs disappearing into the green*
> *Water; and the expensive delicate ship that must have seen*
> *Something amazing, a boy falling out of the sky,*
> *Had somewhere to get to and sailed calmly on.*[142]

If only through Crane, the Wright brothers evidently meant something to Johns too, judging from an anecdote the lithographic printer Bill Goldston told me: Sometime in 1960 after Tatyana Grosman asked Johns to make lithographs at her studio on Long Island, he sent her a postcard from North Carolina of a stone marking the site where the Wrights first took off. Goldston said Grosman interpreted this to relate to the artist's impending venture and "new flight" into lithographs.[143] Possibly Johns knew that Braque and Picasso, another great twentieth-century pair of brothers (of the homosocial variety), liked to call themselves Orville and Wilbur.

In Crane's work, Johns must have found analogues of his own open-endedness. The difficulty of reading Johns's work, frequently expressed by critics, echoes deconstructive critics on Crane. Richard Shiff says Johns creates "conditions for the most active and inexhaustible kind of interpretation, the only dependable 'meaning' that his art signifies [being] interpretation itself."[144] Yingling poses similar "difficulties" for Crane, with the "meaning [of his poems] indeterminate, shifting radically as one reads." Yingling roots Crane's abstruseness in a "homosexual semiotic that is determined to refuse closure."[145] Shiff puts Johns's self-avoidance in a more general historic perspective. He compares his "[failure] to indicate a single position from which to . . . express himself, to mark the 'position' of his person" to a classical approach in which the artist positioned viewers to see a single external authority (God's, the king's, nature's) properly, and to the modernist strategy in which the artist internalized this authority, becoming sovereign himself. Johns's art, according to Shiff, is decentered, privileging neither God nor self. Postmodernist practices force "the viewer to interpret without end and to assume diverse voices, gestures and discourses."[146] Seeing a failure "to mark the 'position' of his person," Johns's postmodernist critics return his painting to itself, as in the old days when his crit-

ics colluded with him in refusing to "frame" the work with anything outside it, with any kind of "home" or "origin." A critic
such as Shiff at the same time expresses both an interest in sources
and a longing for them. "As Johns transforms images and objects,
he renders their origins, their generation, their history, obscure.
They do not originate in *him*. This makes the reception of his
art difficult. One wants to know where things come from."[147]

When Johns was done with the brothers—Crane, O'Hara, et
al.—he cast about for new sources of identification, new icons,
and in 1964 for the first time installed a hero, a "father" of his
trade, in one of his works. In the lower left corner of his monumental painting *According to What* he attached a small canvas on
hinges; its hidden front has a traced profile of Marcel Duchamp
taken from a serigraph by Duchamp himself called *Self-Portrait in
Profile*. As "authorizing precursor" (what Crane had made of
Whitman in *The Bridge*), the Duchamp incorporation is a potent
image in a very big painting, especially as it's concealed (requiring viewers to unlatch the canvas to see it), and it put considerable distance between *According to What* and Johns's previous
work.

Such a singular use of an art father suggests that Johns was attempting an identification that had eluded him while growing
up. Events in his life during the mid-1960s, evidently bringing
about to some extent his "socially prescribed straight identity,"
the most persuasive link with the father after all, support that
view. Like Crane perhaps, who had told his mother "of his vain
efforts to cure himself by attempting normal relationships," Johns
would swing away from the identifying marks of a "flawed nature," as he has described himself,[148] where he had been hurt, and
toward the "proper" (female) object.

With a work dated 1971–72 Johns would, I believe, invoke
his real father, whose age at death, fifty-six, coincidentally was
also the age of Hart Crane's father when he died in 1931.

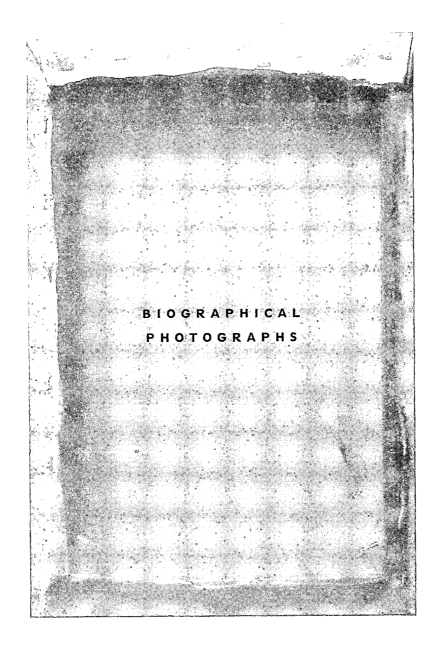

BIOGRAPHICAL
PHOTOGRAPHS

William Jasper Johns, aged 22, graduation photo from Wake Forest Law School, North Carolina.

Baby picture of Jasper Johns, circa 1930.

JAP JOHNS

*good student . . . good artist . . . good actor
all round likable fellow.*
Science Club 1; Press Club 2; Pan-American Club
3; Dramatics Club 4; Hi-Ways Staff 4; Senior Class
Play 4.

LEFT: *Jasper Johns, yearbook photo,
Edmunds High School, Sumter,
South Carolina, 1947.*
BELOW: *Graduation photo from
Edmunds High School, Sumter,
South Carolina, 1947.*

ABOVE: *Sergeant William Jasper
Monument, in Madison Square, Sa-
vannah, Georgia. Photo by author.*
OPPOSITE: *Jasper Johns in the
U.S. Army, 1949, at Fort Jackson,
South Carolina, in an art class with
the soldiers he taught.*

John Cage (left) and Merce Cun-
ningham (right), circa 1964. Photo
by Hans Wild, courtesy of the John
Cage Trust.

ABOVE: *Robert Rauschenberg (left)*
and John Cage (right), circa 1975.
Photo by author.
RIGHT: *Jasper Johns in his studio,*
circa 1980. Photo by Judy
Tomkins.

Jasper Johns at his house in Stony
Point, New York, during the au-
thor's lunch with him in 1983.
Photo by author.

THE GREAT MAN DISCOURSE

I.

My attitude toward art is that of an atheist toward religion,
I would rather be shot, kill myself or kill someone
than paint again.

—MARCEL DUCHAMP

The head the face the human body these are all
that exist for Picasso.

—GERTRUDE STEIN

In art one must kill one's father.

—PICASSO

Little Jap [Jasper Johns] looks a lot like his Daddy.

—SO-SO ALL (LONGTIME RESIDENT
OF ALLENDALE, S.C.)

Sketch for Cup 2 Picasso/Cups 4 Picasso, dated 1971–72, is a small
collage with watercolor, graphite pencil, and ink on paper that
features a profile of Picasso's head with his eyes closed. From the

single image—a photostat of the Spaniard's head glued to a brown paper support—Johns extracted two other profiles. He cut a smaller version out of a sheet of translucent plastic that he'd placed over the photostat, leaving a profile within a profile, and he moved the positive cutout to the right, where it consorts with several sketches for Rubin's figures—vases whose outlines make up double and facing profiles of Picasso. Johns completed these Rubin's figures with Picasso profiles—his first use of them—in two lithographs and a watercolor, *Cups 4 Picasso, Cup 2 Picasso,* and *Sketch,* dated between 1971 and 1973. A decade earlier Johns made a lithograph called *Cup We All Race 4,* both content and title lifted from John Frederick Peto, the nineteenth-century still-life and *trompe l'oeil* American painter admired by Johns. In this litho, the "race" is literalized by the large horizontal imprint of a foot. An outline of a cup refers to Peto's tin cup—an ironic sort of trophy—hanging on a hook. Johns's regard for Picasso might be expressed by an amalgam of these titles, "Picasso, The Cup We All Race 4."

Hidden within the odd construction of *Sketch* are other references, as we expect from Johns. The translucent plastic he used to create two extra profiles in his picture recalls a plaster cast that Duchamp had made for his face in profile in 1959. Duchamp's wife Teeny cast a side of his face in plaster while his cheek bulged with a large nut he held in his mouth. He then placed the plaster cast onto a drawing of his head in profile, calling the piece *With My Tongue in My Cheek.* Johns met the great Frenchman in 1959, introduced to him by the critic Nicolas Calas, who brought him to Pearl Street. "Nico thought Marcel might enjoy seeing our work. Earlier the term neo-Dada had been applied to my work, so I became curious to know who Duchamp was. By the time we met, I had read a good deal about him and had been to see the [Louise and Walter] Arensberg Collection in Philadelphia [in 1954], which stirred my interest strongly."[1] When Johns met him, Duchamp was seventy-two years old. He never got to know him well. He told an interviewer in 1978 that he always played down his relationship "because people have assumed I was very close friends with Marcel, and I was not. I saw him perhaps a dozen times in my life."[2] He usually saw him when he was with John Cage, who was studying chess with him, and he didn't find Duchamp very accessible. "He was not terribly generous about exposing himself."[3] By 1960 Johns had begun collecting works by Duchamp; a decade later he owned as many as thirteen items, including a version of the *Self-Portrait in Profile* created by Duchamp in 1958, an image Johns used on the hidden side of the hinged canvas in his 1964 *According to What*.

Johns made a portrait in profile of himself for a book called *Foirades/Fizzles,* published in 1976, a collaboration with Samuel Beckett. Johns contributed thirty-three etchings to go with five texts by Beckett. One of them was an imprint of his left cheek— a raggedy impression, identifiable by its ear and matted strands of hair. Either by accident or intention, the imprint showed Johns's chin as disfigured—a deep cut or indentation appearing just below his bottom lip.

With its closed eyes, the Picasso head of Johns's *Sketch,* a photo made of the artist as an older man, could be a death mask. In the first volume of his biography of Picasso, John Richardson comments on the artist's quote, "In art one must kill one's father," that "this Oedipal maxim lies at the heart of Picasso's creative process."[4] It's hard to imagine an ambitious artist of whom this could not be said. Picasso's case was dramatic. He thought of himself "as an artistic virtuoso who sprang fully developed from his father's head."[5] Picasso's father, himself an artist, was indeed sacrificed to the glory of his son. An academic painter of pigeons, making his living as a teacher, his sacrifice seemed ordained even before his only son's birth. Richardson speculates that Picasso, still a teenager, "must have realized that compared with other bourgeois families his parents were poor and declassé and that his beloved father was a pathetically bad teacher and painter. This realization would have dealt Picasso's pride a grievous blow. His response was embodied in a determination to exorcise the stigma of parental failure by a triumphant display of his own gifts, something that can only have increased his guilt toward his father."[6]

Picasso memorialized his father's pigeons in his Cubist *Still Life with Pigeons* of 1912—the bird's amputated claws painted with a *trompe-l'oeil* verisimilitude, " 'souvenirs' of the famous claws that launched his career at the expense of his father."[7] Unlike other "failed" fathers, certainly unlike John's, the father of Picasso fully supported his eclipse by his son, supervising his development, "encouraging him to train like a champion"—though he was unable to envision a future for him beyond that of an academic painter of religious subjects.[8]

Johns on the other hand, like Rauschenberg, was hardly an "artistic virtuoso," sprung "fully developed" from a "father's head." There may in fact be no American equivalent to an artist like Picasso, who found himself not only steeped in the European academic tradition, with its institution of apprenticeship, but who was possessed as well of paternal relatives—grandfather and uncles, besides his father—imbued with an interest and practical experience in the arts, especially painting. The only artist in Johns's family was his paternal grandmother, dead long before he was born; she was a Sunday painter of conventional subjects that he occasionally saw in the homes of relatives: "swans on a stream, cows in a meadow, things like that, perhaps they were copied from other things, I'm not sure." He has recalled an artist who stayed with his grandparents in Allendale (where he was living), and decorated "the mirrors of the Greek restaurant with birds and flowers." Johns stole "some paints and brushes from his room," which were missed and "returned . . . by our cook."⁹ There were no artists in Allendale; there was no knowledge of art in the wider world. Johns's father called him a "sissy" for his interest in drawing and embroidering.¹⁰ His youthful work in college was, according to Professor Edmund Yaghian, head of the art department at USC in the 1940s when Johns was there, "not exciting at that time at all." He showed no signs of being a serious artist in school, much less of being a great artist.¹¹ His work then and later in New York, in his early twenties, was tentative and unformed, and without benefit of, say, work from the model, a discipline that Picasso "advocated to his dying day." When Picasso—who once boasted that at twelve he drew like Raphael—arrived in Paris at nineteen he was an accomplished painter, already assimilating modernist influences. It was a background that an American artist like Johns could surely admire and envy; and it was Picasso the giant twentieth-century virtuoso of the figure whom Johns would especially have found awesome. Yet profound differences in background can seem insignificant when similarities in motivation—to surpass and redeem a "failed" father—are considered.

The "reduced" and "degraded" profile in *Sketch* represents, if not Johns's actual father, whom Johns remembers only as "disfigured,"¹² some idea of the "weak and denigrated actual father," as James Saslow describes the father of origins by contrast with the "all powerful male patron, mentor," the "idealized powerful public figure," in his book, *Ganymede in the Renaissance*. Johns's profile of Picasso surely shows "the yearning for eternal union" with just such a "paternal transformation."¹³ The splitting of paternal figures, actual and ideal—a trope of the male consciousness in advancing from family to civic recognition—is especially pronounced in the case of sons unloved or unclaimed by their fathers. Picasso was less split in this sense than even most men. His father handed the tools of his trade over to Picasso when he was very young, sacrificed himself for his gifted son, projected him as a proper successor, and gave him a precocious sense of ascendency, of becoming the father himself. Picasso's early self-portraits show a self-possessed young man, confident and forceful. One was signed Yo el Rey three times, "as if to establish in the world's eyes as well as his own that he, Picasso, was the king, the messiah of the new century."[14] Picasso's many later portraits of himself in the guise of Minotaur seem grounded in an early filial transference of power.

Johns's single self-portrait in his early oeuvre is a photograph of himself printed on a dish attached to the canvases *Souvenir* and *Souvenir 2* of 1964 (one in oil, one encaustic)—mementos of his 1964 trip to Japan, where these dishes are common tourist objects. Posing for the "souvenir" he made a face with the blank and impassive look of a passport or wanted-poster photo. Roberta Bernstein saw a similarity to Duchamp's *Wanted* of 1923—frontal and profile photographs of himself on a "wanted" poster, stipulating a two-thousand-dollar reward, "for information leading to the arrest of [one] George W. Welch."[15] Johns's picture of himself in *Souvenir* seems to be the postmodernist self-portrait par excellence, with the "death of the author" written all over an official face, crying out, catch me if you can.

The description of Johns's father as a man missing his jaw—a result of the auto accident that left his face disfigured—suggests his appearance in the composite portrait *Sketch* in the profile sliced out of Picasso's that leaves a reduced chin. Johns Sr.'s relatives, friends, and acquaintances alike in South Carolina first mention either his accident or his alcoholism in descriptions of him. Charles Shealey, a first cousin of the artist, told me Johns Sr. had "what they call an eggshell fracture," that "he died on the operating table several times," and "he had no jawbone."[16] Geraldine Lewis, a girlfriend with whom Johns Sr. lived off and on during the late 1930s and early 1940s, said that "his jaws had been wired" and that after the accident "he lost his looks" and "was disfigured quite a bit."[17] Curiously, Johns has done some "plastic surgery" on Picasso in his *Sketch* collage.

Johns once told an interviewer a disturbing story about a French clown who broke the legs of his son to make him walk funny, implying a close identification between father (clown) and son. He told it in the context of remarks about making things new. "What's important for us is always what doesn't exist." "If you repeat what you know, it's not really very interesting. When you are making something new you feel more lively."[18] As if to say that a deformed son will inevitably make new things. Johns's father, himself a seriously handicapped son, but unable to escape the locus of family problems, was recreated in a son representing another opportunity, who might end up "walking funny" in a place of profitable exploitation, like the New York art world. Some lore has it that "where a man's wound is, that is where his genius will be."[19]

As a child in Allendale, Johns Jr. replicated essential circumstances of his father's early life by living with his father's father and his father's stepmother. Both father and son, look-alikes with the same name, were orphans in their own town, adrift from immediate family—in the father's case sans wife and child, in the son's missing a home with father and mother. If the diminished profile in *Sketch* represents Johns's father, it may also double for himself, a thought reinforced by the fact that he created two profiles through placement of the positive cutout to the right. The father-son composite idea is perhaps strengthened by association with the deep cut in Johns's chin left by the imprint of his cheek in his etching for *Foirades/Fizzles*.

With his eyes closed in "death mask" fashion and his head disfigured by tampering—given a partial plastic covering and split into two—Picasso is both exalted and presented for revision, a master who had to be mastered. Like Picasso before him, and like all ambitious artists, Johns undertook to tackle and somehow reduce an acknowledged master in making his bid to follow him into the canon. He quite literally demonstrates this in *Sketch* by messing around with Picasso's head, curtailing his profile with the cutouts, cutting him down to size, making him one, if you will, with Johns's disparaged father of origin.

II.

By 1959 Johns happened to answer the improbable question: What would a Duchamp readymade look like if it were a painting?
—MAX KOZLOFF

I have deliberately taken Duchamp's own work and slightly changed it, and thought to make a kind of play on whose work it is, whether mine or his.
—JASPER JOHNS

Me, I'm the father of nothing at all.
—MARCEL DUCHAMP

Sometime during the 1960s Johns had a dream about Duchamp, revealing plans he had for the Frenchman that he would later implement for Picasso. "I dreamed there was a party, with a lot of people. Marcel was lying flat on a table and I saw him from his feet, like that painting [Andrea Mantegna's *Dead Christ*]. The party went on in a very lively way but Marcel did not move. Finally someone began tapping him on the leg, and saying, 'There's something wrong with Marcel, there's something wrong with Marcel.' By then I had moved up to his head, so I saw him from a different perspective. This person kept saying, 'There's some-thing wrong with Marcel.' Then Marcel sat up, very abruptly, and said something extremely funny, and everyone laughed."[20]

Ever the literalist, Johns "moved up to [Duchamp's] head," with his corrective profile of Duchamp's own *Self-Portrait in Profile* on the hidden side of the hinged canvas in the first large panel of *According to What*. Duchamp's original, made out of colored paper from his cast shadow and hand torn around a metal tem-plate, was placed on black paper, providing negative and posi-tive readings of the image. Johns took a tracing of Duchamp's result, the *Self-Portrait in Profile,* hung it from a string, let it cast a shadow of its own, and then retraced it to make his own re-constituted image. The new Duchamp profile corresponds to the old one "as a trapezium does to a rectangle," the way Richard Shiff compares them.[21] Whatever was "wrong with Marcel," ac-cording to Johns's dream, was corrected, seen from "a different perspective."

Duchamp was a kind of godfather to the circle of friends who had influenced Johns the most: Cage, Rauschenberg, and Cun-ningham. He was the living link between the exalted European Dada episode of the late teens and early 1920s and the new Dada sensibility in the 1950s that was spearheaded in the United States by Cage, who "became the channel through which Duchamp's influence was transmitted to a whole new generation."[22] There was an intense revival of interest in Duchamp's work during the late 1950s and early 1960s. Johns read Robert Motherwell's 1951 book on the Dada painters and poets and later owned Robert Lebel's book on Duchamp that was published in 1959 with a frontispiece photo of Duchamp's silhouette from *Self-Portrait in Profile,*[23] as well as Arturo Schwarz's *Marcel Duchamp/Ready-Mades, etc.* of 1964, which includes a color reproduction of the profile.

Duchamp had been living permanently and rather obscurely in New York since 1942, the same year Cage moved to New York. Cage met the older man at Peggy Guggenheim's apartment[24] and was so smitten that he once went so far as to name the whole world after Duchamp: ". . . the things he found [the ready-mades]. Therefore everything seen—every object . . . plus the process of looking at it—is a Duchamp."[25] Johns was later expansive in his own way, saying of the master, "He has changed the condition of being here."[26] He meant that Duchamp's "ready-made was moved mentally and, later physically into a place previous occupied by the work of art."[27] Duchamp's "persistent attempts to destroy frames of reference altered our thinking, established new units of thought, a new thought for that object."[28] Johns himself, having destroyed a certain frame of reference for painting with his flags and targets, "happened to answer the improbable question: What would a Duchamp readymade look like if it were a painting?"[29] Johns has called *Flag* a "handpainted readymade." His dedication to painting, an activity Duchamp stopped by 1918 (unless one counts *The Large Glass*),[30] was a focus around which he could reconcile his love for Duchamp's "new unit of thought"—the ready-made as art. This meant putting Duchamp in his place, or a place where Johns could see him from a "different perspective." In his dream he cast Duchamp as a dead Christ (like the Mantegna painting) and then resurrected him—"Marcel sat up, very abruptly"— once he had that perspective.

From 1959 on, Johns cannibalized Duchamp objects and motifs in many ways—either coincidentally or as conscious citations. Roberta Bernstein said, "Johns once commented on how amazed he was to keep finding references to Duchamp in his work."[31] His very first "magical" act of this nature may have been with *The Critic Smiles*—the sculp-metal toothbrush, its normal bristles transformed into four teeth, set on a sculp-metal base. On April

8, 1959, *The Village Voice* printed an interview with Duchamp headlined: "A toothbrush in a lead box—would it be a masterpiece?" Duchamp is quoted, "I have the feeling that if you put something in a lead box and dropped it in the river with a note on it: Open in 500 years, this is a masterpiece—and if you put a toothbrush in there . . . well all these schools of Africa, isn't that the same thing?"[32] Johns must have seen the interview, then united Duchamp's ironic reference to masterpieces with his own beef against critics, placing *his* "toothbrush" on the outside of *his* "lead box."

His ploy here resonates in a way with the popular story—repeated a number of times in the Johns-related art literature of the 1960s—concerning the contemporary American master Dutch-born Willem de Kooning, who is said to be a favorite of Johns's. As Johns himself put it in 1964, "I heard a story about Willem de Kooning," that "he was annoyed with my dealer, Leo Castelli, for some reason, and said something like, 'That son-of-a-bitch; you could give him two beer cans and he could sell them.' I heard this and thought, 'What a sculpture—two beer cans.' It seemed to me to fit in perfectly with what I was doing—so I did them—and Leo sold them."[33] Johns tells this story with great relish in a film about himself of that time, laughing uproariously.[34] One source of his pleasure could have derived from the sense of topping exlover and rival Bob Rauschenberg's infamously erased de Kooning drawing. Collecting scalps, Johns had a "twofer" here, but the joke on de Kooning over his remark demeaning a common object and defaming his dealer, who did sell the work, seems to have been registered by Johns as a small triumph.

Duchamp's "scalp" was for Johns of course a serious and concrete trophy, a cause for ongoing research, seizure, application, and assimilation. That *According to What* is a vast play on Duchamp's last painting, *Tu m'*, of 1918, is acknowledged by the authorizing self-portrait profile on the hinged canvas at bottom left (in the position of postage stamp if the canvas of three panels were turned around completely). The work shows Johns as a kind of self-appointed torch bearer or baton carrier, wishing to redress Duchamp's history as a "failed modernist," resuming painting where the master left off. The title *Tu m'* suggests any number of verbs that we could fill in after *m'*, including *tu m'emmerdes* (loosely, you bore the shit out of me), one that seems to capture the artist's feeling about painting (done by people who "love the smell of turpentine," as he put it) at the moment he gave it up. A résumé of earlier works and ideas, it was done to fulfill a commission by Katherine Dreier, one of Duchamp's American patrons, fitting a long rectangular space between bookshelves and ceiling in her New York apartment. Duchamp called it "a dictionary of his main ideas prior to 1918."[35] Included are shadows traced from projections of his ready-mades: the bicycle wheel, hatrack, and corkscrew. A realistic hand with pointing finger emerges from the handle of the very elongated corkscrew shadow. A rent in the canvas looks real, but it is painted in *trompe l'oeil* style and "held together" with three real safety pins. Official literature has it that a professional sign painter hired by Duchamp, one "A. Klang," executed the hand, his diminuitive signature appearing just underneath. Possibly A. Klang was as fictional as R. Mutt, the name Duchamp invented one year earlier, in 1917, to "author" his *Fountain,* the urinal entered as a ready-made in the first exhibition of the American Society of Independent Artists.[36] If so, the name would be consistent with the plays on reality or confusion in levels of signification that define the work and Duchamp's postmodernist work generally. Duchamp enjoyed a certain polynonymity, signing various names to objects and correspondence, Rrose Sélavy being no doubt his best-known alter ego. Obviously Johns thought of Duchamp as a kind of coauthor of *According to What,* making an alter ego of the older man, made clear by the "mix-up" of signatures on the small hinged canvas containing Duchamp's traced profile. He mis-signed the outside "J. John," inscribing Duchamp's initials, "MD," on the inside (the side with the profile), along with his own name, "J. Johns" with an X drawn through it.

There is virtually no visual resemblance between *According to What* and *Tu m'*, but Johns appropriated Duchamp's concept completely in making a "dictionary" of his own "main ideas" prior to that time, a number of which were already Duchamp-like, especially Johns's yen for mixing or confusing realities. Duchamp painted his swooping diagonal row of color samples— the image that binds the picture—in perspective, then undermined this illusion of space by "attaching" them to his canvas with a real bolt. The letters of Johns's two juxtaposed and reflecting vertical rows of primary color names are confounded by their appearance as both painted and real, the latter in bent (metal) relief from the canvas. Johns's compendium of motifs from earlier work includes a version of the dramatic leg and chair from *Watchman* of that same year, its shadow projections now more prominently featured, in keeping with the correspondences he intended with Duchamp's *Tu m'*. Not even a hint of slavish imitation, however, characterizes *According to What*. The vertical color chart of circles, the spine of the painting running down its precise middle, is the only concession Johns made to appear to be copying any of Duchamp's motifs in *Tu m'*, and this was also an extension of his own broad plays in previous work with "color charts," limited to red, yellow, and blue. The image in *According to What* that best corresponds to Duchamp's row of color samples, structurally speaking at least, is the diagonal swath of newsprint, so pervasive as undercoating in Johns's earlier work (silkscreened in *According to What*), that links the color names, the chart of circles, and large rectangles of primary colors in the right panel. This ties the picture together the way Duchamp's color samples do in *Tu m'*.

As he reached for the master, Johns both aligned and distinguished himself in the kind of compact that a most ambitious son might strike with a father whom he wishes to flatter and impress, but not to alienate. No artist was better than Johns at the game of "reference, deference and difference" that Griselda Pollock posits as the prerequisite for an artist wishing to make his mark in the avant-garde community.

> You had to relate your work to what was going on: *reference*. Then you had to defer to the existing leader, to the work or project which represented the latest move, the last word, or what was considered the definitive statement of shared concerns: *deference*. Finally your own move involved establishing a *difference* which had to be both legible in terms of current aesthetics and criticism, and also a definitive advance on that current position.[37]

With reference came "recognition that what you were doing was part of the avantgarde project." Summoning deference, the "coveted place" of the father is acknowledged; establishing difference is "the deadly blow by which his place is appropriated or usurped."[38]

Tu m' provided Johns with just the precedent he needed for leapfrogging a figure whose "boom," as Calvin Tomkins writes, "went into high gear" with a major retrospective exhibition of his work at the Pasadena Art Museum in the fall of 1963 (the year before Johns executed *According to What*) and who "found himself hard put to avoid the pedestal on which a growing host of admirers and disciples wished to place him."[39] Max Kozloff expresses Johns's position this way, echoing Griselda Pollock's scheme for advancement: "It is as if Johns had so taken over the contradictory, Pirandello personality of Duchamp that he had no alternative but to outflank and subvert him." "In true Dada fashion Johns is constrained to allude to the older artist but simultaneously to evade him. Under no circumstances can he ... be thought merely to parody or quote his mentor."[40]

Tu m' was ideal in representing equally Duchamp's brief history as a painter and his "deviant" invention of ready-mades, matching dual concerns of Johns's, and for presenting an opportunity to telescope history by dusting the work off and showing it—a kind of self-curatorship to resurrect Duchamp the painter. In a short obituary Johns wrote for Duchamp in 1968 paraphrasing philosopher Ludwig Wittgenstein (his bedtime reading, according to Barbara Rose, during most of the 1960s[41]), he indicated his dissatisfaction with history: "Time has only one direction must be a piece of nonsense."[42] By sleight of mind, Johns contracted forty-four years, making himself and Duchamp contemporaries, both in Duchamp's time and his own. He even lined up the title of *According to What* with Duchamp's, duplicating the sense of omission and question in the latter's incomplete *m'* by appearing to ask a question of his own: *According to What*[?]. Answering Johns's question with an additional question, we might fill in his title thus: According to What Am I the Same as or Different from Marcel? Johns asked this himself in his way: "I have deliberately taken Duchamp's own work and slightly changed it, and thought to make a kind of play on whose work it is, whether mine or his."[43] Answering the question on behalf of Johns, we might fill in Duchamp's title by asserting, "Tu m'es"—you are me.

III.

I'm nothing else but an artist, I'm sure, and delighted to be.
— MARCEL DUCHAMP

Oh yes, I act like an artist although I'm not one.
— MARCEL DUCHAMP

*But that the man [Duchamp] meant more to me than his art is
something that he would have understood, always smiling and
murmuring, 'Cela n'a pas d'importance.' "*
— BEATRICE WOOD

*Art has not the celestial and universal value that people like to
attribute to it. Life is far more interesting.*
— TRISTAN TZARA

*It was beautiful to see J[ohns] and D[uchamp] together. It was
obvious that J admires D as a great genius of our age.*
— ROBERTA BERNSTEIN

In the last decade of his life, Duchamp rose gladly to the occasion of his new public visibility and celebrity, consenting to be
magnified over and over in interviews, public appearances, films,
and publications. Judging from Duchamp's veiled activity for
years on behalf of his future immortality, such as involving himself in byzantine arrangements for the disposition of his work in
a single institution and toiling secretly from 1946 to 1966 on his
last work, *Etant Donnés,* which would become a permanent in-
stallation in the Philadelphia Museum—all the while feigning indifference and inactivity—his revival during the 1960s must have
seemed an unexpected boon to him, especially when his coop-
eration left intact the mystique of his immensely admired withdrawal. Duchamp became an Osiris, and various parties, Johns
one of them, gathered up the pieces of the "dismembered god"—
known as a ruler of the dead—to be made whole as a postmodern icon. The artistic contribution of Johns in this project was
particularly poignant because of its drive toward integration, a

state that evidently eluded him personally, but that he conceptualized here and tried to realize on a grand scale both for Duchamp and for his own relationship to a man nineteen years younger than his grandfather, thirteen years older than his father.

Having steeped himself in Duchampiana, Johns apparently had some special insight into the myth and trajectory of the elusive Frenchman. Of particular interest would be that crucible in his career when he stopped painting, a "moment" for which *Tu m'* is an anagoge representing what he did before, and that Johns similarly commemorated in *According to What*. The first four, telegraphically short sentences of his slight "obituary" (in style lifted from a statement on Duchamp made by John Cage in 1963),[44] with references to three Duchamp works, hint at an understanding of exactly how and why Duchamp gave up painting and in what style he conducted himself during his withdrawal. "The self attempts balance, descends. Perfume—the air was to stink of artists' egos. Himself, quickly torn to pieces. His tongue was in his cheek."[45]

Painting dutifully as a young man in the modernist modes of the time, Duchamp acquitted himself well enough ("the self attempts balance") until 1912, when apparently he did too well for his own good ("descends"). At the age of fifteen he was an Impressionist, showing the influence particularly of Cézanne in family portraits and landscapes. From twenty to twenty-three he was a Fauve. He followed quickly with the subdued palette and flat broken planes of Cubism, so recently inaugurated by Picasso and Braque. Then in March 1912 he sent off the Cubist-style painting he called *Nude Descending a Staircase* to the Salon des Indépendants show. His sister Suzanne Duchamp and his two older brothers, Raymond Duchamp-Villon and Jacques Villon, were also represented in the show. Duchamp said of his *Nude:* "Painted as it is in severe wood colors, the anatomical nude does not exist, or at least cannot be seen, since I discarded completely the naturalistic appearance of a nude, keeping only the abstract lines of some 20 different static positions in the successive action of descending."[46] By the lights of the Paris Cubists, Duchamp's *Nude,* with its study in motion, resembled too closely the style of their Italian competitors, the Futurists. There were other problems. "At that moment in time, in 1912, it was not considered proper to call a painting anything but Landscape, Still Life, Portrait, or Number Such and Such." And "A nude never descends the stairs—a nude reclines, you know."[47] Also Cubism was young, and "a united front had to be maintained against a hostile public." The Cubists called a conference and Duchamp's brothers were sent to ask their younger sibling to withdraw his picture or at least change the title. " 'I said nothing to my brothers,' recalled Duchamp, 'but I went immediately to the show and took the painting home in a taxi. *It was really a turning point in my life, I can assure you.* I saw that I would not be interested very much in groups after that' " (italics added).[48]

As Johns suggested, "the air was to stink of artists' egos." A Duchamp scholar of sorts, Johns invokes "perfume," qualified by the "stink," an ironic allusion to the 1921 "assisted ready-made," a collaboration between Duchamp and Man Ray—*Belle Haleine, Eau de Voilette*—a perfume bottle in an oval box signed "Rrose Sélavy."[49] "Himself, quickly torn to pieces," was Johns's allusion to Duchamp's *Self-Portrait in Profile,* which Duchamp had labeled "Marcel déchiravit," referring to the way he had made the profile that Johns later used—by tearing a sheet of paper along the edge of a metal template corresponding to his cast shadow. Finally, "his tongue was in his cheek" indexed the title of the slight piece Duchamp made in 1959, the side of his face cast in plaster, a large nut in his mouth. The title works to qualify Duchamp's life after painting, as he spoke cleverly under his breath or out of the side of his mouth, mocking the serious, covering serious tracks of his own, ever equivocal and ironic.

This side of the Frenchman, a strong point of identification for Johns, was a side he needed to integrate with the "retinal" aspect of art that Duchamp had disavowed. *Tu m'*, painted by Duchamp six years after his crisis over *Nude,* though done as a kind of throwaway to fulfill a commission, was a revolutionary painting for its time, way in advance of his earlier derivative work, including the Cubist-Futurist *Nude,* and it was critically unrecognized. Johns performed a critical function in bringing the work into contemporary focus, creating the "different perspective" given to him in his dream. If Duchamp *was* a "failed modernist," here was proof that he might have succeeded had he kept going. In his obit statement Johns quoted Duchamp as saying "he was ahead of his time."[50]

Ultimately though, it was Duchamp the "failed modernist" who gave the incipient postmodernist artists of the 1940s and 1950s—John Cage foremost among them—their hero. The alignment of Duchamp's "failure" with the failure of modernism is one of the striking conflations of the twentieth century, testifying to the holding power of an extraordinary cool personality, whose strategies for survival and redemption are perhaps unique in the history of art. A chasm opened in society during Duchamp's youth with World War I, leaving government and bourgeois values on one side, and a new class of angry disenchanted men on the other. In art, Dada of course was their expression. In Dada, the ready-made was the antiauthoritarian gesture that would endure. Duchamp insisted that "there was no concept or intention of any kind involved. He simply took the front wheel of a bicycle and mounted it upside down on a kitchen stool in his studio, where a touch of the hand would set it spinning. 'It came about as a pleasure . . . something to have in my room the way you have a fire or a pencil sharpener, except that there was no usefulness. It was a pleasant gadget, pleasant for the movement it gave.' "[51] But once signed and shown (with *Bottlerack* in 1917[52]) these objects fractured art history, or at least that is the exalted agency accorded them in our time. They are understood to have undermined the bourgeois conception of genius, negating the value attached to individual creation, destroying the distinction between high and low culture, debasing an elite tradition by introducing mass-produced objects into it, ushering in the disturbing novel idea that *all is art*—the "new units of thought" noted by Johns.

By the time Johns discovered Duchamp, Johns was already the kind of artist Duchamp described as different from himself. For Duchamp there was "the artist that deals with society, is integrated into society [painters like Johns]; and the other artist, the completely freelance artist who has no obligations [such as himself]."[53] But Duchamp said this back around 1912 "after his brush with the Cubists" when he wanted "nothing more to do with 'professional painters.' "[54] By the 1960s, in America at least, he himself could be perceived as an artist integrated into society. What was once "antiart" had now been assimilated as art, and he personally engaged with the art world in its courtship of him. Even so, the discrepancy in the histories of the two men highlights their essential differences. Johns was ambitious from the start to enter the pantheon of art deemed dead by Duchamp. "Art," Duchamp said in 1959, "was a dream that's become unnecessary. . . . Painting since 1914 has been . . . superficial . . . not an essential production as in Cimabue, the Renaissance, even the Romantics." As for the Abstract Expressionists: "Just splashes on canvas."[55] So how did he feel about an ambitious painter like Johns who (along with Rauschenberg) idolized him and plundered his motifs, and who enjoyed the kind of commercial success he had decried in artists since at least 1912? An encounter between Johns and the revered older man documented by Roberta Bernstein shows a mutual appreciation—on Johns's side hinting at the kind of father-son compact that he would surely have desired in the relationship.

On March 4, 1968, Johns, with Bernstein's assistance, was putting the final touches on a set of transparent inflatable plastic boxes he had made for Merce Cunningham's *Walkaround Time,* with silkscreened images from Duchamp's *The Large Glass* printed onto the fronts and backs, in readiness to show them to Duchamp and to have them transported to Buffalo for the Cunningham premiere on March 10. Bernstein and Johns picked Duchamp up in a cab at his apartment at 28 West 10th Street to bring him to 343 Canal Street, where they'd been working on the set. It was David Whitney's loft, which Johns had been using as a temporary studio while he lived at the Chelsea Hotel, waiting to move into his Provident Loan Society building on Houston Street. Johns was "unshaven, wearing paint-spattered brown corduroys and torn sneakers" and "nervous . . . as if he wanted everything to be perfect." Solicitous of the older man, "he was worried it might be too cold for Duchamp to want to go out—he mentioned that D disliked the cold weather."

Bernstein reports the first thing Duchamp said as he got into the cab: "Canaday surely didn't know what to say about your show, so he said nothing at all!"—referring to the review in the *New York Times* that very day "where [John] Canaday described the people at the opening of J's exhibition at the Leo Castelli Gallery and hardly mentioned the works." Apparently not mentioning them himself (most likely he had not been to the opening), he nonetheless called supportive attention to the fact of the show, even while observing Canaday's omissive put-down. He had once said, "I don't want to destroy art for anybody else but for myself, that's all,"[56] a remark that Johns included in his "obituary" in 1968.

Bernstein saw Duchamp on this occasion as "gentle, magnanimous, wise, sharp-minded, with a touch of naïveté (similar in a way to Andy Warhol and John Cage—that kind of wonder-at-the-world quality and generosity that is naive, yet within a sophisticated framework)," adding to the myriad descriptions of him by American writers as having "class," a quality distinctly different from the rawness and machismo of, say, the Abstract Expressionists. Commenting on the two men to whom she was playing handmaiden, she said, "It was beautiful to see J[ohns] and D[uchamp] together. It was obvious that J admires D as a great genius of our age" and "D liked the set very much."[57] He had to persuade Johns to take credit for it in the program notes. At the premiere of *Walkaround Time* in Buffalo Duchamp was persuaded to take "credit" on stage, bowing with the Cunningham company.

There's a reminder here of Cage's critical agency in uniting the artists he influenced with the grand old man of Dada, now a figurehead of postmodernism. Cage was influential, if not directly responsible, in all the choices of artistic collaborators for the Cunningham company. Johns's set for *Walkaround Time,* his first venture since becoming artistic adviser to the company one year earlier (a job Rauschenberg held before him), gave him an opportunity to show his respect for Duchamp, to exercise his awe, and in turn to receive a certain attention. He also received a drawing from his idol, in thanks for his efforts, making his Oedipal project more personal.[58] Cage, closer to the age of a son—twenty-five years younger than Duchamp—had been diligent on his own behalf in this respect, "using chess as a pretext to be with him," he said.[59] Since his game was much weaker than Duchamp's, Cage generally played with Teeny, Duchamp sitting at the other end of the room smoking, periodically glancing at their game and making criticisms.

One month before *Walkaround* premiered in Buffalo, Duchamp appeared in Toronto to take part in a festival of art and technology, performing there with John Cage in a Cage piece written specifically for himself and Duchamp. It must have been exciting for Cage to lure Duchamp to Toronto to play chess with him publicly in the "performance" of a piece he called *Reunion*. Duchamp was his teacher, but also a master of the game. He had grown up enthusiastically playing chess with his five siblings; he had played in tournaments in France and the United States, and he had been called a "master among amateurs." In Toronto, Cage had him in his own bailiwick, making "music" the moment he touched any of the chess pieces, which were hooked up to an electronic sound system. Perhaps Cage hoped to beat him at last, with his "environment" as a distraction or decoy, but Duchamp, though he gave himself the handicap of a knight, beat Cage handily, leaving Cage at least the satisfaction of demonstrating a certain intimacy with a much-venerated figure. Cage said he turned to him during the performance and asked, "Aren't these strange sounds?" Marcel smiled and said, "To say the least." Afterward Cage played with Teeny, who had been there looking on, while Marcel remained on stage. The game went on and on; around eleven-thirty they looked up and noticed that everyone in the audience had left. In the morning they continued the game in the hotel. Cage reported that he lost.[60]

With Duchamp's death, Cage inherited his role as chess partner to Teeny, a role he already had, though not to the exclusion of her husband. Conceivably, he imagined also succeeding Duchamp as grand master of postmodernism, a mantle he probably did receive from his own postmodernist world—the wide-flung international group of neo-Dada composers, choreographers, and artists, along with latter-day converts, who had so thoroughly fallen under his influence during the 1950s and early 1960s. Johns and Rauschenberg were of course among the earliest.

Duchamp underestimated his importance to this group when he said, "In Europe the young always act as the grandsons of some great man—Victor Hugo, or Shakespeare, or someone like that. Even the Cubists liked to say they were grandsons of Poussin.

Duchamp, a "father" of postmodernism. "Dada in any of its manifestations, and modernist painting, are antithetical to one another. Where the former aspires to obliterate all distinctions between works of art and other kinds of objects or occurrences in the world, the latter has sought to isolate, assert and work with what is essential to the art of painting at a given moment."[62] Johns had adopted both men as "ancestors," featuring profiles of them as well as their motifs and titles in his work. Now he would make them converge in a picture singling out Picasso's profile along with an emblematic representation of Picasso's *Straw Hat with Blue Leaf* (1936), placed on a tracing of Duchamp's abstract Cubist work *Bride* of 1912. Johns had been tracing or copying both works during the 1980s. For another *Untitled 1988* he reversed the figure of Duchamp's *Bride* and turned it on its side. Thus his own "bride" is recumbent, if you will, and he has converted her head into a chalice containing the familiar facing Picasso profiles in negative. The one to the right "holds" the rectangular "picture" of *Straw Hat with Blue Leaf*—a still life with a book, a vase, a base, and some leaves (on the hat) "worn" by a bald head in profile consisting of two eyes, a mouth, and three rounded protuberances. Downsized as part of the "head" of his drawing, the *Straw Hat* image has been "miniaturized . . . and then . . . inserted into another world, as it were," as Johns has mused in general on his preoccupation with relationships between parts and wholes.[63]

Johns, who told me he likes the Picasso for being "more than one thing," has also said, "it's informed with sexual suggestion and very complicated on that level, but it seems offhand."[64] Minus the hat and leaves, the surreal head looks as male as female (though the prominent eyelashes reinforce its femaleness)— which is perhaps partly what Johns meant by "very complicated." It certainly appears he intends this kind of complication himself. For instance, he's given Duchamp's *Bride* a complex head consisting of three heads and other accessories. Lining up the nose-profile of the *Straw Hat* head with the negative Picasso profile "cut out" of the right side of the chalice, Johns has inserted Picasso's metaphorical female, *Straw Hat*, into the profile of Picasso himself, impregnating him or filling up his head with an image from his best-known subject—Woman. In the context of Johns's untitled painting, *Straw Hat* becomes a "bride." But she is also Picasso, taking up the space of his whole (imagined) head, forming, as it were, its cranial contents. Duchamp occupies the left side of Picasso's brain, the ground of his *Bride* invading the profile, though Johns was careful there to darken the area within the profile, making the Picasso outline stand out. The doubling of things, typical with Johns, is intense. The chalice or vase of the Rubins image doubles with the vase of *Straw Hat*. Picasso is "married" to Duchamp in the picture, reminding us that Johns's deepest emotional projection involves twinning two men. This is a serious interest, but Johns is not often at a loss for humor, and here he has tipped his chalice just slightly to the right, a drop of water falling out of it and hovering immediately over the blue leaf part of the hat, as if of course about to water it.

If *Untitled 1988* concerns the marriage of two "fathers," it must also represent the two fathers as lodestones who were able to obtain what Johns found elusive, namely brides. I wouldn't underestimate the emotional strength of the *social* yearning for marriage, especially for those who, like Johns, have grown up siding with society against themselves, and were hardly touched by the politicized gay community. In 1988 Barbara Rose told me that Johns was always saying two things: "He doesn't want to live in New York, and he wants to get married."[65] In 1912 when Duchamp painted *Bride,* he was rather far from having such an object himself. Done in Munich where he spent three months after his debacle over *Nude* in Paris, *Bride* was a mechanomorphic study pointing toward *The Large Glass,* or *The Bride Stripped*

Bare by Her Bachelors, Even, the strange and singular project that would occupy Duchamp between 1913 and 1923, an abstraction on glass that he felt was one of only "4 or 5 things" he did in his lifetime that were "actually worth anything"—a work he prized for showing "no direct influence."[66] Duchamp didn't marry until 1927, when he was forty years old, and then only for seven months (to a young Frenchwoman). He realized he was "unable to bear the bond, moral burden and responsibilities of marriage" and found "it [was] an absolute necessity for him to regain his liberty and that he [wanted] a divorce."[67] Not until he was sixty-seven did he have a bride again, the American Alexina (Teeny) Sattler. As for Picasso, he had one bride (Olga Koklova) he could never get rid of (she refused to divorce him)—until she died and he married Jacqueline Roque.

Johns first traced *Bride* in 1978, turning it into an ink on plastic picture called *Tracing.* It was only his second tracing, the first executed one year earlier, and also called *Tracing,* but clearly revealing its source in Cézanne's *Les Grandes Baigneuses,* the group of women bathers, which he later gave to David Shapiro, a straight poet friend. Johns's model for his *Bride* tracing was a 1930 aquatint he owned, done after the Duchamp original by the artist's brother Jacques Villon. He did nothing further with *Bride* until 1986. Then, in another Cage-linked project, he made eight untitled ink-on-plastic tracings, this time using a reproduction of the original *Bride* painting in a book. He made them to be used as the basis for gravure illustrations in a series of seven books projected for publication by Osiris Editions of Cage's mesostics, *The First Meeting of the Satie Society,* a homage from Cage to Duchamp's friend, French composer Erik Satie.[68] Mesostics, a poetic form that can be read both side to side and vertically, was used extensively by the composer as a "spine"—a "row down the middle"—in organizing appropriated texts, shuffled or mangled by chance operations. The volume in this series with the

Johns *Bride* tracings includes Cage's mesostic or central vertical word reading "relâche" (suspension of performance)—the title of a ballet presented in Paris in 1924 by Duchamp's Dada confrere Francis Picabia, with music by Erik Satie and featuring Duchamp as a performer. Duchamp's role in the ballet was to impersonate Adam, and he performed nude except for a fig leaf, along with a nude Eve (her left hand covering *her* crotch in the extant photo). His part was modeled on the painting *Adam and Eve* by the sixteenth-century German painter Lucas Cranach. While in Munich in 1912 Duchamp had been inspired by both Cranach and the nineteenth-century painter Arnold Böcklin. He said if there was an influence for his *Bride* it had to be Cranach and Böcklin, but especially Cranach. "I love those Cranachs . . . I love them. Cranach the old man. The tall nudes. That nature and substance of his nudes inspired me for the flesh colour."[70] Cranach (1472–1553), incidentally, was a pupil of Grünewald's.

A dizzying confection of associations is suggested by this aggregate of names in the project for a volume of Cage's mesostics. The "duet" of Adam and Eve is as nothing next to all the males who are paired off: Johns and Cage, each with his dyadic interest in Duchamp, the creator of *Bride* (1912), here himself "stripped bare" in a ballet (the only historic reference putting him in company with Merce Cunningham, a "bride" of Cage's, but also of Johns's insomuch as he "dressed" the dancer with decor and costumes in his role as artistic adviser to the company); Duchamp and Picabia, like Johns and Cage exemplifying the patriarchy's homo*social* alliance of brothers; Picabia and Satie in the same kind of bond to produce *Relâche;* Duchamp and Satie, who were friends; Cage and Satie, paired on the son–father order, admirer and chosen dead mentor; Duchamp in the "grandson" relation to Cranach; Cranach the pupil of Grünewald, whom Johns of course extensively adopted, and so on. Eve in *Relâche,* the only woman in this group, is unidentified in both Robert Lebel's

1959 book on Duchamp and in Arturo Schwarz's later 1963 compendium.

Commenting on a painting he did in 1912 before *Bride,* called *Passage from the Virgin to the Bride,* Duchamp cast himself in the two roles of his title in terms of being an artist. "[It is] not a physiological passage but a passage in my life of painting, one after the other."[71] In another comment the sense of identity with his *Bride* is reinforced, as she appears in *The Large Glass:* "The Bachelors serving as an architectonic base for the Bride, the latter becomes a sort of apotheosis of virginity."[72] It was as an artist determined not to be "taken" (by the world of art) that he decamped from Paris, took up residence in Munich (a "scene of complete liberation", he said[73]), and experimented with forms that would lead him to *The Large Glass*—something "showing no direct influence." The full sexy title of *The Large Glass, The Bride Stripped Bare by Her Bachelors, Even,* doesn't describe what you see in the picture: the "bride" in the glass section above strictly segregated from her "bachelor" forms (the "malic moulds") below. One critic sketched the scene as "highly esoteric, disjointed, [a] satiric story about a female, her nine suitors and their interaction of mutual arousal, rejection and frustration; *their union remain[ing] an impossibility."*[74] Of course if you read or heard nothing about the work you would see only some abstract forms. Told what they represent, you would agree that "their union" is "an impossibility." Writing about Duchamp in 1980, Paul Matisse, son of Teeny Duchamp by her previous marriage, said of *The Large Glass:* "There is a bride, which we cannot really see, who is being stripped bare, also not pictured, of her clothes, also invisible." Duchamp himself said extraordinary things about the picture, which he published in something called *The Green Box* in 1934. Echoing him, as many writers have, Matisse went on, "There is a desire-magneto, a ventilation, scissors that open and close, air current pistons that waft back and forth in a draft, a cannon that fires, water that falls, a mill wheel that revolves, a wasp that kicks and sometimes spurts, rams that go up and down, sparks, explosions, crashes and splashes."[75]

In essence it seems *The Large Glass* represented, as André Breton put it, "the trophy of a fabulous hunt through virgin territory," or as Duchamp said, "a passage in my life of painting," which he cast interpretively (by title and descriptions) as an erotic onanistic enterprise, yet invoking the language of cultural imperatives for male designs upon women. He was just twenty-five at the time. He had art and no doubt women on his mind, not brides, except himself metaphorically speaking—the "infinitely seductive Bride [who] . . . can never be truly possessed," as Calvin Tomkins frames him.[76] Referring to *The Large Glass* in his brief "obituary" Johns mentioned "the Bride, held in a see-through cage—'a Hilarious picture.' " Hilarious presumably on account of the utter irony of its title and descriptions, the fun it thrust at representational art, even to the extent of its title exposing the literal desire behind much realism: "The Bride Stripped Bare."

Duchamp "stripped bare" was clearly appealing to both Johns and Cage, in the sense that this particular "father" was a straight man who could take off his clothes, that is, expose his female side. His body alone was admirably lithe, hairless, and unmuscular, an ectomorphic Adonis, a poetic ideal—quite unlike the square brawniness of the hirsute Picasso, small yet built like a fire plug, an apotheosis of masculinity as we have known it. In Duchamp, Johns and Cage and their kind found an androgyne like themselves who happened to be straight, and who as such had been able to get away with acts and exposures unimaginable to them: cross-dressing (as Rrose Sélavy), perpetrating female aliases (not only Rrose but Sarah Bernhardt and indeterminate names like Totor and Dee), appropriating and defacing a female icon (the Mona Lisa), not to mention withdrawing from art, the effect of a rejection by a group of men—two parts of a condition that have perennially afflicted women under patriarchy. Here Johns and Cage, being outsiders to the large group of men who define the normative male, could identify, subconsciously at least. Cage could make a parallel professionally, having experienced rejection as a composer. And he could identify further through the "masculine" solution of survival by perseverance and wit, including the creation of an antiart movement of his own.

Activity under cover was common to Duchamp, Johns and Cage, albeit in varied forms. These were men who knew exclusion and retreat, but were "manly" enough never to give up. Of the three, Johns had been blessed professionally, if instant and sustained acceptance by peers and authorities in a traditional medium is counted lucky. Herein, at any rate, is where he parted company with the men with whom he otherwise had so much in common—a difference accounting for his eventual Picasso obsession.

Johns's tracing of *Bride* in his *Untitled 1988* is occluded in a critical way by the overlaid Picasso images. The Duchamp "body" of the work—both as ground and as body of the "bride"—is given the head, the brains, the crown, the portrait, of Picasso. Johns early on identified Duchamp as a "conceptual" source of inspiration, also citing Cézanne as "important in terms of the visual aspects" and Leonardo as balancing "the visual and the conceptual."[77] But with *Untitled 1988* Duchamp is represented by a picture pinning him to his "bride stripped bare," his mental function dismissed, and incarnated instead in an artist considered a brute by comparison. One observer saw "Marcel Duchamp . . . a few centuries more developed as a human animal than our beloved Picasso."[78] Another saw Duchamp as a "dandy [who] concealed the complex artist striving for a higher freedom, questioning the very purpose of art."[79] Duchamp has also been called Picasso's "bad conscience,"[80] a reference to his renunciation of art, perceived (by many) as an abhorrence of the rising commercialism in the market. But whether Picasso was a "barbarian" or not, insomuch as Duchamp's *Bride* was executed in the Cubist style coinvented by him, the bodies of both men form the ground of Johns's *Untitled 1988*.

The picture shows a certain ascendancy in Johns's mind of the hugely remunerated Spaniard, due perhaps mainly to his own awesome market success during the 1980s—approaching even Picasso's posthumous market value—but also to his absorption with *Straw Hat with Blue Leaf,* as he found countless uses for it in his work of the late 1980s and early 1990s. The older Johns is much less the child of Dada and Duchamp than a grown-up part of the tradition of painting epitomized by Picasso, no longer interested in "questioning the very purpose of art," if indeed he ever really was. He marries off his heroes in *Untitled 1988,* not as two men or equals but conventionally, as a dominant man and a submissive woman, with Picasso obviously on top.

If the *Bride* tracings project a "mature" desire for marriage—having in mind Freud's pronouncements on the puerility, the stunted development, of the homosexual state—an earlier quotation of a Duchamp icon by Johns shows what probably remains his authentic sexuality (an ambivalence between aspirations for normality and a true, however secret, homosexual identity). This is a color lithograph of 1969, *Figure 7,* from the series *Color Numerals,* with the face of the Mona Lisa nestled coyly in the lower part of the bottom stroke of the number "7," interrupting its progress there; and an imprint of the palm of the artist's right hand in the lower left corner, a big masculine hand, unmistakably positioned with respect to the Mona Lisa to signify a greeting on her part. She's smiling her famous sly, inscrutable maidenly smile and saying "Hi" like a man.

It's the closest perhaps that Johns has come in his work to "camp." He brought his Mona Lisa out of the closet, so to speak,

when he featured her in his big 1983 encaustic and collage painting on canvas, *Racing Thoughts,* as a kind of pinup, imprinted
(silkscreened) on a poster-style rectangle "taped" to the canvas,
her name boldly printed in a caption redundantly identifying the
world-famous image. She is not alone. In *Figure 7* she was given
the company of the artist's hand, but in *Racing Thoughts* she's acquired the conventional companion of a handsome man—a
silkscreened photograph of the youngish Leo Castelli. And with
the Rubins image profiles of Queen Elizabeth and Prince Philip
appearing in the same picture, Johns's burgeoning interest during the 1980s in traditional coupling, in the bourgeois solution
to sex, is here announced and emphasized.

Johns of course from the beginning "corrected" Duchamp's
Mona Lisa, returning her to Leonardo, a proper female sans
moustache and beard. But with his hand imprint in *Figure 7* he
retained the masculine association, keeping somehow the spirit
of the Duchamp, who said of his desecration: "The Gioconda
was so universally known and admired, it was very tempting to
use it for scandal. I tried to make that mustache very artistic. Also,
I found that the poor girl, with a mustache and beard, became
very masculine—*which went very well with the homosexuality of
Leonardo"* (emphasis added).[81] With Duchamp's title:
L.H.O.O.Q., whose sound pronounced phonetically in French
becomes "Elle a chaud au cul," or "She has a hot ass," the gender slippage seems complete. Duchamp evidently acted on a certain lore of the Mona Lisa's androgyny—the legend that the
painting actually represents a man, perhaps Leonardo himself.

Duchamp himself "corrected" his *L.H.O.O.Q.* in 1965 with
a ready-made (a playing card featuring the Mona Lisa mounted
on folded note paper) called *L.H.O.O.Q Shaved,* referencing his
early defacement while returning her to Leonardo.

Johns updated his own Mona Lisa in 1985, one year after her
appearance in *Racing Thoughts,* by including her in *Summer,* the

third painting in his *Seasons* series. At that time he was also developing a unique female face created in part of features borrowed from Picasso's *Straw Hat with Blue Leaf*. By 1989 he had titled one of these faces *Montez Singing,* a direct reference to his paternal stepgrandmother with whom he lived during most of his first nine years. From the *Mona* Lisa to *Montez,* Johns made a big jump, both personally and artistically—from an icon owned by the world, universally recognizable, to an unprecedented-looking image, art historically, with a name known only to the artist; from the appropriated ready-made to the individualized invention; from replication to representation; from art history aborted to, more wholeheartedly, the bourgeois conception of genius; from the gesture of rebellion against the fathers to a place at their side.

With Montez and her numerous look-alikes, mostly titled "Untitled," Johns the "(sur)realist" forged an image he had been missing in his long quest to enter art history: Woman, with a personal imprimatur. And with Montez also he signaled an interest in his maternal background, counterpart to the patristic claim he made for *Flag* in 1979 when he asserted that he and his father were named after a Revolutionary war hero. Besides indicating personal history, Montez betokens a seizure of the *cultural* image of Woman.

THE EVOLUOF MONTEZ

I.

Johns is the first artist to have used the handprint as a repeated motif with a wide range of meanings.
—ROBERTA BERNSTEIN

In Jasper Johns the hand is a kind of voice. Where others draw persons, things and objects, he draws intrinsicality.
—DAVID SHAPIRO

He was born, he went to school; and then this hand started painting, this disembodied hand starts making this work and there's no person or life or anything behind it.
—JULIE MARTIN

His tour de main . . . is to make his viewers feel dumb.
—ROBERT HUGHES

On his mother's side Jasper Johns is a Riley. On June 6, 1989, during my fourth trip to South Carolina in search of the artist's family, I met his mother's brother, Edward Patterson Riley, a longtime resident of the small, pleasant city of Greenville, an hour and a half's drive northwest from Columbia. I found Mr. Ted, as he told me he was called, in his offices on the twenty-seventh floor of something called the Daniel Building on North Main Street. Garrulous and lively, still handsome and practicing law at the age of eighty-eight, he told me much more than he was supposed to. He hadn't yet been informed by his niece Owen, one of Johns's younger half siblings, that I—or anyone, I presume—wanting information about the artist should be kept in the dark, a restraint I would later discover for myself. When I saw him again on November 10, 1993, Mr. Ted was wearing two hearing aids, and his upper back was somewhat humped, but he was still keen at ninety-three. Now he told me he was under orders not to talk. But he wasn't entirely able to check himself. He told me that his sister Jean Riley, Johns's mother, had died a year ago, and he conveyed quite a few other things as well. He even got out of his chair to give me a hug after he recognized me.

Mr. Ted, I knew already, was now the proud father of the U.S. Secretary of Education. His second son, Richard Wilson Riley, born in 1933 and governor of South Carolina from 1979 to 1987, had been appointed by President Clinton to the post in 1992 when he took office. Mr. Ted told me that Dick and Bill were close friends as governors. Dick Riley's governorship and new appointment reflects a long distinguished history of Rileys in South Carolina as planters, soldiers, and people who, the way Mr. Ted put it, "messed with local politics." Active in politics himself, in 1960 Mr. Ted delivered South Carolina to John Kennedy in his capacity as chairman of the South Carolina Democratic Party and state chairman of JFK's campaign for president. By 1962, having decided his son Dick was ready for politics, he coached him in a bid for the House in South Carolina; after fourteen years in the legislature, Dick had run for governor.

The first time I met Mr. Ted, in 1989, he nonchalantly handed me a book I could take home with me called a *Historical and Genealogical Record of the Riley Family and the Barker Family,* showing how he and his sister Jean could trace their ancestry in America back to one Miles Riley, from a Protestant Irish family of Ulster, Ireland, who had settled in Beaufort Province of South Carolina by the 1740s, founding a plantation called Fiddle Pond, which consisted of about three thousand acres. His son Miles Riley Jr., born in 1779, fought in the 1812 war against England and married a Kirkland, some of whose family lands had been grants from George III. One of Miles Jr.'s sons, James Wilson Riley, a "successful planter" and "influential citizen," a captain in the state militia and Confederate soldier, was the great-grandfather of Edward (Ted) and Jean Riley. The present Secretary of Education was named after the father of Edward and Jean, Richard Wilson Riley, born 1867, a dentist who became county auditor, following a "famous campaign speech"—which Mr. Ted read aloud to me from another book he had in his office called *The Town of Allendale.*[1] "Fellow citizens, ladies and gentlemen: I'm running for the office of Auditor because it's an easy job and pays a very good salary—and I need the money. Keel's had it [a past holder of the office], Moody's got it [the incumbent] and I want it. I thank you." He was elected overwhelmingly and died in office years afterward, in 1922.

Jean Riley, born in 1906 in the town of Barnwell, seventeen miles west of Allendale, with the name Meta Jeannette, was sixteen years old when her father died. Her mother Meta Dowling Simms died when she was an infant, her brother Edward Patterson Riley being about six at the time. Their father then married a widow who brought a daughter two years older than Jean into the union. Jean's daughter Owen, Johns's half sister, was given the middle name of a brother older than both herself and Edward, George Owen Riley, born in 1898, who was very successful in the insurance business and who, remaining childless—Mr. Ted told me—helped Johns go to college and left trusts to both Jean and himself.

A Riley legend linking the family with Ireland involves a reference as striking as the flag in Johns's paternal mythology, and an icon perhaps even more common in Johns's work, if without the flag's national significance. The Riley family's coat of armor, according to a note in the *Historical and Genealogical Record* that Mr. Ted gave me, bore an emblem that was a favorite device of the province of Ulster—Lamh dearg Erien—the "Red Hand of Ireland." The story goes that its use was connected with one Niall or O'Neil, ancestor of the princes of Ulster, who was in a company of seamen searching for new territory. "When the green isles of Ireland were sighted, his boat was far behind his competitors, but to carry out his ambition to be the first to touch shore, he severed his hand from his wrist and flung it ahead of them, and was awarded the lands of Ulster." The note ends, "Many Irish families use 'The Bleeding Hand' as their family symbol."

Johns certainly has "flung" many hands (imprints mainly of his own right one) onto paper and canvas during his career. Claiming territory figuratively through the individual stamp of the handprint is an ancient practice. In contemporary terms, it may not be as persuasive as a signature in identifying ownership of a painting, but it's still a signature with impact, carrying a kind of sacred symbolic power. In Johns's case we could say that the handprint was a means as significant as the flag in claiming or proclaiming a space that was his. Simon Rodia, the Italian tilesetter who made Watts Towers in Los Angeles his life work, impressed the wet cement of the wall surrounding his construction with prints of his hand. But for Johns, with of course evolving and re-contextualizing meanings, the handprint has been a motif equal to the flag, the later heads and Grünewald figures, shadowed self-images, and cups or pots, in constructing new narrative fragments by cubist-collage treatments.

His probable first handprint, actually a painted hand, appears in a small painting, tempera on silver foil mounted on tissue, 18 1/4 inches tall by 6 1/4 inches wide, circa 1952, belonging to an early pre-*Flag* body of work that he did his best to destroy. Called *Spanked Child,* it's a Dubuffet- or childlike figure of a child blending with a Klee-like compartmentalized ground, which Johns later used in various works, outstandingly to organize some of his number or letter series. The work has never been exhibited in New York, nor possibly anywhere else.[2] It shows Johns early on to be very interested in both the figure and its expressive attributes and possibilities. A black-and-white ink drawing called *Idiot* of the same apprenticeship period features two hands and part of the "idiot's" moonface, which is falling off the picture edge. The hands are realistically drawn, the right hand appearing to cup the chin, two fingers touching what passes for the "idiot's" mouth. In *Spanked Child,* the hand of the child's disciplinarian is applied in red to its bare bottom, the child's tears falling schematically in vertical dashes from eye to reddened hand.

Here, oddly and astonishingly, is a "bleeding hand," although it seems unlikely that the artist either knew of this Riley coat of arms emblem in his maternal family background or, if he did, drew on it for *Spanked Child* or for that matter the later hand imprints that proliferate in his mature work. The probability is that he felt confident in making use for his own purposes of a motif he had seen in the work of such admired established artists as Picasso, Magritte, Miró, Man Ray, Duchamp, Jackson Pollock, and his mentor Robert Rauschenberg, whose images and themes often found their way into his work. Yet if it's true that Johns is "the first artist to have used the handprint as a repeated motif with a wide range of meanings,"[3] it's as tempting to link his handprints with that numinous emblem of Riley ancestral lore the "Bleeding Hand" as it is to join his flags with the Revolutionary war hero Sergeant William Jasper. At some future time Johns might insinuate a parallel distaff relationship for his handprints, should he happen to read the words of, say, a critic identifying the Riley coat of arms emblem the way Charles Stuckey pointed out the coincidence of Johns's name, his flags, and Sergeant Jasper.

There is no evidence to date that Johns has painted or reproduced or specifically indicated any images, consciously or not, derived from his maternal background. Montez, whose name figures prominently in work of the late 1980s and early 1990s, was the second wife of his paternal grandfather; and *Spanked Child,* with its red hand so seemingly pregnant with the maternal mythology, can be more convincingly referenced to Johns's family on his father's side, who raised him. Two anecdotes suggest for the picture a self-pitying memory of a humiliating experience or experiences at the hand of his grandfather. "As a young child living in his grandfather's house, [Johns] remembers being dressed in the kitchen, by the cook, in a new white linen suit. He didn't want to wear it, and threw off the suit, which landed in a skillet of hot grease on the stove. His grandfather came in and began throwing him in the air, catching him, and spanking him as he fell. He was terrified."[4] In 1990 an old friend of Johns's who had recently had dinner with him and others at a midtown Manhattan restaurant reported that Johns had held up his plate, the meal finished, saying that when he was a little boy he cleaned his plate, held it aloft, and announced, "Look how clean my plate is, it doesn't need to be washed," and his grandfather gave him a whipping.[5]

Aside from the red hand of *Spanked Child,* I am not aware of any other artistic use of hands by Johns during the 1950s, excepting the cast of a hand in a compartment along with eight other casts of body parts domiciled in individual compartments, each equipped with a wooden flap for viewing the parts or hiding them, all set in a row like amusement-park souvenirs above the painted target of *Target with Plaster Casts* of 1955. Handprints abound in Johns's work of the 1960s, when his hand became "a kind of voice," a vital cog in his lexicon of images, performing several basic functions: expressive (as in *Land's End* or *Study for Skin I* or *Figure 7*); marking the artist's presence *(Arrive/Depart);* bearing witness, cautioning or warning, delimiting spaces *(Periscope [Hart Crane]);* indicating intention or destination *(Diver)* and location; pointing at featured objects, illustrating the tool (hand) used to make the work.

During the 1970s, when Johns's crosshatch or herringbone patterns were sovereign in his work, when he was asserting himself as a master of abstraction, it was noted that these measured bundles of lines creating the patterns resembled stylizations of the human hand.[6] By 1977, having noticed this analogy himself, or having read it in criticism of his work, Johns reversed the implication in an untitled of 1977, in ink, watercolor, and crayon on plastic, in which angled handprints echo his directional crosshatch forms. A year later, with another untitled, a large acrylic on paper, he used his fingers to apply paint, making a "fingerpainting" to create the by then well-known crosshatch patterning. The earlier untitled work shows Johns's great virtuosity in compounding images and meanings derived from different periods of work. Here he intermingles his handprints with the handles of paintbrushes stuck in a Savarin coffee can, establishing a "formal homology among the artist's hand, his tools, and the marks they create,"[7] both recalling his *Painted Bronze* Savarin can and brushes of 1960 along with their many variations in other mediums, and evoking the "signature" of his hand in its many manifestations, creating "a dialogue between an image's past history and its present appearance."[8]

The dismemberment of Johns's reproduced hand or hand-*cum*-forearm, often pointed out by critics when referring to the body parts in general that litter his work, is perhaps its most distinctive feature, telling of both loss and discovery, the divestment necessary for invention, the sacrifice that precedes and accompanies breakthrough or new blood—a gestalt so perfectly illustrated by the apocryphal tale of the ambitious Riley ancestor who severed his hand from his wrist and flung it ahead of him, succeeding in being awarded new lands. In his "Sketchbook Notes" of the early 1960s Johns wrote of an "object that tells of the loss, destruction, disappearance of objects. Does not speak of itself. Tells of others. Will it include them? Deluge."[9] "Tells of others"—presumably the things "it" (for instance, a dismembered hand) brings into being. A "deluge" of things. The founding of entities, of new forms, is at stake.

Around 1973, visiting Antwerp for the first time, I happened to see the amazing fountain representing Brabo, the hero of that city. Sculpted as a beautiful Adonis atop a castle held aloft by three graces, Brabo runs and throws the hand of Antegoon, the giant who dominated the city and collected taxes, now sprawled in a parabola around the base of the fountain, both handless and decapitated. The founding of Antwerp, which takes its name from the hand, reverses the manner in which some Riley ancestor supposedly established holdings in Ireland. The Antwerp hand is thrown away into the sea. The giant represents the "old father" or unconsciousness; his destruction makes way for the modern city. In the Riley story the hand comes out of the sea, so to speak, and "invades" or "impregnates" the land.

There is no father per se in the Riley story; presumably in "the search for new territory" the "father" was simply left behind—a style that corresponds to Johns's personal story. In Mr. Ted Riley, the artist's uncle, we can get some idea of what such a father, call him the "giant" of the Antwerp tale, the one who traditionally holds his son(s) back by repression or abuse, or by neglect and abandonment, might think about a son who got away, founding a strange sort of power base far from the remains of the old Confederacy where such deeds tend to be of a political nature, word of this "son's" triumphs having drifted back to him. Johns's own father died of course on the eve of his discovery by his dealer-to-be, and one year before his stunning overnight success. Mr. Ted had two children, both sons, both lawyers like himself, the elder having continued to work in his firm with him—a defense firm with civil cases, having 180 lawyers and offices in seven southern cities. Naturally I wanted to know what he thought of his nephew the artist, whom he barely knew and had not seen for years, probably not since the late 1940s when Johns was a college student in Columbia, not far from his mother's house in Sumter, where he had finished high school while living with her and three half siblings.

Without much prompting Mr. Ted told me that once when he went to see his sister Jean at Edisto Beach (where she lived in a house Johns had had built for her on the vacant lot where his own house burned down in 1966), she pointed to one of her son's paintings on the wall and said it was worth fifteen or twenty thousand dollars, making him say, "What *is* it?" He laughed hard as he told me this. I asked him, "What *was* it?" He replied, "The number 1." I said, "Oh well then, it was very clear what it was," following up this tautology by mentioning Sergeant William Jasper the Revolutionary war hero, linking him with his nephew's painting of a flag by which his public first knew him—hoping evidently to see if or how he would respond to my rooting the artist in some glorious piece of South Carolina history. Ignoring South Carolina history, Mr. Ted, laughing hard again, declared, "And the second [by which his public knew him] was the beer can!"

The next day, as I was visiting the artist's uncle at his modest white frame house with a lawn somewhat gone to seed, in a quiet Greenville suburb, he tried without success to find a watercolor Christmas card that Tump (a family nickname of Jasper's on his mother's side) made once for his Aunt Martha, Mr. Ted's wife of over fifty-two years, who died a number of years ago. According to Mr. Ted, "When she found out what it was worth she was even more proud." He remembered Tump as "shy and reserved." Four years later, in 1993, Mr. Ted added more from his fund of impressions, this time observing greater respect, perhaps out of regard for his deceased sister, the mother of Tump, and for her daughter Owen, whose warnings could have made my project seem more real or serious to him. Now he said, "I admired Jasper's success. I've had occasion to brag or admit that he's my sister's son."

During my first interview with Mr. Ted in 1989 he remarked that "Jasper was rid of his family for some time." In our 1993 meeting, indicating another state of affairs, he said, "Jasper was very good to his mother." While Montez was a maternal figure on his father's side, her appearance in his work during the 1980s seems to symbolize a growing closeness to his mother in her last years.

II.

*[Jean] never discussed what happened between
her and Jasper [Sr.]*
— MR. TED RILEY

You can learn what you need to know from Jasper himself.
— OWEN RILEY

*They were just fine people . . . very well
thought of in Allendale.*
— MRS. ERNIE STEVENSON

*[Jean is] pretty, charming, bright, and with a most winsome
personality . . . whose only regret in her marriage is that it will
remove her a slight distance from the home town in which she
has always been so popular.*
— THE PEOPLE'S SENTINEL, BARNWELL,
SOUTH CAROLINA, SEPTEMBER 15, 1927

*I don't think you could get close to Jap Sr. [Johns's father].
He stayed to himself.*
— VICTOR SPIGNER

*In a way it's a tragic family, the Johnses . . . because of
the alcoholism.*
— MRS ERNIE STEVENSON

By the time Montez became Johns's surrogate mother, Jean
Riley had left Allendale. At first, she took the baby with her.
Then she relinquished it; she lacked the resources of the Johnses,
who could provide aunts and an uncle willing to assume responsibility for the baby and a grandfather's household that included servants and a titular mother at least in the grandfather's
wife Montez.

Jasper Johns's cousin Charles Shealey says his mother Gladys—
Jap Sr.'s older sister who lived with her husband Frank Shealey
and four sons on Lake Murray, some sixty miles northwest of Allendale—was an intermediary mother, receiving the baby in di-

apers when he was eight to ten months old. He was brought to her by the baby's father, and he was "trained" before being returned to Allendale to live with his grandfather and Montez.[10] Johns went back to live with Gladys in 1939 when he was nine, after his grandfather died, staying with her until 1946. He attended school in the one-room schoolhouse in Climax where Gladys taught all the grades and then attended the Batesburg-Leesville high school, before going to his mother in Sumter and finishing high school there. Charles Shealey, a longtime resident and mortician in Batesburg, claims that Johns's mother left Allendale and her son behind before he was one. Mary Young, daughter of Jap Sr.'s other sister Eunice, has also said Johns was "still in diapers" when his parents abandoned him.[11] But her story varies from Charles Shealey's on what happened then, or else she simply omitted the part involving Charles's mother Gladys. She reported, "His father [Jap Sr.] found himself with a failing farm and a failing marriage. He brought his young son to our grandfather, W. I. Johns, and it was with him and his second wife, Tezzy [Montez], that Jasper made his home." In September 1990, when I asked Mary Young to tell me what happened, she said, "Jean Riley left for a vacation with the baby and didn't want to come back. Uncle Jap and my mother Eunice went to get the baby. She didn't want to keep it, [was] unable to care for it."[12] Presumably it was after this that Jap Sr. brought the baby to Charles Shealey's mother Gladys, before he was delivered back to his grandfather.

Although Mr. Ted had told me Jean "never discussed what happened between her and Jasper," I decided, with some trepidation, to try to make an appointment to see her. When I called her at Edisto Beach, from Columbia, she readily agreed to meet me. She was very gracious on the phone, but then, remembering that her daughter Owen, who lived with her, would not be back until the following day, asked if I could come then. I was concerned that her daughter could be the kind of formidable family guardian that many writers seeking biographical information encounter and realized she could compromise or block my appointment. I went anyway, taking note of a sign I saw before entering Edisto proper that said, "Beware of Alligator." And indeed, I was turned away at the door by Owen, who said she had met me once in New York when she "used to work for Jap" and who told me, "You can learn what you need to know from Jasper himself."[13]

Charles Shealey had said the separation of Jean and Jap Sr. was the least talked-about thing in the family.[14] The marriage of a Barnwell Riley to the younger son of W. I. Johns, a leading citizen of Allendale and a founder of Allendale County, was described as "an outstanding event of social interest" by the *People's Sentinel* of Barnwell on September 15, 1927. The wedding took place at the Barnwell Baptist church, which was decorated with "palms and ferns, clinging vines and high white and gold cathedral candlesticks" and "was attended by a large throng of friends." There were also four ushers, two pairs of groomsmen, and maids (among them Mr. Ted Riley and Martha Dixon, his wife-to-be); a matron of honor, Eunice, sister of the groom; a maid of honor, Mary Roberts, half sister of the bride; a flower girl, a ring bearer; the best man, W. I. Johns; the bride's other brother, George Owen Riley, the successful insurance man, who gave her away. "Her wedding gown was of shimmering white satin with an overdress of tulle petals on which rested lightly tiny orange blossoms. The long filmy veil was also sprinkled with orange blossom petals in a billowy mist forming the long train. White satin slippers adorned with tiny clusters of orange blossoms and bouquet of bride roses and valley lilies completed this exquisite toilette." Jean was described as "the lovely young daughter of the late Mr. and Mrs. R. W. Riley . . . an exceptionally attractive girl in every way. Pretty, charming, bright, and with a most winsome personality . . . whose only regret in her marriage is that it will remove her a slight distance from the home town in which she has always been so popular." Her groom came off as "a splendid young representative of a family which has always been known for the moral strength and mental ability of its men . . . [who], with his father, has large farm interests in Allendale County." At a prenuptial supper for twenty-four, the bride presented her attendants with pearl pendants, the groom his groomsmen with silver pencils.[15] If the bride's "only regret" in her marriage was that it would "remove her a slight distance from [her] hometown," it could be said that she had high hopes for herself.

Her son, Jasper Johns Jr., was born May 15, 1930, two years and eight months after the wedding. It seems more than likely that Jap Sr.'s alcoholism played havoc with the relationship. The birth of a baby, especially of the first one, an event that normally puts pressure on a couple, probably pushed Jap Sr. even closer to the edge. He was a binge drinker, so he may have abandoned his bride for periods of time, leaving a frightened young mother to fend for herself in an unfamiliar town. If a common background—both left motherless at a young age—had drawn them together, the strain of a husband feeling deprived of his new wife turned mother of his child, and a wife needing succor herself and becoming divided between two needy males, could also have driven them apart. Jean's mother died when she was one; circumstances impelled her to leave her son when he was around that same age. Jap Sr.'s "failing farm" and the onrushing Great Depression couldn't have helped. Finally, add to alcohol the lethal ingredient of violence, and I believe you have enough reasons why Jean Riley Johns abruptly left town.

From Geraldine Lewis, Jap Sr.'s girlfriend during the late 1930s and early 1940s, I learned that Johns's father could be an abusive alcoholic, prone to both physical and verbal violence. I had already heard something about this from Geraldine's son Jerry, who was born in 1938 when she was eighteen, around the time she got together with Jap Sr. I found Jerry Sineath in September 1990 at his convenience store called Jerry's Fireworks, next to a Kentucky Fried Chicken on Route 301, which runs through the main street of Allendale. When I asked him what Jap Sr. looked like, he said, "Like an alcoholic." Since he quickly added a note about the famous accident, which "happened . . . on the road to Savannah, [when] he crashed into a bridge," he seemed to imply that he thought Jap Sr. was driving while intoxicated. He told me his mother left Jap Sr. "cause he beat up on her"; his mother's brothers "caught him beating up on [his] mother and that was the end of the relationship."

Bill Johns, son of Jap Sr.'s brother Wilson R., told me his uncle was a binge drinker. "He'd drink as long as he could stand it health-wise," then he'd have to quit for a while. Geraldine Lewis, a roundish pleasant-looking woman of seventy when I met her, thought Jap Sr. had been a "social drinker" until he went to see "old Dr. Boyd" to obtain additional morphine for the pain he sustained after his accident and the doctor produced a jar of white lightning (moonshine), saying, "Son forget about morphine, take the liquor."

I was brought to Geraldine's modest, cozily outfitted house on a nice tree-lined street by Joe Topper, a popular Allendale photographer-*cum*-paramedic, who had taken it upon himself to drive me around introducing me to people. When I called Geraldine months earlier, she had said, "I just don't care to talk about that . . . I don't care to reveal my personal life." Now, although reserved and suspicious, she was willing to talk, encouraged perhaps by the sponsorship of Joe Topper. She said her "Daddy," a blacksmith in town, "and Wilson [Jap Sr.'s older brother] were very close friends." She had an affair with Jap Sr. in Savannah during the war, where they shared an apartment and worked in the shipyards, he in the toolroom offices as a clerk, she as a guard, then later in the toolroom offices herself. She admitted reluctantly that Jap Sr. was not always "loving toward her," saying he "was very possessive, dependent, and violent." She had fond memories of his son Jasper as a "sweet" boy, with "charm," a "very loveable child," and "a good cook, always trying to please." The boy's father, she said, called him a "sissy" for embroidering flour sacks, which he would rip open, then bleach and convert into dishtowels by hemming them. Then he embroidered drawings he had made of fruits and vegetables on them. Geraldine said he gave her the finished products, and that she bought paper and crayons for him.[16]

On my next visit, two and a half years later, in November 1993, Geraldine appeared warmer and more relaxed, if still somewhat reticent in her dignity. This time she gave me a more complete interview, feeling heartened perhaps by a communication she had had recently from Jasper through his cousin Mary Young, wanting to know if she could provide a sketch of the floor plans of the house in Martin (several miles outside Allendale) where she and his father had lived for three years. Geraldine didn't remember Jasper visiting them there, as she did him staying with them in Savannah for a week or so at a time. (Perhaps it was on one of these occasions that Jap Sr., walking with his son in Madison Square, pointed to the statue of Sergeant William Jasper and told him that they were Jasper's namesakes.) She also remembered Jasper going to stay with his mother during the summers. Geraldine made the sketches, and Jasper had sent her a letter of thanks along with a *Seasons* catalogue, which she brought out to show me, saying she was proud of it.[17] I was able to tell her he was sure to be making use of the floor plans in his work, as he had already incorporated such plans from his grandfather's house in a painting.[18]

In Martin, Jap Sr. grew a lot of watermelons, Geraldine told me, and had "a colored family" to help him, the husband a chauffeur, the wife a cook and maid. She felt "sure he was raised by a black nanny . . . he always liked to be waited on by them." She was quick to add that "he appreciated what the blacks did. He cared for them. They were human beings to him. He let them have barbecues." But apparently it wasn't easy living with him. "He was broody, withdrawn. . . . I could tell by the way he acted he was motherless—possessive, jealous . . . he didn't even want Jerry to see me." And finally impossible. Geraldine recalled Montez's father, John Bramlett, saying, "Why do you put up with him, he abuses you all the time." In 1946 Geraldine got away from him by decamping to Savannah. In 1950 she married and had two daughters. Before I left her this time, I poised myself to ask her if Jap Sr. was her son Jerry's father. Jerry's birthdate and other vital information—he told me he grew up not knowing who his father was and had been told he was killed—had made me wonder.[19]

After meeting Mrs. Ernie Stevenson in Allendale, I had concluded that Jap Sr. probably was. Mrs. Stevenson, one of the townspeople Joe Topper introduced me to, is as lovely looking in her butch-cut white hair, apple-pink skin, azure-blue eyes, ready smile, and beautiful teeth as is her big old house, which sits on Main Street, Route 301, right across from the site where Jasper's grandfather's house once stood. Her view of the Johnses encompassed in a nutshell both their good standing in town and their family difficulties. "Wilson Sr. was a lovely, lovely person. They were just fine people . . . very well thought of here in Allendale." And, "In a way it's a tragic family, the Johnses . . . because of the alcoholism." When I asked Mrs. Stevenson about Geraldine and her son Jerry she said that Buster Lewis, an Allendale classmate of hers, whose uncle had married Geraldine, told her he went out to visit Geraldine and Jap Sr. once in Martin and that Geraldine was pregnant then: she inferred from this that Jerry became their issue.[20] Joe Topper said Dr. Boyle told him that Jerry was Jap Sr.'s son. But Ernie Stevenson's brother Victor Spigner said, "Jerry is *not* Jap's son. I can't tell you who his father was." And he added an impression of the putative father of Jerry: "I don't think you could get close to Jap Sr. He stayed to himself."

Geraldine echoed Victor: no, Jap Sr. was not Jerry's father. She seemed neither embarrassed nor affronted by my question. She recalled a trip she made with Jap Sr. and Jerry to visit Jerry's father in the mountains in North Carolina. (An incident on the trip, Jap drinking and clowning around on a little rocking chair he had bought for Jerry near Asheville, stood out in her mind.) Geraldine's impression of Montez as a lady who liked to drink and party was echoed by other people who knew Johns's step-grandmother.

Bill Johns's word for Montez was "different"—pronounced "diffrunt." It was with Bill and his twin sister Betty and their parents that Jasper lived for a year during the 1930s. Bill went bankrupt in 1984, losing all his land in Allendale as well as his house. I found him in a nicely furnished trailer on the muddy banks of a small river, near the towns of Sheldon and Yemassee, a forty-minute drive from Allendale. He and his wife Mary rented the trailer from "a colored lady." Bill pronounces the "er" at the ends of words as "uh." He said "I don' remembuh" frequently. He seemed like a sweet man who'd gone downhill gently and was resting in resigned quiescence at the bottom, living for the eight or nine Miller Lites that his wife allows him only on weekend evenings. His replies were very slow and monosyllabic or minimal; yet there was nothing unclear about what little he said. His most complete utterances were reserved for the alcoholism of his Uncle Jap and father Wilson R., men who went on long benders followed by long droughts in recovery. He said his father used to tell him his Uncle Jap "was real smart," that he knew what he was doing. "He'd be good for six months, eight months, then all of a sudden, he'd get on a drunk." I interjected, "That must have been difficult for your Dad [who supported Jap, he had put in]" and he said, "No, not too much. . . . My father was the same way." I got the impression that every Johns male was a heavy drinker. Bill's eldest son, Wilson R. III, died in a car crash aged twenty-one, following a party. Debbie, the exwife of Bill's other son, Allan Dale, implied that alcohol was a factor in their divorce.

I asked Bill, how was Montez different? He answered, "She wasn't liked by us then." I pressed on, "She wore different hats? . . . She dressed differently?" And Bill confirmed, "Right." Suddenly he came up with a certain otherness: "She talked diffrunt." I asked him where she came from; he didn't know. I tried: "She was different from your mother," causing him to reply decisively, "Right."[21]

How different was she, I wondered, from Evelina, W.I.'s first wife, who died in 1906 at the age of thirty-four—the mother of Gladys, Eunice, Wilson R., and Jap Sr. All that appears to be known about Evelina, apart from her parentage, place and dates of origin, her marriage and time of death, is that she liked to paint. Charles Shealey suggested that she died of complications in childbirth, saying that he had heard that. It was her death, in any case, that gave rise to Montez, who married W.I. Johns in 1911, and ultimately to Jasper Johns's use and public identification of her in his first invented image of Woman, features of which he seized from Picasso's *Straw Hat with Blue Leaf*.

*If one recognizes that there is an interior to a work by Johns, the
viewer must then discover what it holds or it might disclose and
what the appearance of its contents is.*

—MARK ROSENTHAL

*Certainly [Proust] realized, if ever anybody did, how the
recapture of time gone by can create an infinite future.*

—JAMES LORD

*[He] . . . had fallen into the trap of Picasso's stare . . .
a sensation that all the artist's friends would sooner
or later experience.*

—JOHN RICHARDSON

The first impression one might have of Johns's Montez images
is that they're "different." They're as different as Picasso's double faces can still seem to be, with their features shown both
frontally and in profile. Quarrying the eyes and nose from Picasso's *Straw Hat with Blue Leaf*, Johns first constructed this face
in an untitled drawing on paper in 1984. For the nose, Johns
didn't use the Picasso nose—a protuberance in profile with no
bridge indentation—but rather Picasso's wavy line indicating the
area of the mouth.

Montez was not introduced until 1988, when Johns made two
pictures called *Sketch for Montez Singing*, one in charcoal on paper
and one in ink on paper. It was as if he had made a face that was
waiting for a name, a name that occurred to him once he linked
the face with a memory he had of his step-grandmother singing.
He removed her name from works where the face wasn't
"singing," falling back on "untitled." In all the paintings, whether
called *Montez Singing* or untitled, the face is rectangularly
bounded, its two eyes grafted to the inner perimeters, one filling the right-angled upper left corner of the rectangle, the other
adhering to the lower portion of the rectangle's right vertical bor-

der. The mouth of the face—a pair of Little Lulu-like lips—lies near and beneath this lower eye, a "twin-peaked" mouth suggesting a piece of landscape along the "horizon" of the rectangle's bottom edge. The nose, simply a cipher or ideogram, a slight line arabesque, describes the nose's base contour seen frontally in its pendant curve rising and curling on either side around each nostril. Off position for a nose, it's situated above but way to the left of the mouth. Every feature in fact is off position, the eyes walled and disposed at different heights (just as Picasso has them in *Straw Hat,* though reversed), the nose floating in cheek-jaw space, the mouth placed to the side and missing all that comes below by way of chin and jowls. This is a "funny face"—a caricature or travesty, a kind of flattened cartoon of the features and proportions that we associate with the human visage, like something a child might do. Having long demonstrated his refusal to draw or to tackle the human figure in any straightforward way, choosing instead to work indirectly through the use of surrogate imprints, tracings, and photographs, Johns here reiterates that unwillingness by rendering the face as a perverse pictogram with appropriated features.

In his perversity he had a plan, one quite consistent with his methods to date: to establish an image that he could repeat over and over, in a variety of colors, design variations, and mediums. The face is unique, however, in Johns's repertoire of images. Peripheralizing its main features to the outermost limits of the rectangle, where they adhere to the frame, he has created a certain synonymity of frame and face-defining traits. This produces an emptiness of sorts within the frame. The flag, target, and Grünewald tracings, to mention three well-known Johns icons subjected to a tremendous range of treatments, including their use as pawns in collage moves, represent another order of things—being the things themselves that fill up the spaces within frames.

Johns rarely superimposed an extraneous image on any of his primary images such as the flags, targets, or numbers. Offhandedly I can recall only the small vertical strip of four photo-booth countenances of a man (Johns told me he found the strip on the street) very discreetly incorporated into *Flag above White with Collage* of 1955. His crosshatch motif was a special case, an abstraction that evolved into a surface to be adulterated by various superimposed images, until finally the figure erupted from its lineaments. Johns's face-frame image invented in the 1980s summons up an early preoccupation with frames. In *Canvas,* 1956, a frame is introduced into the center of a canvas, while the space both inside and outside the frame as well as the frame itself is painted grey. Three decades later, with the face-frame, he set out to fill it up with his trove of signature images of common articles, along with details from his own past work, sometimes just paint itself, as in the 1956 *Canvas,* and new images of a more personal nature.

The face generically serves to illustrate its function as a frame to hold art, and by analogy the idea that Johns's head is full of art. But his main purpose with these pictures it seems was to recycle or update his interest in framing as a device for excluding the world, for illustrating anew how a "common object"—here a face—can hide or destroy its function and contents. Here is another subject that frames itself. It both represents its subject and exists as the subject represented, forcing attention to the works as self-sufficient art objects, turning them into abstractions. Like *Flag,* the outer edges of the face images correspond to the perimeters of the frame framing them. Is it a face or is it a painting, Johns might like to have us ask. As with the Grünewalds, he has flattened out a dimensional image, only in this case not obscuring the results. Picasso's *Straw Hat* image, itself quite flat, is further abstracted by Johns, with its formerly normal feature placements (despite its surreality) now radically rectangularized and eliminated. Still, there is a face there. And because of its intense in-wardness, its isolation (as art object) is more pronounced, or more forcefully asserted, than ever before. The eyes are the thing; as "frame" they turn their gaze to the center, toward their con-tents, scrutinizing the freight of memory, fastened as if navel-gazing on the productions of the self. Nobody else needs to look; the artist, we surmise, has been self-sufficient in this respect for a long time, perhaps since the beginning. All we as observers need to notice are the marvelous surfaces, the intelligence guid-ing complex, often stunningly contradictory, relationships, the utter virtuosity in the transplantation of images from one con-text or established theme to another.

Johns's first face, the 1984 pastel and graphite pencil drawing, contains an inner rectangle—a picture nailed illusionistically to the picture and featuring an upside-down version of the traced Grünewald victim from the *Temptation of St. Anthony* panel of the Isenheim Altarpiece, filled in with opposing groups of stripes. The space between the Grünewald picture and the outer face-frame is carpeted with pencil shadings. In 1985 Johns painted two more face-frame works, both oils on canvas, using the same framed Grünewald "nailed" down, one showing the victim in the same capsized position as the 1984 drawing, the other re-versed and flopped as well. In the latter, which Johns titled *A Dream,* he thought to add something else, a hanging watch, also "nailed," an article that became popular with him as time went on. The watch appears outside the upper right corner of the rectangle-enclosed Grünewald figure.

In 1986 he characteristically reversed the properties of this work—always trying to "make paintings about paintings"[22]—to see how his face would look as the *inner* rectangle. He filled the space between its perimeters and the outermost border of the pic-ture with the now greatly enlarged Grünewald victim (still up-side down), painted in the familiar opposing-stripe patterns, partly covered by the face-frame rectangle, here empty of contents other than paint. That same year Johns's watch grew bigger in two more face-frame works. In 1987 he overhauled his face, the rectangle becoming a skewed quadriform, a "nailed" hanging cloth or veil shape, with eyes, mouth, and nose disposed in the same positions they hold within the rectangles proper. Now he had two basic face constructs by which to regard himself, as it were.

The eyes shun us by gazing inward and staring us down at the same time. Not for nothing are they Picasso's eyes, which both in life and in art were instruments of penetration, command, engorgement, and intimidation, as well as of introspection. John Richardson speaks of the *"mirada fuerte* power"—the "magic power"—of Picasso's eyes, and how "Picasso capitalizes on his amazing eyes: the area of white above and below the pupil [being] no exaggeration" in a particular self-portrait.[23] Jaime Sabartés, Picasso's longtime amanuensis, was once waiting for him in a café, feeling "lonely and dejected." Suddenly Picasso arrived, "eyes blazing voraciously as he drank in the spectacle of his pitiful friend." Sabartés, who became Picasso's inspiration for one of the first pictures of his Blue period, commented that he "had fallen into the trap of Picasso's stare"—a "sensation," as Richardson puts it, "that all the artist's friends would sooner or later experience."[24] Jasper Johns, a man with a covert gaze, eyes that narrow and stare from a head averted or from under a portcullis lowered to keep others from looking, appropriated eyes painted by an unembarrassed voyeur. His "framed" organs of sight and taste show his own rapacity, the power of ingestion, to gormandize the world, to eat self, yet hidden in a way behind some eyes that are not his, at least by reference.

As female images the frame faces are so generic and ideogrammatic that the emergence of Montez, just as a name (in 1988), gives us some sense of a physical presence, of the idea of a person that could animate and historify them, and serve possibly as guideline for Johns's view of women. With the title *Montez Singing,* obviously referencing the frame faces outside the works themselves, Johns overruns his abstract and exclusive program for the faces, suggesting these are works that can only be completed biographically. That critic who wanted "at all costs to return this orphan [any picture by Johns] to its proper owner"[25] would here seem to have a solid permit by the artist himself to do so. While the untitled faces are not devoid of varied moods and emotions, there is a sense in the progression of the pictures that they change with the introduction of Montez, that the untitled faces *after* her become moodier, more individualized. The two 1988 pictures called *Sketch for Montez Singing* laid out his plans for her diagrammatically. His first Montez following them is *Montez Singing* of 1989, a crayon and watercolor on paper that exaggerates the eyes and mouth of his face, bringing the face out as more decidedly female, stereotypically or farcically understood. The "twin peaks" of the mouth, for instance, are two exuberantly bobbing waves, apparently quite "made up," the maw's right side positively beginning to lift off the bottom edge of the rectangle upon which the lower lip tends in most pictures to lie flat. Now a little square containing a tiny sailboat that Johns had drawn in his two *Sketch* pictures the year before appears upper center in the "empty" face area, the forehead or third-eye region, one of three distinguishing features in every face-frame painting with Montez's name.

The tiny red sailboat illustrates, metonymically, the "singing" part of the title. Montez, the artist has explained, used to sing "Red Sails in the Sunset" while playing the piano. Above the sailboat within its square is a minute sun on a horizon line, with rays, and below it a wavy line representing water. With *Montez Singing,* his frame face becomes more fully figurative, with the addition of slightly curving lines sketched off the left side of the rectangle indicating hair, and two three-quarter moons sketchily drawn underneath the mouth, outside the rectangle between its bottom edge and outermost picture limit, suggesting breasts. None of the untitled face-frames have hair and breast emblems. Only the Montez paintings have these attributes, along with the boat. Now the face has a place reference as well, in the vertical stretch of *faux bois* almost flush to the right side of the rectangle, used by Johns since the early 1980s. Here it probably signifies Johns's grandfather's house, in which Montez played and sang. It's clearly a section of floor in any case, as seen from above, with its wood graining and line showing where two planks meet, and the heads of six nails drawn in. In another *Montez Singing* of 1989, an encaustic on canvas of considerable size (75 by 50 inches), the representation of a wood floor is gone, making room for the curling hair lines that appear on the left side. Now the face is "framed" with hair as faces normally are. The face here is glummer, darker, than that of the crayon and watercolor painting. Her lashes resemble nails, or spermata swimming toward her eye-wombs; her mouth is sullen, not buoyant as in the other picture. The eyes in all the face-frame pictures, always crossed as they look inward, seem simply crossed in the Montez works, making her seem ridiculous, or a bit nutty.

Johns's memory of Montez places him as a child between one and nine, but presumably not older than nine, when his grandfather died and he went to Lake Murray to live with his Aunt Gladys. In one *Sketch for Montez Singing* he shows a virtual stick figure we assume to represent himself: hands and feet with fingers and toes, but awkwardly drawn, the way a young child might do them; no torso, legs like pipe stems running directly from neck to feet, head a tiny lifesaver; the image falling away from two small minimal diagrams of the picture he intends to make called *Montez Singing*.

A later, partial, version of the sticklike figure appears in the big oil *Mirror's Edge* (1992), placed in a part of the floor plan of his grandfather's house and overlaid by a cruciform. Three stick figures that descend directly from the "predella" of the ink on plastic *Perilous Night* are also accommodated in *Mirror's Edge*,[26] as is the tracing of a child's shadow from the *Seasons* painting *Summer*. By 1992 Johns was making no bones about his autobiographical project involving childhood. Two years earlier he told an interviewer that "no-one ever talked about family history and only lately, with hardly anyone alive to ask, has he begun to wonder about it."[27]

Mirror's Edge can be transcribed literally as Johns the child (in several versions) situated in his grandfather's house, with the heads of household—W.I. and Montez—represented by shadow profiles of Prince Philip and Queen Elizabeth II. The threefold child in the painting faces in toward several pictures contained within a large "picture" made clear as such by the painted pieces of tape "taping" it to the "ground," and curling corners revealing bits of the "back" of the picture. The left hand, primitively rendered, of the large middle stickish figure, appears to be *presenting* the big picture with its inner pictures, as if saying, "Here, look." One of the two featured inner pictures is a detail of the falling foreground soldier from Grünewald's *Resurrection* panel of the Isenheim Altarpiece, traced of course, and filled in in mauve, green, blue, and ocher colors. Johns has turned the figure one quarter clockwise, making it appear upright, and he has occluded its bent left knee and stiffened right leg, so the soldier now can be read as both upright and *charging,* sword held high. Johns the shadow or stick-figure child in *Mirror's Edge* is looking in at a powerfully embodied grown warrior, a figure with signature impact—representing his accomplishments as an artist. "From early childhood," Johns has said, "I was going to be an artist. I was always going to be an artist. That was my intention."[28] His accomplishments are well demonstrated in this subtle conversion

of the Grünewald soldier in *Mirror's Edge,* having him play an active role in the artist's mythology of success. Here is another reminder of the many uses to which he has put his repertoire of
images, making them play both aesthetically and theatrically, in
mininarratives that link up with other such narratives in tangled
webs of cross-references.

Mirror's Edge is one of Johns's best-developed narratives,
though it speaks only minimally of a child in a house, and
grandiosely of the child's future. A weakling male child conquers
all and wins an exalted place in society, it seems to say. The soldier, coming across more realistically and accessibly than ever before, is the hero of the future, or the one who makes the future
possible. Johns is the child in his abased stick-figure realizations,
witness of the past, of the story in his grandfather's house. A ladder emerging from the floor plan and from behind the "pictures,"
and thrusting upward diagonally to meet the top edge of *Mirror's
Edge,* could represent a vehicle of escape, or of construction. The
floor plan of the house, with an overlaid cruciform, is the foundation both for seeing ahead and for regarding the past. It is also
the foundation for Johns's building of *Mirror's Edge:* a "house"
composed of four planes, one laid down, as it were, on top of
another—the "topmost" the swirling white nebula in a black sky.
Acknowledging venerated artists besides himself—Barnett Newman, Grünewald—the picture of pictures reads as the artist's future, seen from the child's point of view as he imagines it, quite
splendidly, or as the artist's present, looking back on his days in
his grandfather's house where he existed marginally but watch-
fully within an ordered floor plan.

So what was Montez doing in the house besides singing "Red
Sails in the Sunset" while playing the piano? And what else did
she mean to her young step-grandson? Why is she the first relative he has identified in his work? What would Montez think?
Would she say—to paraphrase Dora Maar's description of

Picasso's portraits of her—"They're all Johnses, not one is Montez"?

One thing that can be said for certain about Johns's view of her is that her attention was captured by something other than himself. We can also infer that her absorption in singing and playing the piano was a cultural model that was meaningful to the future artist.

IV.

*Montez was a stately, well-dressed person . . . big brim hats
. . . she seemed very distinguished.*
—GERALDINE LEWIS

*[Jasper] didn't want to do a lot of things that had to be done
. . . he didn't like bringing in the wood, he liked all
the indoor stuff.*
—CHARLES SHEALEY

During the 1930s Montez was a woman in her forties; she had been married to W.I. for over two decades and had raised their two daughters. W.I. was one of the largest producers of cotton in the state, a businessman, and a member or chairman of various boards. Montez was a woman of leisure who enjoyed having bridge parties, as well as singing and playing the piano. Geraldine Lewis remembers Montez being upset when her parties with W.I. made the house reek from the chitlins he liked to eat. If Mary Young's memory of Jasper sharing the same room and sleeping in the same bed with his grandfather is accurate,[29] Montez was probably no longer intimate with her husband—a man in his sixties at the time and twenty-one years older than she was. She was a woman on her own in a large house containing servants, an older man, and a boy. She had interests and distractions that encompassed friends, keeping her busy and self-absorbed.

Once, while asking him about the little red sailboat in his *Montez Singing* works, I inquired, "Montez was a mother to you . . . ," making him scoff at the thought. He exhaled a slight noise akin to a harrumph, waved his hand and rolled his eyes.

Geraldine Lewis, decisive on the fitness of Montez to parent, said, "She was *not* motherly." Having lived with Jap Sr., who acquired Montez as a stepmother in 1911 at the age of eleven, Geraldine was not without authority on the subject. It was Charles Shealey's understanding that when Jasper lived at his grandfather's house in Allendale he spent a lot of time with his Aunt Eunice and her daughters Mary and Dimmey.[30] Mary Young has corroborated this, saying, "Jasper came home with us to spend the school-day afternoons, until granddaddy picked him up at bedtime." In her account of their childhood in Allendale, Mary casts herself in relation to Jasper as an affectionate older cousin or big sister. "He became my shadow. I took him for haircuts, bossed him around, and played 'devil in the ditch' with him. We shared numerous childhood adventures. Riding horseback, watching a mule-drawn contraption grind the juice from sugarcane and tasting the boiling syrup from the huge outdoor pot . . . swimming in the shallow streams, making pets of goats and jumping from the barn rafters into mountains of cottonseed."[31] Allendale was "such a small town . . . you went out to play, you didn't even have to say where you were going because everybody took care of you, and nobody locked their houses . . . we didn't even have a key to our house."[32]

Mary Young told me that Jasper and Montez were close, and she didn't think Montez "sang out of the ordinary."[33] Presumably if Montez had had a maternal interest in Jasper, he might have continued living on with her after his grandfather died, instead of going to his Aunt Gladys. But her "difference," as Bill Johns characterized her, and as Jasper renders her in his *Montez Singing* pictures, probably lay precisely in her lack of such an interest, with an attendant focus on matters of relevance mainly to herself. It seems possible to conclude that she was identified with the traditional female role chiefly in its ornamental aspect, as one whose contribution to a man and his household is to look good, to lend a sense of culture and refinement that may enhance the man's image, with reciprocal expectations of support and appreciation. As the second wife of a successful man, Montez had a certain classic profile—the wife who comes from afar (she was from Beaufort, in another county, whereas Evelina was home-grown), is younger (she was eighteen years younger than Evelina), costs more, and expresses by her idleness or hobbies and "higher" tastes the prosperity and largesse of her husband.

Called Tezza or Tezzie, Montez sang in the choir in church as well as at home, and she liked dances. She lived from 1890 to 1976. Geraldine remembers her as "a social figure," who "could *afford* to do the things she did."[34] She was a "stately, well-dressed person . . . big brim hats . . . she seemed very distinguished." Charles Shealey confirmed that she was "a stylish dresser."[35] Most recollections embrace her hats. For Geraldine, "hats were her trademark." Katherine Grubbs, a longtime resident of Allendale, says she wore the biggest hats she could find. "She was tall and slender . . . [with] a beautiful face, she was a pretty sight." Montez could also drink "real bad, right along with W.I. and the rest of 'em you know"—when they had "the big parties." Mrs. Grubbs used to go to the house to help out when they had the parties. "I seen her so drunk she couldn't walk."[36] Lest I think that all these people did was drink and have big parties, Mrs. Grubbs hastened to compliment the Johnses, saying how charitable they were: "They didn't shun a poor person, they loved everybody, and I imagine W.I. gave more money and helped more people in Allendale County than any other man ever done." Mrs. Ernie Stevenson, the lovely woman who lives across from the site where W.I.'s house once stood, and knew "Tezzie" as "a good friend," portrayed her as a "southern belle," an evocation that fits Mrs. Stevenson as well, and that perhaps best sums up the Montez of the various attributes ascribed to her.

The Johns women—Eunice and Gladys, and their mother Evelina no doubt, also Elizabeth Oswald, Wilson R.'s wife—were not southern belles like Montez, nor was Allendale a place where they were commonly bred or imported, though they might have been admired and their stations coveted. They could also be scorned, and Bill Johns expressed that sentiment when he said, "[Montez] wasn't liked by us then," a view not necessarily shared by the future artist. Of course how Jasper viewed Montez then and now could be very contrary things. From his paintings bearing her name, we deduce that he shared Bill's view of her as "different." Yet her difference would have meant different things to both of them, with what was an abstraction to one being a liability or loss to the other. But there was also clearly something to be learned by the motherless boy from Montez's "absence." Apparently he could see a model of the self-absorbed artist in her. Jasper himself has been described by several (male) relatives as having been "different" when he was a child. His father classified him a "sissy" for his interest in drawing. Bill Johns said he was "quiet" and "didn't hunt or fish or ride horses like the rest." Charles Shealey, who feels that his cousin Jasper has been ungrateful for everything Charles's mother, Gladys, did for him (and is "shocked" by the kind of art he makes), said, "He didn't totally fit in, no—he didn't want to do a lot of things that had to be done. . . . He didn't like bringing in the wood," adding that "he liked all the indoor stuff," comparing him unfavorably to himself and his three brothers, who were all "outdoorsmen." Johns has confirmed this in an interview, saying that when he moved into his Sixty-third Street townhouse he had most of the fireplaces removed because they reminded him of his boyhood when firewood was the only source of heat, and lugging logs from the yard was a daily and deeply resented chore.[37]

That Johns's "funny face" portrays himself as well as Montez and some idea of women in general is borne out by the face-frame "contents," which are all self-referential. They represent his art and sometimes a watch, the latter coming tagged with a childhood memory: "Once his father promised him his watch when he was grown up. Soon after, Johns decided that he was grown up; he went to his father's house and took the watch. His father came and took it back. 'I guess I wasn't grown up, after all.' "[38] The funniness of Johns's face may have been unintentional, the inadvertent result of making the eyes turn inward to indicate, in his inimitably literal way, what they are looking at, and of the faithful transposition of Picasso's discrepant heights of his two eyes in *Straw Hat with Blue Leaf*. There is, in any event, nothing "funny" about the contents of the faces, except perhaps for the tiny red sailboat in its picture frame in the Montez-named works. Behind the watch we can read something quite serious, if it is linked to the anecdote involving the artist's father.

The watch looks electrifying in a 1990 watercolor and pencil work included as one of twelve pictures made for a 1991 calendar.[39] Slotted for May, Johns's birth month, the watch is set in the upper center of the face on a grey and white "ground," lines radiate out from it to the frame holding the mouth and the eyes, which are secreting prominently visible teardrops. The lashes are galvanized as wavy spermata. The watch, which the face is apparently "thinking about," seems to be implicated, as if it has elicited these tears, this "outburst" of emotion. Other face-frame pictures featuring a watch present it neutrally or as a happy object of desire—the feeling obviously aroused in Johns the boy by his father's "promise." The miscarried pledge is apparently the subject of the calendar picture showing the face crying over the timepiece. There's anger and humiliation in the little story. Jasper "went to his father's house and took the watch," acting on the promise, but miscalculating his age, imagining he was grown-up enough. "His father came and took it back. 'I guess I wasn't grown up, after all.' " To a child, the time it takes to grow up can transpire in a matter of minutes or hours. Though innocent in his theft, having entertained the opinion no doubt that enough time had elapsed after his father's promise to justify his heist, he had to have felt caught out. The watch was his father's; he had incurred his father's displeasure; his father was the authority. Like a girl, whose sense of rage at injustice can be transformed into self-reproachfulness and tears, the boy, or the man looking back at the boy, is similarly affected. The watch in Johns's story and in the 1991 watercolor symbolizes the much larger grievance concerning a father who, having had him, reneged on the social obligation of raising him. The boy went to get a piece of him, his watch, had it briefly, and had it taken away from him, symbolizing the main story.

Another frame face, also a 1991 calendar picture, this one designated for April, features the vertical watch with a yellow strap surrounded by five crosshatch clumps; it is on a "ground" painted dominantly in red and orange hues and could be construed as angry.[40] The whites and rims of the eyes are painted orange, and the mouth looks very glum in this picture. The mouths and eyes change in mood from picture to picture as they're affected notably by color schemes and paint treatment, and in minor ways by the slightest alterations in design.

There is a certain identification between Montez and the generic frame face that Johns may not have intended. Despite the ideograms that set Montez apart—the tiny sailboat, hair, breast circles—all the faces, Montez's and untitled ones alike, are united by their common structure. The evidence too shows that Montez the woman was leading a life as abandoned, isolated, and self-involved in the big house as Jasper the boy was. They both had *social* lives of course, but emotional starvation drove them inward, seeking sustenance in fantasy, culture, or inventions of the mind. The child and the woman would have shared also the sense of being in the wrong. This I believe is where Johns's female identification would chiefly lie. His lot was not his fault, but he had no other recourse in thinking about himself if, as is most likely, his circumstances were never explained to him. No rationale could have been forthcoming regarding his father's defection, his mother's flight, and his step-grandmother's failure of attention. One avenue of hope for the damaged male child turned adult lies in the recognition of the cultural stereotype of woman as different, as "other," and thus seeing oneself reflected in another while denying any involvement of the self. Montez and the frame faces generally bear this reflection. They are objects of derision, yet at the same time serious containers for thoughts and activities of the subject camouflaged to self and others.

V.

It seems [Picasso] was always surprised by the fact that
he didn't dissolve, like a lump of sugar.
—JASPER JOHNS

The first time [Picasso] saw one of de Kooning's Woman
paintings, he turned to someone and said "melted Picasso."
—JASPER JOHNS

Could de Kooning's paintings of women be seen as his wanting
to get into the ring with Picasso?
—PAUL BRACH

On the surface Johns seems to have so little in common with a man like Picasso as regards women that his appropriation of Picasso's *Straw Hat with Blue Leaf* for purposes of constructing a female face makes a case for a study in irony, if not pretension. He not only owed his frame face to *Straw Hat,* but also his use of the entire image, which he moved around from picture to picture, either in its totality or sans blue leaf, vase, book, and base, Picasso's metamorphic head often appearing naked, without its accessories. But for an artist of Johns's stature, approaching sixty during the 1980s, and not yet seen to be boasting a female image in his bag of themes, except for the Everywoman Mona Lisa, Picasso—acknowledged master of every form of woman—would have seemed the perfect source for a belated acquisition of this indispensable badge of admission to the society of great artists, present and historical. A complementariness was suggested by Picasso's very pronounced experience in dealing with forms of the female. During the 1980s Johns got serious about plundering all manner of things Picasso, and while he was busy rifling two Picasso works for images to deploy in his *Seasons* paintings—*The Shadow* and *The Minotaur Moving His House*—he was at the same time helping himself to *Straw Hat,* trying it on for futures in the woman market. Both *Straw Hat* and *Minotaur* are dated 1936, a year of which Picasso has said, "That was the worst time of my life."[41] His personal life was in turmoil and his native country embroiled in a civil war. *Straw Hat* is a perversely contorted surreal form standing at the frontier of Picasso's extraordinary portraits of women throughout 1937, most notably the *Weeping Woman* series linked with *Guernica.*

In 1975 Johns titled a big three-panel crosshatch painting rather mysteriously as *Weeping Women,* no weeping women being observable in the canvases. A female presence can be deduced by association with the four steam-iron imprints appearing in the central panel (two suggesting breasts), along with a reading of very abstracted figures embedded in the crosshatch patterns. A real presence was perhaps behind the title in the form of a Japanese woman called Emmy Fukazawa, reportedly intimate with

Johns at some point during the mid-1970s, who was finally heart-broken that he wouldn't marry her.[42] His *Dutch Wives,* painted the same year as *Weeping Women,* as wanting in wives as the latter is in weeping women, may reflect on the artist's predicament that gave rise to his *Weeping Women,* a Dutch wife being a wooden board with a hole used by sailors as a surrogate for a woman. By 1982 Johns had introduced a handkerchief into his work (with *Perilous Night*), said to be quoted from a Picasso *Weeping Woman,* though there is no resemblance whatever between Johns's handkerchief and those in any of Picasso's *Weeping Woman* series.[43] Johns did however borrow a cloud of Picasso's, incorporating a piece of tissue paper that he had torn in the shape of the cloud in Picasso's painting *Head: Study for a Monument* of 1929[44] into a 1987 collage-drawing called *A Souvenir for Andrew Monk.*

The appeal of *Straw Hat* for Johns lay assuredly not only in its being "informed with sexual suggestion," as he said,[45] but in its formal simplicity and emotional emptiness, for use in his own associative or expressive programs. *Straw Hat,* weird as it may be for a head, is a model of reductiveness and vacancy compared to Picasso's monstrous and polymorphic heads of the following year that represent two mistresses who were tearing their hair out and "weeping" over him in 1937.[46] For Johns, apart from the way he used it as a collage component, the head never became anything more until its transformation in a large 1988 encaustic on canvas. Here Johns reached an apotheosis with *Straw Hat,* showing the whole Picasso image, head with blue leaf hat, vase, book, and base, against a "nailed" towel, in the process of dissolving, blurring, and melting away into what we can assume is a bathtub, given the tub fixtures painted just under the image and contiguous with the bottom edge of the picture.[47]

Two anecdotes that amused Johns are behind the painting. According to one, "it seems [Picasso] was always surprised by the fact that he didn't dissolve, like a lump of sugar," and according to the other, "the first time [Picasso] saw one of de Kooning's Woman paintings, he turned to someone and said 'melted Picasso.' "[48] In illustrating these stories, Johns deals with Woman, Picasso, and de Kooning in one stroke, having them all go down the drain, as it were. The faucet, after all, is "running" in his tub fixtures. A variation on the second anecdote has Jackson Pollock being called "melted Picasso" by critics who once ridiculed him.[49] It's better, of course, having Picasso himself call an artist that. For Johns in any event, though Pollock has undoubtedly meant a great deal to him (his first crosshatch work, Scent, 1973–74, bears the name of Pollock's last painting), the critically noticed and expounded association of de Kooning's portraits of women with Picasso's makes de Kooning the perfect reference. Writing about de Kooning in 1990 the artist Paul Brach, quoting Lillian Ross on Hemingway in a New Yorker profile as "wanting to get into the ring with Tolstoy," asked, "Could de Kooning's paintings of women be seen as his wanting to get into the ring with Picasso? Queen of Hearts and Pink Lady, both early 1940s remind me of the Dora Maar portraits from the Guernica period."[50] And the question could be pushed along: Can Johns's Straw Hat pictures of women be seen as his wanting to get into the ring with Picasso and de Kooning?

When Johns was finished with his Untitled 1988 and other, similarly derived, work in which he has Straw Hat melting and disintegrating, he laughed and said, "Now that I've done these paintings, I won't have to think about the anecdotes any more."[51] Nineteen eighty-eight was his big year for Straw Hat, appearing as it does in another untitled painting in conjunction with the Rubins cup profiles of Picasso and the tracing of Duchamp's Bride, in a third untitled painting as a feature in a work Johns did for an auction to benefit AIDS, and in two works called The Bath. Done with the paintings and the anecdotes, Johns may have been glad to get rid of *Straw Hat,* though that was not exactly the end of her. He had tag-end uses for the image. For instance she's featured in his 1991 calendar book in the picture for August, a charcoal sporting a piece of her blue leaf hat but no other accessory, shown against a "nailed" veil or towel, on a crosshatch ground, all within the face-frame. Her inclusion in the calendar is apparently meant to exhibit the source of his face-frame features, which structure each calendar picture.

The Bath pictures of 1988, one a big encaustic and collage on canvas, the other a smaller charcoal and pastel on paper, both with the *Straw Hat* image (one "melting", one not), show the most poignant juxtaposition of his female figure with the figure I assume to best represent the artist himself—the Grünewald victim. In *The Bath* pictures the Grünewald floats in the watery element of "the bath," above the familiar tub fixtures, a projection of the artist imagined lying in the tub stretching invisibly toward us. Turned two quarters to the right, the profile of the victim's head is made to line up with the "profile" of the major portion of the *Straw Hat* image, the rest of the Picasso image split off and appearing to the left. The victim is framed by the Picasso, which, being flopped on the right side, turns away from him while being identified with him at the same time through the matching profiles. In the encaustic both victim and *Straw Hat* appear to be melting together, while in the drawing both figures are vividly drawn, not dissolving, their structures maintaining their integrity. Running out in the bath or not, Johns seeks identification of woman and victim, even while the woman turns away.

In general, *Straw Hat,* appearing either whole or in parts, is used emblematically, as a simple stand-in for Picasso; as a study in disappearance; or as a laughingstock, the latter most evident in the face-frames, which also provide a space for meditation on the past. In another pair of pictures of 1986, prebath, the victim sprawls in a Siamese-twin version of himself, doubled and consuming the whole ground of the picture. Emblematic forms of Johns's three women of the 1980s are "nailed" as "pictures" to parts of his body—the face-frame, the whole Picasso head minus accessories, and his crone (incorporating the young woman). Twinned, the victim feeds (on) itself. The three distaff images are isolated and self-sufficient. They're simply "nailed" unwittingly to the victim figures of the ground. And they are nothing but pictures. They could represent the various women in Johns's background who by his lights no doubt had better things to do than to raise him or give him the unconditional love and attention of a mother, or to make the sacrifice culturally associated with mothers.

Montez Singing seen this way is quite a sad picture. The "face" peers in at a tiny red sailboat under a wee sunset hanging on a "wall," an object of curiosity and a token of exclusion, at the same time a cause for identification. A woman and a boy are both left to their own devices, one performing for herself, the other watching this redemptive exercise in narcissism. The woman is a lively model for Jasper Johns, the family outsider, who is well kept yet abandoned within his own family, looking to the future for his salvation as an artist.

LOVE'S BODY: THE FIGURE IN THE CANVAS

I.

A Dead Man. Take a Skull. Cover it with Paint. Rub it
against Canvas. Skull against Canvas.
—JASPER JOHNS

I was thinking about issues like life and death, whether I could
even survive. I was in a very gloomy mood at the time I did
[Dancers on a Plane], and I tried to make it in a
stoic or heroic mood.
—JASPER JOHNS

Johns distributes colors the way Merce Cunningham
distributes bodies in chaste space.
—DAVID SHAPIRO

Beginning in 1977, the year Johns had his big Whitney Museum retrospective, he launched a series of paintings, drawings, and prints with the title *Usuyuki*, a word in Japanese that means thin or light snow and that is also the title of a Kabuki play—a story of love and loss involving the melancholy relationship of an aging man and a beautiful young geisha, whom he can desire but not possess.[1] With the *Usuyuki* works, then *Cicada* of 1979, two paintings called *Dancers on a Plane* of 1979 and 1980, and *Tantric Detail I, II,* and *III,* of 1980 and 1981, Johns explored the theme of love and death in exquisite crosshatch abstractions with "incidents" and painted fragments of the body. It was in 1982, immediately following all this art, that Johns found a way to make his crosshatch motif work for him as a container or vehicle for the human form, transforming the motif into webs with which he could both delineate and mummify his two Grünewald figures.

Usuyuki of 1977–78, a large encaustic and collage on canvas in three panels, painted entirely in flesh colors, was finished during the year he quit his responsibilities as artistic adviser to the Cunningham company, a position he had held since 1967. Johns explained to Mark Rosenthal that the overall hatch pattern of *Usuyuki* was predetermined and based on a plan of repeating sections—twenty-seven in all—with the arrangement of imprints on the canvas also preassigned, a scheme close in spirit to the systems compositions of Cunningham and John Cage. "[Here] Johns wants to create a two-dimensional approximation of the appearance of two systems of marks, on a donut-shaped object, as each spirals in opposite directions. One recalls here his interest in 'the rotating point of view' of Cézanne and Cubism, except that Johns's intention is based on a stationary viewpoint from which to witness a painted, quickly moving object."[2]

The "stationary viewpoint" was Johns's precise position as a longtime audience member at Cunningham performances. The "quickly moving object" is obviously the dancer on stage, while equated at the same time with the "movement" of paint on canvas. The dancer-spectator aspect of *Usuyuki* could only be extrapolated from the later title, *Dancers on a Plane,* which evolved

ship. In 1961, the year of their break-up, Rauschenberg, who had designed sets and costumes for Cunningham since 1954, became romantically involved with dancer Steve Paxton, who had been invited that very year to join the Cunningham company. Paxton was twenty-two years old, Rauschenberg then thirty-six. By coincidence the dancer who interested Johns in 1977, Jim Self, was himself twenty-two years old. When he joined the Cunningham company that year Johns was forty-six, an age difference that qualified him to be a kind of Jupiter figure in some version of the myth of Ganymede—the beautiful Trojan boy abducted by Jupiter and borne to the heavens where he became cupbearer to the gods. Rauschenberg's 1959 painting *Canyon* is spiked with Ganymede references; it even bears a stuffed eagle (fastened to the canvas), the bird Jupiter was disguised as when he snatched the boy up and carried him off.[4] Ganymede himself is represented by a photo of Rauschenberg's son Christopher as an infant, reaching and gazing appropriately skyward. Johns of course would never be so graphic, not even in his late work so populated with readable images. His own antiphonal reflex to the Jupiterish predicament he found himself in in the late 1970s was to create covers for his real object in beautiful abstractions with mysterious titles requiring specialized knowledge to be understood (like the Kabuki play reference for *Usuyuki*), esoterically depicted abridgements or schematic indications of the body, and citations such as *Dancers* or "Merce Cunningham" (Cunningham's name appears along the bottom edge of one *Dancers on a Plane*). Not surprisingly, Jim Self, when looking at that time for signs of himself in his lover's work, was unable to find anything.[5]

Cicada, like *Usuyuki*, has a background reference specifically denoting the brevity of beauty and passion. In the life of cicadas, a fantastic moment occurs when these astonishing insects emerge from seventeen years underground (there is a thirteen-year species also; they're both called periodical cicadas) and swarm into trees, where they spend only a few weeks before dying, the males in choruses of song, a vibratory clamor for which they're famous. The cicadas of southern Europe were much esteemed by the ancient Greeks and Romans, who often kept them in cages to furnish entertainment with their music. During 1979 Johns created two brightly throbbing works called *Cicada* in abstract crosshatch schemes of primary colors—an oil painting, and a watercolor, crayon, and graphite pencil work on paper. The latter contains a "predella" full of doodles and drawings that include four small renderings of a cicada, two seen in profile, two from above, drawn from an entomological text.[6] Johns said he "was interested in the fact that the cicada contains another version of itself inside its shell, an insect that eventually becomes winged and flies away."[7] Other images in the "predella" beneath the gorgeous fully soaring crosshatch cicada are a skull and crossbones, testicles, a yoni, a burning Tantric lamp or funeral pyre, a necklace of skulls, a reference to a newspaper photograph captioned "Pope Prays at Auschwitz/Only Peace" and a tiny stick figure, its arms signaling SOS. All appear to be reminders of the long underground "death" that brackets the insect's brief flight and transfiguration.

By the fall of 1979, Johns and Jim Self had separated, though they were together sporadically during 1980. The *Cicada* paintings are like the husk of an affair, the aesthetic immortal remains. Johns seemed to know that such an affair would be over practically before it began. The single continuity in his life was his work. Self left the Cunningham company at the end of 1979. In May of 1980 Johns turned fifty. More splendid husks were forthcoming. During 1979 and 1980 Johns painted *Dancers on a Plane,* and in 1980 he commenced the *Tantric Detail* series.

Dancers on a Plane were not only entities disported on canvas but people who traveled internationally in the Cunningham troupe. There's an allusion also, according to Barbara Rose, to "an old gag of Johns's, who suggested that [Leo] Castelli, who made his artists world famous, buy an aircraft, to be called the Picture Plane, to transport gallery members and their works around the globe."[8] With the painting's title and its structure of mirrored vertical halves, with marks at the left and right edges of the canvas that suggest the edges could be joined to form a cylindrical composition—the skin of a human torso, a dancer, is created. With the addition in the second *Dancers on a Plane,* of 1980, of a dotted midsection vertical line and schematically rendered testicles, vagina, and section of penis, the figure is more fully promised. Both the *Dancers on a Plane* and *Tantric Detail* series are inspired by a painting from Nepal that Johns saw reproduced in a book by Ajit Mookerjee on Tantric art representing the Buddhist deity Samvara, a dancing figure of many arms and heads similar to the Hindu Shiva, copulating rapturously with his goddess-consort.[9]

It would have been hard for Johns—an adept at construing parallels between himself and things around him—not to find in this exotic example of the ancient equation of dancing and sex a correspondence with his relationship to the Cunningham company and with one of its dancers. Below the site of the god's sexual union with the goddess, a garland of skulls and heads, joining the goddess's necklace of pearls, encircles Samvara's prominent testicles. Three beaded tassles hang directly down from the god's testicles through the goddess's "necklace." The beads or pearls, as dotted lines, are what Johns transposed to his own *Dancers on a Plane,* functioning in some suggestive way very similarly to the Nepalese work, linking his (schematic) testicles with a line we can imagine continuing where it breaks off not yet midway up the painting to its extruded penis penetrating a vagina within the top border. The right and left borders of both *Dancers* works contain the eating utensils of knives, forks, and spoons, painted in the 1979 work, cast in bronze in the 1980 version. Associated "with the many-handedness of Shiva and his [consort],"[10] a readier use comes to mind: "Take, eat, this is my body," the body of both the painting and the dancer.

With a third *Dancers on a Plane,* 1980–81, which Johns gave to Merce Cunningham, perhaps actually made for him, the border of utensils is gone, and gone also are the schematic genitals, though not the dotted line reinforcing the idea that the vertical midline of the painting is the spine of a dancer. Gone definitively by 1981 from the life of the artist was the dancer who apparently inspired this body of work, although with his gift to Cunningham, Johns acknowledges a generative source, the master under whose aegis the young dancer appeared and became available to him, and who after all was a longtime associate and would continue to be important in his life. In a kind of postscript, in 1982 Johns made a final *Dancers on a Plane,* a graphite wash on paper, restoring utensils and genitals, the latter in fact appearing more realistically here than before—a work he kept for himself.

With the *Tantric Detail* paintings Johns brought his testicles out of the closet, so to speak (no casual observer would identify them in the *Dancers* series), though hardly as the homoerotic subject that prompted their display in the first place. David Shapiro reported that when the *Tantric Detail* paintings were shown in 1982 at the Blum Helman Gallery in New York, "they caused a sensation. For many, the use of the testicles and partially hidden phallic images was too loaded, too sudden . . . and was horrifying in the context of what had become the more serene norm of his crosshatching."[11] No homoerotic reading would have been made then, and none is possible now without recourse to biographical sources. This is the nature of that expediency called "secrets-in-view"[12]—one of the shelters known to homosexual artists and noteworthy in the artistic histories of Johns and Rauschenberg.[13] In Johns's case, his *Untitled 1984,* featuring the two Resurrection soldiers with a tracing of Grünewald's spiked tool between them enlarged and shaped to resemble an erect member, can be counted as a vivid exception.

In general in his *Dancers* and *Tantric* series, with his reference to the classic Nepalese image, Johns has used the familiar cover of heterosexual sex, which his straight critics have glossed with an appeal to the universality of the artist's interests, for instance in "an acceptance of potentially apocalyptic catastrophe," or in remaining calm "despite the agitation of a disintegrating, corrupt, and violent world," or his awareness that "death was as much part of the reality of life as sex."[14] The decoy of Cunningham's name attached to the *Dancers* series is another stock device providing biographical cover. At closer range, such evidence as a personal quote by the artist that begs potentially embarrassing questions is left unexplored by critics. Johns "indicated that when he painted [*Dancers on a Plane* of 1979] he was going through a difficult time. He was looking at Tantric art, 'thinking about issues like life and death, whether I could even survive. I was in a very gloomy mood at the time I did the picture, and I tried to make it in a stoic or heroic mood.' "[15]

A "disintegrating, corrupt, and violent world" is easily suggested in the *Tantric Detail* pictures by the boldly painted testicles, replete with hair, all now very visible, coupled with the image of a skull appearing below, poised or impaled atop the dotted vertical line of dashes. The face that was missing from the previous paintings is now a death's head. Ironically Johns is burying a figure that is now more explicit, having been inferred much more obliquely before. It's a figure that he had already buried in different ways. Of his 1980 *Dancers on a Plane* he said that the vertical dotted line that bisects the canvas is "all that is left" of a string of pearls around the neck of the goddess,[16] really quite a sad statement, it could be said, though of course he was merely referring to his appropriation and abstraction of the goddess's pearls with his own dotted line. In *Tantric Detail III,* of 1981, his last in the series, a remarkable white or fade-out along the whole right side of the painting is occurring, the crosshatching appearing in ghostly, sometimes virtually invisible forms. And the skull here is whitened, made chalky. Johns set this up beginning with *Tantric Detail I,* of 1980, where herringbone patches are losing both form and color, then in *Tantric Detail II* with the right side, top to bottom, a fade-out that becomes complete in *III.* It's curtains for this particular figure—case closed.

It's been said of *Cicada,* which heralded the *Dancers* and *Tantric* series, that "the image presaged a period in which many observers felt that Johns himself was at last emerging into day."[17] It does seem that by this time Johns had begun researching himself in a way preparatory for his dramatic autobiographical work of the 1980s and 1990s, which would at last include full representations of the figure. Richard Elovich, one of his assistants in the late 1970s, said he never met anyone outside academia who had read as much psychoanalysis as Johns had. As far as he knew, Johns had read almost all the major works of Freud.[18] Studying Freud was surely a big shift from such demanding reading fare of the 1960s as the rigorously abstract Ludwig Wittgenstein. Johns had begun seeking reflections of himself in the cognitive literature of psychology, a development that evidently led him to speak, in 1978, of dropping his "reserve," and ultimately to a greater integration of self and work. "In my early work," he explained, "I tried to hide my personality, my psychological state, my emotions."[19]

Johns was indeed "emerging into day," and the death of a former self was commemorated in all the work he did between 1977 and 1981. Of his *Cicada* works he said, "The Cicada title has to do with the image or something bursting through its skin which is what they do. They have shells where the back splits and they emerge, and that basically splitting form is what I am trying to suggest."[20] Moreover the pictures (along with the *Usuyuki,*

Dancers, and *Tantric* series), accompanying him in a perilous life passage, afforded him an indispensable means of steadying himself, of balancing and enduring. He suggested as much when he said he painted *Dancers* "in a stoic or heroic mood." Roads to or through this maturation stage included a destabilizing affair and at least one other known confrontation with mortality—an encounter with a European curator that would mean a great deal to him, especially as it led him to Colmar and to his first sight of Grünewald's Isenheim Altarpiece.

II.

The childhood of creative people seems . . . burdened by their awareness of their being "different," with all the implications of guilt and ambivalence over being "special."

—HANS KLEINSCHMIDT

I had no power, no money, I wasn't interesting enough. . . . I felt like the only difference I could make in his life was to hurt him.

—JIM SELF

In 1971 Carlo Huber, director of the Kunsthalle Bern, presented *Jasper Johns: Die Graphik.* Johns had known Huber since 1969 when Huber was curator at the Kunstmuseum Basel and he exhibited *Jasper Johns, 30 Lithographien 1960–68,* which had been organized and shown at MoMA in New York. Some time after the Basel show Huber became ill, at length dying of leukemia in July 1976 at the age of forty-four. He was two years younger than Johns. For a book he was writing about the artist's prints, Huber had traveled to New York several times. He knew he was dying, having been in remission on several occasions, and he was desperately trying to finish the work. When he was no longer able to travel, Jasper managed to make the trip in his direction, com-

bining seeing Huber with a visit to the Basel Art Fair where
Foirades/Fizzles, his collaboration with Samuel Beckett, printed
by the Petersburg press, was on display. Jasper was accompanied
by Mark Lancaster, the English artist who had been his chief as-
sistant and amanuensis for two years by then. Lancaster told me
that Huber, whom they visited in the hospital, was in extremely
bad shape when they saw him. This was in June of 1976. They
stayed in Basel three or four days, and on one of those days went
to Colmar, not more than an hour's drive from Basel, both of
them seeing the Grünewald Altarpiece for the first time.[21] The
following month Carlo Huber died.

From both Lancaster and Christian Geelhaar, who became curator of modern art at Kunstmuseum Basel a year later, in 1977,
and who was a close friend of Johns's, I gleaned that Huber had
had the kind of heavy investment in his book project that the
dying can have in any final undertaking. Lancaster mentioned his
"devotion to the project,"[22] and Geelhaar, confirming my speculation that it meant a lot to Huber, especially perhaps as it was
his last involvement in the work of an artist, said, "I agree with
what you say about Carlo's involvement in Jasper's work."[23]
Jasper, in turn—according to Lancaster—"was affected by this
man's death."[24] Judging from his sensitivity to those in distress,
those at least whom he already knows or with whom he has some
special contact or history, Johns was more than likely to be
touched under the circumstances: a man of proximate age to him
whose dying months were consecrated to the very thing closest
to his own heart—his work. It was perhaps also Johns's first experience of the death of someone he had grown to consider a
friend, and beyond that a meaningful professional associate. In
all likelihood he came away from Huber's hospital bed in June
1976 vulnerable to the feelings of awe and helplessness that over-
came him upon first glimpsing Grünewald's Isenheim Altarpiece
in Colmar.

Johns next visited the Altarpiece on April 7, 1979, this time on the occasion of an exhibition, *Jasper Johns: Working Proofs,* at the Kunstmuseum Basel, curated by Geelhaar. Now he went to Colmar in a group that included Carlo Huber's widow Helga, Teeny Duchamp, and Aldo Crommelynck, along with Lancaster and Geelhaar.[25] Crommelynck, Picasso's printer, had worked with Johns on the intaglio prints for *Foirades/Fizzles* in his Paris atelier earlier in the decade. Presumably he had come to Basel to attend the opening of Johns's *Working Proofs.* Sometime between April 7, when the show opened, and June 2, when it closed, Jim Self was in Basel on tour with the Cunningham company. He said he was unable to get into the show and didn't make it to Colmar either—assuming he wanted to after hearing Jasper rave about the Altarpiece. "Jasper started talking about the Grünewald the spring of 1979, [saying] it was the most incredible thing and I had to see it."[26]

It was during the following summer, in 1980, that Johns received the portfolio gift from German dealer Walter Wittrock of Altarpiece reproductions published in Munich in 1919 that he used to make his first tracing—the detail from the Crucifixion panel showing John the Evangelist supporting the swaying Virgin, her hands clasped in grief.[27] Unknown to Johns, as he began tracing images from an Altarpiece designed in the early sixteenth century to function as a healing program for sufferers of a plague then sweeping Europe, another killer, which was causing what would also come to be called a plague (ignominiously labeled a "gay plague" early on by the gay press) was quietly stalking three continents—Africa, where victims have been mainly heterosexual, Europe, and North America. In 1981, when Johns made the first tracing and was beginning to trace the St. Anthony victim and Resurrection soldiers, came the first reported death in America of a young man suffering from a mysterious immune deficiency disease, later to be known as AIDS. Eventually, surveys would show that by the end of 1980, 55 young men in the United States had been diagnosed with some infection linked to the new virus, and four Americans, all identified as gay men, had died of the disease.[28] In 1981 there were 108 cases nationwide, and 43 had died.[29] It was learned that people had begun getting sick in 1978 and 1979. Johns would have known nothing of this new disease afflicting homosexual men until 1983 or 1984; in 1985 Rock Hudson died, and the news reached every household in the Western world. By then 12,000 Americans were already dead or dying of AIDS and hundreds of thousands more were infected.[30]

Johns's personal vulnerabilities, having recently left him more exposed to feelings of helplessness and abandonment, had intersected with a still-underground event of general social magnitude. Embracing images from a famous "religious machine" made in an era when disease was thought to indicate the presence of sin, particularly sexual, Johns revealed deep affinities with the past, if only his immediate past in a southern Baptist family, though somehow it seems hard to imagine such "anachronistic" thoughts crossing his mind at the time. But then, during the 1970s (and mid- to late 1960s) he had been active in his own corner of the so-called sexual revolution. In the late 1970s Johns was part of a small group of men who were quite intimately involved with each other.

At the time of his Whitney retrospective the fall of 1977, with the art establishment and the heavy media machinery poised to turn him into a superstar, Johns was introduced to a large public as a man with no family, no intimate life at all. That is, none was mentioned, except his family of origin. Such tremendous exposure, with its imprimatur of a stratospheric success, could only be accomplished in the case of homosexuals by the firmly closeted, in a well-known collusion between the subject and "everyone who knows." It is impossible to imagine how this enormous discrepancy between personal reality and public perception would not affect an artist as sensitive and intelligent as Johns in some way adversely, making him feel at the least like an impostor, or a frighteningly triumphant thief. "Emerging into day" had to be an emotionally complex passage for him, encompassing guilt, fear, anger, and perhaps a new compassion for himself, if his subsequent identification with the St. Anthony victim is seen in this perspective. With his first retrospective in 1964, at the Jewish Museum, Johns apparently went through an early version of this conflict between knowledge of self and the sense of how others saw, or wanted to see, him. In that instance he escaped afterward to Hawaii and Japan, and upon return, tried to line himself up better with the forces that promoted him, one might say, by pursuing various intimate associations with women.[31] During the late 1960s, the art world generally was disappointed with his work, which had lost the focus of his flags and targets, and had yet to reclaim a signature image, which came in the 1970s with the impressive crosshatch abstractions. Johns's sexual identity issues were complicated both by his fame and his background of neglect; those close to the exalted one, or those wanting to get close, are often unable to see the true person for the glorified object.

Ideas in a paper that Richard Elovich obtained for Johns by New York psychoanalyst Hans Kleinschmidt, called "The Angry Act: The Role of Aggression in Creativity," may have illuminated issues for him in personal relations that were endemic to his past and to the place his history had brought him in this respect.[32] According to Elovich, Johns wanted Kleinschmidt's number, with the thought perhaps of seeing him, but apparently he never did.[33] In the paper Johns would have read how "the childhood of creative people seems . . . burdened by their awareness of their being 'different,' with all the implications of guilt and ambivalence over being 'special.' " The key to this state is a "very early and severe deprivation," for which Kleinschmidt of course chiefly blames the mother, who is burdened also with any damages sustained through the father. His thesis is that the future artist with such a background withdraws from social relations or from the possibility of emotional dependency on others and develops a severe independence, an exsanguinating self-reliance, a perfectionism that he ends up investing in his products. "Only the perfect work of art merits [his] fantasied ideal love." Alliances or associations in which emotional realities are mutually recognized are not possible, except in the idealized love state.

Fame, obviously, is one perfect condition for perpetuating an early concept of being different and incomparable, a state reinforcing the individual's isolation. Fame has been neglected in its function as a repository for the unwanted—a stigma of surpassing human invention, the apparent or obvious rewards making its stigmatic status an unsurprising oversight. Public attention can be a heady drug, also a means of keeping people away, confirming any early sense of alienation. Growing testimony by Hollywood and rock stars reveals fame to be a poor substitute for intimacy or the sustenance of interpersonal communication. Johns showed one tendency of the famed and bereft to see desirable objects in the same (proto-)renowned, and wanting light, when he told Jim Self that Self was "very special" and that he "should never forget who [he] was."[34] It isn't hard to guess at Johns's predicament in 1977, his need for intimacy at that point placing a strain, as it had in the past, on his greater need to be solitary, to be left alone with his work. With its illusion of perfection, of "oceanic blending," romance has built into it its own ablative agency—the capriciousness and incertainty of the loved one. Self helped to fulfill the promise of *Usuyuki* as a story involving the melancholy love of an aging man for a beautiful young geisha he can desire but never possess. According to

Self, "I gave him everything, I completely devoted my life to him. . . . I saw it as a long tradition of passing knowledge from a mentor to a student." But when he got together with Jasper, Jasper told Self he would probably leave Jasper in some awful position. Self was restless—"I had to go explore other things."

Young, attractive, intelligent, Cunningham's sempervirent star, Self was the "new kid" on the dance and art block. In fact, both Richard Elovich and Mark Lancaster had been intimate and in love with him before he became involved with the famous artist, and he continued his intimacy with Elovich during and after his break-up with Johns. So two of Johns's assistants had feelings for the young man who became Johns's. And there were others; most unacceptable to Johns was the rising performance artist star Robert Wilson, with whom Self lived for five years after leaving Johns. The romantic alliance of a powerful, established older man with a still socially impotent, rebellious figure the age of a son is not generally thought to be a contract promising the best outcome. While Self appreciated what he learned from Johns, he also saw him as more dominating and controlling than his own parents. "I was so pissed off at him for telling me how to behave all the time . . . how to sit, how not to sit, you know if I'd sit there in the car with my legs open, he'd say don't sit like that . . . it's suggestive of something." Self said he "would go to parties and sit on somebody's lap, that would just freak him out. . . . I think he thought it was confusing . . . so I kept getting confused by the confusion." But most disturbing to Self was the secrecy of their relationship. There was never any "public display of affection. . . . We shook hands if we met at a party. . . . I wanted to have some public acknowledgment of our relationship and he said, I'm not interested in doing that . . . we're already that. He said we know what we have and fuck everybody else. I understood what he meant." In the end, says Self, "I had no power, no money, I wasn't interesting enough. . . . I felt like the only difference I could make in his life was to hurt him."[35]

It seems that Johns's life between 1977 and 1980 or 1981 was overdetermined by events he had little or no way of controlling, once certain choices were made. The oldest choice—to be an artist—had culminated in a giant retrospective that made him attractive to people who didn't know him and exposed him to a large public as a man with no private life, leaving open the possibility of the question of his right to inhabit the new Olympian aerie into which he was thrust. His choice of lover made him vulnerable to reexperiencing feelings of loss and abandonment rooted in early life, powerful emotions that work could compensate—indeed was designed to compensate—but never assuage, once the agents of such primary feelings had been unleashed.

Johns was not very well set up to be a Jupiter, the god whose history as an unwanted, unloved son made him supposedly admirably suited to deliver a son with a similar background once he attains his riper years. The role of deliverer is self-abnegating and forbearing—one who loves unconditionally and is prepared to lose control, to let go. Johns still needed emotional deliverance himself. This is clear from the way his work was about to go; though he was uniting self and work at a whole new level, at the same time he was turning himself into a kind of corpse in a trunk, well delineated (holding good form) but impossible to see or find. Critics in 1984, seeing the skulls and crossbones and death from avalanche warnings and amputated arms in some works, heralded Johns's show in universalist doomsday terms, not realizing that there were sealed-off bodies in the paintings and that a death of rather a personal nature was being glorified there. Within the one medium in life over which Johns could exercise unequivocal control (at least until the work left his studio) he had installed a new set of controls—images he could play with and exhibit without critics or public knowing the images were loaded.

Johns's discovery of the Grünewald Altarpiece was perhaps the best thing that happened to him then. The foreground plague victim in the Temptation of St. Anthony and the foreground soldiers in the Resurrection panel seem to express feelings of defenselessness and defeat, reflecting events in his life. Both the plague victim and the soldiers are subdued and overawed by the scenes stretching above them—the devouring monsters in the St. Anthony panel, the rising Christ of the Resurrection. Stupefied and amazed, himself, by the paintings, Johns sought a means to subdue the Grünewald masterpiece and the feelings that vibrated so intimately with his essential vulnerability. Just like the cicada, which briefly "emerges into day," singing in radiant summation in trees, Johns "died" and went underground again, there to research his autobiographical iconography in bloodless privacy, all done behind the facade of gorgeous colors and surfaces and collage complexities that his public had come to expect of him.

III.

I thought it was of no particular interest that [an image] was one thing or another or something else.

—JASPER JOHNS

And if some of the pictures may take a lifetime to unravel— well, that lifetime will have been well spent.

—JOHN RUSSELL

As a witless member of the public in 1984, I recall vividly the gourmet spread of choice morsels from the artist's palette in the fourteen big paintings that constituted Johns's Castelli gallery exhibition on Greene Street in January—*Racing Thoughts* and *Per-*

ilous Night the most majestic among them. One critic called them "shamelessly beautiful";[36] another, commenting indirectly on the overwhelming sense of mystery, said, "These new works seem to demand completion through biographical information."[37] *Vanity Fair*'s headline for an article on the show read, "The Painter Who Celebrates the Inscrutable."[38] Another, more peevish heading was "Jasper Johns's Beautiful Banalities."[39] A combined richness and mystery in the work created a tension that could hold viewers in a state of satisfied bedazzlement and perplexity, yet at the same time enable them to carry away the feeling that the artist had fulfilled one of the great purposes of art, to convey certain universalities, like "a heroic confrontation with mortality."[40] I walked away with some vague impression of that nature myself. The subject matter was so specific—the images of the Mona Lisa, of Leo Castelli, faucets and pots for instance—and out of all the specificity, the severed forearms, skulls and crossbones, and avalanche warnings projected the most or perhaps only accessible meaning, which could be thrown like a net around the whole show.

It was in this 1984 show that Johns concealed his two veiled Grünewald images: the plague victim from the Temptation of St. Anthony and the pair of falling soldiers from the Resurrection; only the latter was identified, appearing, with here and there a special mention, on a kind of laundry list of all the icons in the work. Much later, the victim also having been identified,[41] Johns made two remarkable statements explaining his intention in using the Grünewalds. "I thought how moving it would be to extract the abstract quality of the work, its patterning, from the figurative meaning. So I started making these tracings. Some became illegible in terms of the figuration, while in others I could not get rid of the figure. But in all of them I was trying to uncover something else in the work, some other kind of meaning."[42] And, "I was attracted to the qualities conveyed by the delineation of the forms and I wanted to see if this might be freed from the narrative. I hoped to bypass the expressiveness of the imagery, yet to retain the expressiveness of the structure."[43] By this time he would also chafe at the public knowledge of the source and identity of his figures, disturbed and "annoyed that pictures were being discussed in terms of imagery that could not be perceived."[44]

What "other kind of meaning" was he after? He seems to be identifying meaning with "patterning" and "structure," in a program to turn the figures abstract, move them into the neutral places of the postmodernist design for the picture as object. He wanted to free the figures from Grünewald's narratives, get rid of their "expressiveness" in their religious settings, make them expressive in his own abstract terms. It seemed *"moving"* to him to "extract the abstract quality . . . from the figurative meaning." Johns speaks here of the surface value of his tracings, how they are seen simply as patterning—as one critic put it in 1984, "the crosshatching . . . resulting in a surface like a jumbled parquet floor"[45]—prior to any understanding of them as *figures*. This was how he wanted them, or thought he wanted them, to be seen. Evidently he continues to see them that way himself. "I thought it was of no particular interest that [an image] was once one thing or another or something else."[46] Others, of course, seeing and identifying the figures, can be hard put not to see them in expressive figurative terms, whether in the original (Grünewald) context or in his own. A critic substantially in Johns's pocket (one of his collectors, after all) backs up the artist: "As Johns had once directed attention away from himself, saying that his work was not meant to be an expression of his feelings, he now directed attention away from the origins of the imagery he employed."[47]

In 1989 Johns committed himself to tracing an image of unmistakable human and animal features, blatantly both an explicit and mysterious "figure," whose identity this time he was determined to keep a secret. Its very purpose appeared to be to tell his curious public off. Commenting with conspicuous sophistry on his new dialectical venture, he said, "From my point of view, my perception is altered by knowing what it is, even though what it is is not what interests me. . . . So when I made this picture I decided I wasn't going to say what it was."[48] It's hard to understand how an image that has altered his perception by his knowledge of it is not of interest to him for what it is—considering how it has altered his perception. Easier to understand is his desire to exclude his public. *His* perception is altered by knowing what it is; he doesn't care about ours—whether, in this case, we have one or not: "I decided I wasn't going to say what it was." In his paranoia, Johns has emphasized the importance of the figures' identities himself, and seemingly underestimated the sophistication of his viewers, who at best should be capable of appreciating both form and content, of embracing this classical duality in art, and who would not even begin to care about the figures if they were not aesthetically clothed. Beauty, as a means and not an end, is what makes the content of art powerful to the beholder.

Feeling cornered, Johns cornered himself, threw a blanket over his head and yelled a muffled message from inside: *I know who I am, but you'll never see or find me; anyway the pattern on the blanket that covers me is all there really is. I'm dead, these are my remains.* With his unknown image, he comes full circle: from mundane icons immediately recognizable for what they are—flags, targets, and so on, with which the spectator has so many associations that the object becomes in an important sense meaningless—to exotic images not only not immediately recognizable for what they are, but not recognizable at all without some supplementary mode of identification, yet intended also to be just as "meaningless" as his early icons. Whatever was tacitly hidden by or behind targets and flags is now hidden by proclamation behind patterned figures. Johns appears to regret the artistic choices that brought him to this pass. He let something out of the bag and feels misunderstood. Where he once agreed with Cage and Duchamp that the spectator completes the work of art, he came to object to the way some of his works have been "completed." He's been lucky though in having, on the whole, understanding and collusive critics. "Johns's attitude is certainly consistent with the artist who has worked to break images free of clear context and associations, and to locate them in a new region of ambiguity and doubt."[49]

"A new region of ambiguity and doubt" can be read as, "Let's not intrude on these regions with troublesome, perhaps embarrassing, interpretations." Assuredly, Johns was interested in breaking his Grünewald images "free of clear context and associations." The project was to re-place them in expressive settings of his own. Johns himself may have great ambiguity and doubt toward his critics and public, none at all in the way he has expressively deployed images that he wishes we would see only as "patterning." By extracting his figures from Grünewald's pictures and placing them in his own environments and painting them again and again, Johns has tamed them, decathected them, turned them into emblems. Yet he has created "scenes" of his own in which they perform expressively. He moves the dying St. Anthony figure around virtuosically, situating him in little "plays" in which he is a kind of "chorus" commenting on other elements in the picture, or an emblematic protagonist, commented upon in turn. He's "figure" or he's "ground" or both, in boundless permutations, over seventy of them.

An untitled watercolor and ink on paper of 1988 featuring the St. Anthony victim, in a play with Picasso's *Straw Hat* image stripped of accessories, movingly illustrates a primary motivation of Johns's (and perhaps most artists) in making art—to establish in it a paramount source of sustenance. In the picture, Johns has "nailed" two sheets (veils?) of fabric to a light blue sky filled with cumulus clouds. The sheets or veils are decorated in the brightly colored striations of the twinned plague victim, seen on the left-hand sheet in violet and green in the original Grünewald position, and on the right in yellow-oranges and green, but inverted and flopped. The color green functions to outline the figures and also to fill in the spaces so outlined, alternating striping with the violets, yellows, and oranges. Of course we don't *see* these handsomely clothed figures, unless we have prior knowledge of their identity; outstandingly visible on the other hand is Picasso's bald *Straw Hat* head, consuming a good portion of the right-hand sheet. Johns has ingeniously slipped the lower protuberance, capped by an eye, "behind" the left-hand sheet so that its eye, now easily read as a nipple, rests against the chest wall of the upright Grünewald victim. Johns's inscription and signature lower left upon one of the cumulus clouds says, "For Jane Meyerhoff/Jasper Johns Feb. 1988, N.Y.C." Robert and Jane Meyerhoff, of Phoenix, Maryland, are longtime Johns collectors. For Jane Meyerhoff, he turned the Picasso protuberance crowned by an eye into quite a realistic-looking breast, which is *feeding* his victim. The "breast" and eye-nipple breach part of the bloated stomach and leg of the victim in order to extend to the sufferer's chest wall. The collector literally feeds the artist—a comment on the collector as furnishing the means, the financial support, for the artist to survive. And the artist's picture feeds on itself, as well as providing a reason, by virtue of the artist's name and mastery, to be fed.

In other pictures, Johns has not only twinned but "siamesed" his Grünewald victim tracing, demonstrating an even greater self-sufficiency on the part of this condemned figure—a capacity to feed itself. This sort of transformation of the victim in a large untitled encaustic and collage of 1988 is very apparent as parts of one victim are distorted and elongated to merge with parts of the other, as if both are floating in a common amniotic fluid. Doubling, mirroring—devices used repeatedly by Johns throughout his career—embody a principle of nourishment. Having embraced and adopted this Grünewald figure—dying, deformed, turning into an animal, clearly helpless before his fate—*rescuing* him in a way, bringing him "home," Johns has kept him alive: giving him playmates, often a twin, enclosing him in amniotic situations, further protecting him with "guardian" figures such as the old crone or his dealer Leo Castelli. He also allowed his victim to fly or swim; in short he gave him plenty of attention. Johns establishes him in fact as a kind of basso ostinato to a whole body of work, insinuating him everywhere, not leaving him out of any grouping of icons, in many instances making him the protagonist, who during 1988 was seen frequently with Picasso's *Straw Hat* image: Woman and Victim paired.

Having "drained . . . the Grünewald . . . of illusionism, reduced [it] to pattern," as Johns has said, he understandably hates to see his accomplishment reduced or negated through the possibility of having the Grünewald reconfigured in naturalistic visions of his own. For people to know the source of the soldiers and plague victim in the Altarpiece is one thing—essential knowledge in fact for fully appreciating Johns's achievement in converting highly expressive figures into abstractions, into pure structural components. Quite another thing for Johns is the critical interpretation that such knowledge is bound to elicit at some point, a development clearly unacceptable to the artist, certain as he is that such exercises are sure to direct "attention away from the work." He wants to stay personally hidden behind his oeuvre. "I need darkness to work in," he once told poet David Shapiro, adding, "Poets need audiences too much, and they . . . release too much."[50] He would insist that audiences are free indeed to "complete the work of art," in fact they inevitably do, as his mentors Cage and Duchamp pointed out, but he further insists that they have no right to information beyond or outside the picture itself to help them out. All such information of course unavoidably dilutes the artist's formalist inquiry, threatens to expose his reasons for his undertakings, originally founded on feelings and events in life for which there had seemed no other outlet.

As the life of an artist as successful as Johns unfolds, a brief of biographical data is built up, accompanying his progress, providing the possibility of insights that can seem to the artist to menace his one reliable defense: the work that was erected as boundary, as buffer, *between* its foundation—the biography—and the rest of the world. Yet Johns has made that very boundary line between self and world very thin, even porous, even as he postures in protest over any erosion of purely artistic concerns with his great concealment dramas and the biographical brief he has been building up himself (as in the constant reiteration in paint of his possessions, both private and work-related). With his Grünewald venture, he risked the collapse of that line altogether. So far, many of his critics have struggled to help him maintain the integrity of the barrier, leaving unasked any of the obvious questions surrounding Johns's extraordinary decision to render and conceal figures of such overtly sentient resonance. The critical alliance with the artist here exactly reproduces *his* repressive intentions in tackling these figures. Lying inert within the genesis of the project, the figures slumber on, remote from their highly visible revelatory sixteenth-century glory as sufferers in pictures made to serve the people.

The isolation of contemporary artists, of an artist like Johns especially, drenches his Grünewald effort in pathos. Clearly he approached the Altarpiece in the late 1970s in a reverent spirit, and he seems to have prostrated himself before it anachronistically, experiencing feelings it was originally designed to call forth. All this is understood in his use of it. All this is engrafted in the figures as they lie hidden in their tremendous variegated wardrobe of decorative motifs. And all this can be sensed when the figures are "unclothed," imaginatively resituated in the Grünewald context or cast as protagonists in Johns's own scenarios. But the disguises and deceits also tell us that the artist stuffed his feelings, converted them to the pleasures of art, in which he expects to be joined.

IV.

Throughout his life my father waged a war with himself,
between, on the one hand, the impulse to be private, secretive
. . . and on the other, an enormous need . . . to unmask, to
reveal, to disclose all.

—MUSA MAYER (DAUGHTER OF PHILIP GUSTON)

He is an autodidact, intuitive, undisciplined, and very
sophisticated, who gives the impression of having tuned in on the
important themes of his time by a kind of inspired accident.

—MAX KOZLOFF

In coming to rest on this embodiment of suffering, Johns
(perhaps unintentionally) has evoked the context that originally
provided the Altarpiece with its reason for being

—ANDRÉE HAYUM

The religious theme is divested of the story which had given it a
place in the heritage of the Church, and is rearranged in an
entirely new dimension: an elitist and personal sense of refined,
solitary, private piety.

—SALVATORE SETTIS

In 1988, fifty-five thousand, three hundred and eighty-eight Americans died of AIDS. Many benefits were held to raise funds for treatment and research, and one of them, the Auction Benefit for AIDS, the idea of Mrs. William Buckley, was organized for the sale of paintings to help the St. Vincent's Hospital Supportive Care Program in Manhattan. Mrs. Buckley teamed up with collector Thomas Amman, her neighbor in Switzerland, to put the auction together. Some of the artists besides Johns who donated work were Richard Artschwager, Ross Bleckner, Francesco Clemente, Eric Fischl, Barbara Kruger, David Salle, Julian Schnabel, and Cy Twombly. Johns's contribution, an untitled work of 1988, was sold for about three hundred fifty thousand dollars and was turned into a poster that sold for five dollars.

The Grünewald St. Anthony victim appears on the left side of this picture, upside down but otherwise in Grünewald's position, with parts of its thigh and its bloated pocked stomach hidden by the familiar *Straw Hat* image enclosed in a rectangle, two dark dots on either side at the top indicating nails "pinioning" it to the Grünewald, telling us it's a picture (within a picture). Johns outlined and colored in the stripes of his contoured spaces in the same greens, oranges, and yellows of the victim as he did on the right side of the untitled 1988 watercolor in which he contrived to have a protruberance of the Picasso turn into a breast. These colors in the AIDS-auction picture seem especially appropriate, suggestive of sickly greens and jaundiced yellows. Contrasting vividly with these hues are the red, white, and blue of two stacked American flags on the right side of the work. Just underneath the bottom flag Johns painted the top of his bathroom laundry basket and to the right of that his taps and faucet—those signature images of the artist's intimate presence, invisibly regarding (from his tub) the pictures he is reproducing for us. *Straw Hat,* flags, and the skull and crossbones with part of the lettered warning about avalanches are "pictures" he "nailed"—a device as familiar as the images themselves, letting us know what we should or might already know, that the artist is quoting himself. Included in these quotes are the Rubins cup profiles of Queen Elizabeth II and Prince Philip superimposed on one of the flags, signs of the nation's concerned "parents," but here as in all cases harking back to the old country with its reassuring ancestral continuity, symbolized by royalty.

New and singular in the work is a silkscreened copy of part of the front page of the *New York Times* of February 14, Valentine's Day, 1988, with a headline reading "Spread of AIDS Abating but Deaths Will Still Soar." Johns silhouetted elements of a photograph in the *Times* on the XV Olympic Winter Games opening in Calgary to the left of this article and made the caption headline unreadable. Perfectly readable is an election article headline: "The Run in New Hampshire Is Now a Run for the Money." In the far upper right of Johns's silkscreen, he uncharacteristically altered something, changing a headline that appears in the *Times* as "Clash over Drugs as Reagan Meets with Mexico Chief" to read "President Meets with Mexico Chief." Parts of the "picture" upon which the skull and crossbones are depicted bridge parts of both the newspaper clipping and the topmost American flag, obviously uniting them as place and communications signifiers in the AIDS epidemic. And the skull picture begins just below Johns's headline alteration: "President Meets with Mexico Chief." Omitting "Clash over Drugs," (a reference to illegal drug trafficking) and eliminating the president's proper name by substituting "President" for "Reagan," the men with their titles as heads of state now appear to function as responsible, concerned parties in the AIDS disaster. Their "meeting" is not over (illegal) drugs now, but over the subject headlined in the article just to their left, "Spread of AIDS Abating but Deaths Will Still Soar," the topic dramatized by the artist's various "pictures."

The "picture" of the Grünewald plague victim, which could be said to be the true subject of the painting, is strikingly excluded in this scenario by virtue of its concealment. Johns couldn't, of course, sacrifice the place of the plague victim in his canon and expose it just because its visibility would have been ever so appropriate for an AIDS portrait. He went as far as he could simply by including it. Making up for its omitted identity, the painting is hardly lacking otherwise in signifiers of the epidemic. To imagine this figure "out of the closet" in any setting at all is to conjure the aesthetically unrecognizable, and a whole new diagnosis of Johns's overall purpose in making art. With his AIDS picture, he demonstrates support and sympathy for an embattled cause, withholding at the same time vital information that could convey his message more powerfully, more expressively. Not surprisingly, his ambivalence is compatible, psychologically speaking, with his strategies in art. As it was, he risked questions by informed critics concerning his use of the Grünewald in general.

The authors of the catalogue for the retrospective exhibition of Johns's drawings at the National Gallery in Washington, D.C., in 1990 told him that a number of people had asked them "whether the afflicted demon in the St. Anthony panel functions as a contemporary witness to the plague of AIDS." They added that its appearance in the "beautiful watercolor for the AIDS auction encourages this thought."[51] Johns answered, "As concerned with the disease as our society is, it is easy to have such a thought." Then the authors, knowing already the date of his first tracing, when no one was aware that an epidemic was brewing, asked if it was "something [he] intended in the first place." And Johns said, "No, but it is probably an unavoidable association at the moment." More probingly, a writer in the New York Times in 1988 wondered, "Why would Johns, who is in good health, be moved to confront his own mortality with such directness and urgency?" Johns told her, "I suppose I've become increasingly aware of the way things can be cut off. . . . I don't know whether it's the loss of friends . . ." Then, as the writer commented, "[Johns] stops, and retreats to safer ground." In conclusion Johns said, "I think my early work exposed me just as much as any other bit of my work."[52]

In August 1990 I asked Johns when he registered AIDS as a phenomenon. Filling in his silence with another question, "When someone you knew died?" I had no better luck. My last question, "Have you lost many friends?" also went unanswered. But when I mentioned the AIDS-auction picture he seized the opportunity to accuse me of "concentrating on only this one aspect of the imagery," thus "seeing the work less clearly." He was alluding to the St. Anthony victim, and spoke with such vehemence that he seemed to be unloading feelings he had stored up over my identification of the victim three years earlier. His remark here I believe sums up his fear of what he has to lose through the public identification of his suffering plague victim. Seeing "the work" less clearly means seeing "this one aspect" *too* clearly. His obsessive renderings of a particular body lead us away from the work and toward his own person. Yet he seems protected by the universalizing tendency of critics, who thoughtfully reduce the figure to a commentary on AIDS, an association made more palpable by the auction picture. With the dates of Johns's first tracings of the figure obscured, the strange and remarkable possibility that he had "tuned in on [an] important theme of his time by a kind of inspired accident" as Max Kozloff once characterized a special ability of the artist's as he saw it, can be ignored. Such divinely "inspired accidents"—suggestive of sources deeply personal—seem to many to be best left unnoted when such sources appear unavailable.

But another kind of "accident," which shows Johns reaching back inadvertently to Grünewald's time, when artists (though not Grünewald), particularly in Italy, concealed subjects to appeal to a privileged few, seems even uncannier, and points the way toward a fuller, more searching discourse concerning Johns's use of the Grünewald. By secularizing and privatizing aspects of a religious Renaissance masterwork, Johns precisely entered into the spirit of the most advanced artists of Grünewald's period.

With the gradual shift from religious to private patronage during the quattrocento, artists began making work for an exclusive community of men initiated into the wonders of science, familiar with the Bible, and educated in the classics and pagan antiquities. These aristocrats, commissioning paintings for their private houses, enjoyed subtle allusions to religious iconography that were only too easily understood in church settings. A distinction had developed between public devotion, the practice of the masses, and private piety, a license of the new man and sign of his evolved individuality, his recognition of an inviolable inner life. Artists working for the learned client, wishing to avoid the obvious iconography that could associate him with the ignorant masses, strove for ambiguities and hidden references. Religious subjects were transposed and altered for clients who might ferret out the sources, guess at concealed meanings, or link dramatis personae with acquaintances, friends, family, and often themselves. In his treatise on the Venetian artist Giorgione (1478–1510), one of the first "modern artists," Salvatore Settis shows how the painter iconographically disguised, among other subjects, Adam and Eve and their expulsion from Eden in *The Tempest*. He turned Adam into a man of his times, giving him modern dress and making him a *homo interior,* a figure with whom Giorgione's patron could identify.[53] The "mysteries" of the elite—their private communications with God and their knowledge of the language of the ancients—were considered treasures that should be preserved within select cliques. The cleverest artists became a part of that elite.

Jasper Johns in our own time has risen outstandingly to be this kind of artist. Like the Renaissance painters, he has inserted portraits of his truest patron, his dealer Leo Castelli, into his work, and invariably linked him with that hieroglyph so closely related to himself—the Grünewald plague victim. And like the best of those earlier artists, his dealer and collector-patrons are his friends, and his lifestyle resembles or duplicates the richest of them. Like many famed, successful public figures, in his older years he has undertaken to delineate his memoirs, however vestigial due to the limitations of his medium and restricted by the dictates of privacy. This is a condition he shares with the elite of the art establishment, whatever their different origins. The critical branch of the art establishment has of course been seduced from the start not only by Johns's painterly surfaces but by his subtleties of allusion, his intriguing stratagems for mystifying and challenging viewers that gratify their professional appetite for insider information and qualify them for membership in some tacitly recognized art cognoscenti.

It seems strange perhaps that as yet Johns's use of the Grünewald Altarpiece has not engaged the art critics (other than myself) and has in fact seemed to turn them off. The reason may lie in the suspicion that Johns has found in the Altarpiece a serious devotional object that he could privatize but hardly contain once the secret of his source was revealed—a matter much more public than in Grünewald's time. There were no news media then; there were no phalanxes of critics coming between artist and patron to disseminate their hardwon information to a broader public. For an artist of Johns's postmodern stature to be revealed in a religious light could be disconcerting at the least. If this is the case, his accomplishment in requiting one of the great tasks of modern artists—to subvert outworn or familiar iconographies—has so far been lost on the majority of his critics, as they hold him to the obvious, immediately recognizable, and "meaningless" icons of his postmodern past. In the revived figurative period of the 1980s, Johns outflanked all contenders by appropriating two very dated, but highly emotive, human forms. He made it difficult yet not impossible to see them, and behind this cover turned them into stylized, purely pictorial elements in groups of compositions where they play both heraldically and in narrative, once recognized. Considered *the* artist of his times during the late 1950s and early 1960s, circumstances once again united personal issues with events at large to show Johns leading the way amongst artists in the 1980s. Such a judgment has not yet even been floated in the critical writings of the art establishment.

Arguably the most consummate strategist of the postmodern era, after Duchamp, Johns masterfully merges figuration and abstraction by the elegant concealment of embarrassingly expressive bodies—an unprecedented move in the canons of contemporary realism. He has thus deconstructed both abstraction and realism, fabricated a brand-new way of looking at them, and pitched the art game to another level. The heightened affect of concealed bodies is a factor to ponder, for instance. The discovery of the unknown or the hidden, the inaccessible, has always been a great imperative for people. In literature, the big traffic in mysteries devolves principally upon the attraction of unfolding identities—the bodies (often hidden) and the criminals (innocent until revealed). It isn't just the proper names that people are looking for, of course. Identity is like tree bark that can be peeled to disclose many layers, rings of matter, imprinted with a vast matrix of experience and memory and relationships, within which there lies a core, the biggest mystery of all. Johns's ontogenic development recapitulated a certain twentieth-century evolution of interest in psychology, in the inner workings of the mind, the origins of knowledge, and the effects of personal history and brought him up against an art tradition steeped in formalism and the very lack of this concern. But being well grounded in formalist issues himself, Johns went about fooling, or trying to fool, the custodians of art—those who established him—with his move to clothe extremely intimate figures in the trappings of surface delights. He had at the same time, we can imagine, the provisional hope that once the figures were "unwrapped," his new achievement would be understood. In lieu of that outcome, he could count on the figures being ignored—even better, condemned. The repeated description of the St. Anthony victim as a "demon" in late-1980s and early-1990s literature on Johns, a word rooted in some historical usage and one that the artist has employed himself in describing it, has the effect of distancing us from the figure as a suffering human.

Pursuing his inner life under cover, Johns conforms to postmodernist expectations of the artist. His responsibility is to keep looking aesthetically like himself, in order to maintain his market value, and while doing this to introduce something new at every showing—if not a novel play upon flatness, an unfamiliar icon and an original setting for it. Private issues, he assumes, are his own business. Critics may duly note his personal icons but may never pursue them to any biographical end. A photograph in a lithograph of 1994 could put this approach to the test. With his most blatantly biographical image to date—a Johns family portrait circa 1904—Johns recontextualizes his Grünewald Resurrection soldier, upright and charging, which consumes the body of the work, reinforcing the impression of him in *Mirror's Edge* as the mythic heroic projection of Johns the successful artist. It also strengthens the point that soldier and plague victim evolved into polarized self-portraits: the soldier the outward, upwardly mobile, and worldly representative; the victim the inner reality of the past, the agent of reconnaisance into lost horizons of the interior, the keeper of archaic feelings.

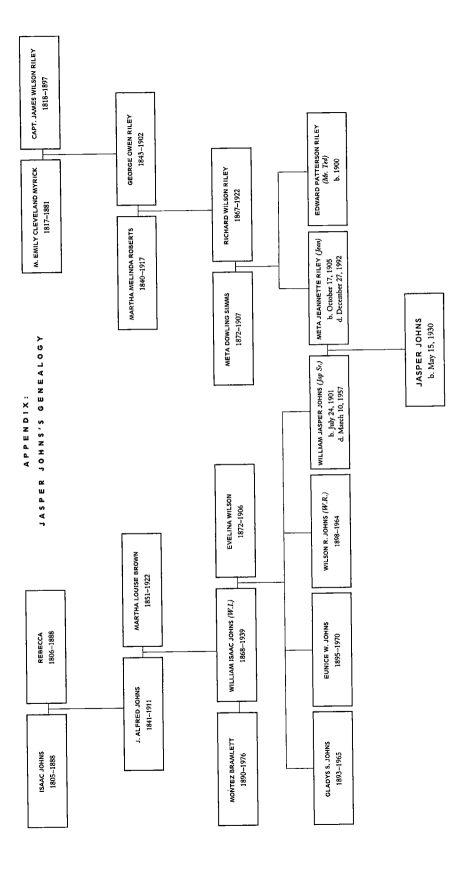

APPENDIX:

JASPER JOHNS'S GENEALOGY

NOTES

CHAPTER 1:
THE GRÜNEWALD CONNECTION
I.

1. Michael Crichton, *Jasper Johns*, rev. ed. (New York: Harry N. Abrams, 1994), 68.

2. According to Roberta Bernstein, these pairs of circles, triangles, and squares refer to a brush painting of a circle, triangle, and square by the nineteenth-century Japanese Zen master Sengai, which made Johns think of Cézanne's advice to "treat nature by the cylinder, the sphere, and the cone." Roberta Bernstein, *Jasper Johns's The Seasons: Records of Time,* cat. (Brooke Alexander Editions, 1991–92, New York), 13.

3. Jed Perl, "Jasper's Seasons," *New Criterion* 5, no. 10 (June 1987): 58; Steven Henry Madoff, "Jasper Johns: A Seasonal Lull," *ArtNews* 86, no. 5 (May 1987): 158.

4. Barnaby Ruhe, "Jasper Johns' 4 Seasons; David Salle at Whitney," *Art/World* (Spring 1987): 1, 4; Perl, "Jasper's Seasons," 58.

II.

5. Roberta Bernstein, *Jasper Johns' Paintings and Sculptures 1954–1974: The Changing Focus of the Eye* (Ann Arbor, Mich.: UMI Research Press, 1985), 68.

6. John Russell, " 'The Seasons': Forceful Paintings from Jasper Johns," *New York Times,* 6 February 1987.
7. Barbara Rose, "Jasper Johns: The Seasons," *Vogue* (January 1987).
8. The panels are grouped into three structures or frameworks that open and close. The Resurrection is part of the group that includes the Annunciation, the Angelic Concert, Madonna and Child, and the Lamentation, the last in a predella (see Illustrations).
9. John Russell, "Jasper Johns Show is Painter at his Best," *New York Times,* 3 February 1984, section III, p. 22; Roberta Smith, "Jasper Johns Personal Effects," *Village Voice,* 21 February 1984: 89.
10. Richard Francis, *Jasper Johns* (New York: Abbeville Press, 1984), 102–103.
11. John Ashbery, "A Tortoise among Hares," *Newsweek* 103, 27 February 1984: 81.
12. Nan Rosenthal and Ruth E. Fine, *The Drawings of Jasper Johns,* cat. (Washington, D.C.: National Gallery of Art, 1990), 45, and Ostar Hagen, *Grünewalds Isenheim Altarpiece in neum und voerzog Aifmajem* (Munich, 1919).
13. Vivien Raynor, "Conversation with Jasper Johns," *ArtNews* 72 (March 1973): 22.

III.

14. Francis, *Jasper Johns,* 107.
15. The photograph was a Christmas gift from someone in the gallery. April Bernard and Mimi Thompson, "Johns about Painting, on . . . Poetry, and Himself," *Vanity Fair* 47 (February 1984): 65.
16. William Rubin, "Younger American Painters," *Art International* 4, no. 1 (1960): 24–31.
17. Max Kozloff, "Traversing the Field . . . Eight Contemporary Artists at MoMA," *Art Forum* 13, no.4 (1974): 44–49.
18. Rosenthal and Fine, *Drawings of Jasper Johns,* 39.
19. Ashbery, "Tortoise among Hares": 81; Jeanne Silverthorne, "Jasper Johns," *Artforum* 12, no.10 (1984): 86–87.

IV.

20. J. K. Huysmans, "Two Essays on Grünewald," in *Grünewald,* E. Ruhmer, ed. (New York: Phaidon, 1958), p. 20.
21. Andrée Hayum, *The Isenheim Altarpiece, God's Medicine and the Painter's Vision* (Princeton: Princeton University Press, 1989), 155.
22. Huysmans, "Two Essays on Grünewald," 19–20.

23. "Only in 1597 was this disease discovered to be alimentary in origin and its cause isolated as ergot, or poisoned rye," Hayum, *Isenheim Altarpiece,* 21.

24. John Fuller, *The Day of Saint Anthony's Fire* (New York: Macmillan, 1968), 75.

25. Ibid., 117.

26. Huysmans, "Two Essays on Grünewald," 21.

27. Hayum, *Isenheim Altarpiece,* 21.

28. Fuller, *Saint Anthony's Fire,* 1–2.

29. "The only other Old Master artists [besides Leonardo] I have heard Johns express admiration for are Dürer and Grünewald," Bernstein, *Johns' Paintings and Sculptures 1954–1974,* 224, n. 3.

30. Author's conversation with Jasper Johns, New York City, October 1988.

31. Tim Marlow and Bryan Robertson, "Jasper Johns," *tate-the art magazine,* 1 (Winter 1993): 40–47.

32. Crichton, *Jasper Johns* (1994), 72.

33. Peter Fuller, "Jasper Johns Interviewed, Part II," *Art Monthly* 19 (September 1978): 7.

34. Jeff Perrone, "The Purloined Image," *Arts Magazine* 53 (April 1979): 135–39.

35. *Jasper Johns: Ideas in Paint,* a film produced and directed by Rick Tajada-Flores, WHYY, Inc. Production in Association with WNET/NY, 1989. The director made his field footage log available to the author.

36. Mark Rosenthal, *Jasper Johns: Work Since 1974,* cat. (Philadelphia: Philadelphia Museum of Art, 1988), 69, 102.

37. Paul Taylor, "Jasper Johns," *Interview* 7, no. 20 (July 1990): 100, 121–23.

38. Rosenthal, *Jasper Johns: Work Since 1974,* 94.

39. David Hickey, *The Invisible Dragon* (Los Angeles: Art Issues Press, 1993), 44.

40. (She is part of a trick double image, the other image being that of a fashionable young woman who is looking away from the viewer. It comes from a drawing by W. E. Hill, "My Wife and My Mother-in-Law," which was published in *Puck* in 1915 and used by the American psychologist Edwin Garrigues Boring as an example of a perceptually "ambiguous figure.")

CHAPTER 2:
THE PATERNITY OF FLAG

I.

1. Leo Steinberg, *Jasper Johns* (New York: George Wittenborn, 1963), 8.

2. Taylor, "Jasper Johns," 100, 121–123.

3. Steinberg, *Jasper Johns,* 8.

4. Robert Rosenblum, "Jasper Johns," *Art International* IV, no. 7 (25 September 1960): 75.

5. John Bernard Myers, "The Impact of Surrealism on the New York School," *Evergreen Review* 4, no. 12 (1960): 75–85.

6. Fairfield Porter, "Jasper Johns," *ArtNews* 56, no.1 (1958): 20.

7. Steinberg, *Jasper Johns,* 8, and Hilton Kramer, "Month in Review," *Arts Magazine* 33 (February 1959): 48–51.

8. Hilton Kramer, "Johns's Work Doesn't Match His Fame," *New York Times,* sec. D, 18 December 1977: 33.

9. *Ideas in Paint,* Tajada-Flores, field footage log.

10. [no author] "Trend to the Anti-Art," *Newsweek* (31 March 1958): 94–96.

11. Peter Fuller, "Jasper Johns Interviewed, Part I," *Art Monthly* 18 (1978): 6–12.

12. [no author] "Five Young Artists," *Charm* (1959): 84–87; and Leo Steinberg, *Jasper Johns* (New York: George Wittenborn, 1963), 8.

13. [no author] "His Heart Belongs to Dada," *Time* 73 (4 May 1959): 58.

14. Steinberg, *Jasper Johns,* 15.

15. Ibid., 10.

16. All quotes in this paragraph: ibid., 10, 10, 12.

17. An untitled 1983–84 drawing; watercolor, charcoal, and crayon on two sheets of joined paper.

18. Steinberg, *Jasper Johns,* 31.

19. Ibid., 31.

20. Ibid., 31.

21. Harold Rosenberg, "Jasper Johns: "Things the Mind Already Knows," *Vogue* 143, no. 3 (February 1964): 175–77, 201, 203.

22. Calvin Tomkins, *Off the Wall, Robert Rauschenberg and the Art World of Our Times* (New York: Doubleday and Co., 1980), 117.

23. Author's interview with Rachel Rosenthal, Los Angeles, 4 February 1991.

24. Bernstein, *Johns' Paintings and Sculptures 1954–1974,* 1, 215.

25. Max Kozloff, "The New American Painting Post-Abstract-Expressionism: Mask and Reality," in Richard Kostelanetz, ed. *The New American Arts* (New York: Horizon Press, 1965), 88–116.

26. Steinberg, *Jasper Johns,* 12.

II.

27. Charles F. Stuckey, "Johns: Yet Waving?" Letters to the Editor, *Art in America* 64, no. 3 (1976): 5; Michael Crichton, *Jasper Johns,* orig. ed. (New York: Harry N. Abrams, 1977), 67, n. 34.

28. Mark Stevens with Cathleen McGuigan, "Super Artist Jasper Johns, Today's Master," *Newsweek* 90 (October 24, 1977): 66–68, 73, 77–79.

29. Barbara Rose, "Modern Classics: Johns and Balthus," *Vogue* 174, no. 2 (February 1984): 362–65, 417–18.

30. David Shapiro, *Jasper Johns: Drawings 1954–1984* (New York: Harry N. Abrams, 1984), 56.

31. John Cage, *A Year from Monday* (Middletown, Conn.: Wesleyan University Press, 1967), 78.

32. Taylor, 100, 121–23.

33. Dumas Malone, ed., *Dictionary of American Biography,* vol. 5, part 2 (Charles Scribner and Sons, 1932–33); David R. Chesnutt, *Sergeant Jasper—Hero of the Revolution* (1976 pamphlet).

34. Charles C. Jones Jr., "Sergeant William Jasper," address delivered before the Georgia Historical Society in 1876 (Georgia Historical Society, 1876): 5–36.

35. D. R. Rickborn, "Art's Fair-haired Boy," *State Magaziner* (Columbia, S.C., 15 January 1961).

36. A process in which brushes and collage material, newsprint and cloth are dipped into hot pigmented wax and applied side by side in short, Cézanne-like strokes to the surface before the wax cools and solidifies.

37. *Ideas in Paint,* Tajada-Flores, field footage log.

III.

38. Probate document for William Jasper Johns, County of Allendale, State of South Carolina, 10 March 1957.

39. The exception was the appearance in 1955 of one of his pre-Flag works of 1954 that he did not destroy, called *Construction with Toy Piano,* at the Tanager Gallery, an artist's cooperative on Tenth Street; and the curious presence of a little flag in a painting of Robert Rauschenberg's at the Stable Gallery in 1956, placed behind a door in his canvas.

40. Robert Hughes, "Jasper Johns's Elusive Bulls-Eye," *Horizon* 14 (Summer 1972): 21–29.

41. Judith Goldman, "35 Years," in Susan Brundage, ed., *Jasper Johns/35 Years/Leo Castelli,* cat. (New York: Leo Castelli Gallery, 1993).

42. Hughes, "Johns's Elusive Bulls-Eye."

43. Author's interview with Leo Steinberg, New York City, 4 February 1993.

44. Author's interview with Bill and Mary Johns, a cousin of Jasper Johns and his wife, Sheldon, S.C., 20 November 1988.

45. *Ideas in Paint,* Tajada-Flores, field footage log.

46. Meryle Secrest, "Leo Castelli dealing in myths," *ArtNews* 81 (Summer 1982): 66–72.

47. Goldman, "35 Years."

48. Susan Cheever, "Johns & Castelli, Inc.," *Harper's Bazaar* (January 1993): 76–81, 137.

49. Fuller, "Johns Interviewed, Part I," 6–8, 10, 12.

50. Cheever, "Johns & Castelli, Inc.," 137.

51. Mary Lynn Kotz, *Rauschenberg: Art and Life* (New York: Harry N. Abrams, 1990), 98.

52. Jill Johnston, "The World Outside His Window," *Art in America* 80, no. 4 (April 1992): 114–24, 183.

53. Robert Rauschenberg's father was the son of a German immigrant father and a Cherokee mother. He was a lineman for the Gulf States power company in Port Arthur, Texas.

54. Author's interview with Leo Castelli, New York, 28 February 1990.

55. Rosenthal and Fine, *Drawings of Jasper Johns*, 70.

56. See genealogy, appendix.

IV.

57. David Revill, *The Roaring Silence, John Cage: A Life* (New York: Arcade Publishing, 1992), 85.

58. Ashbery, "Tortoise Among Hares," 81.

59. Jones, "Sergeant William Jasper," 5–36.

60. The sword was broken off when author saw the statue in spring 1992.

61. Kay Larson, "Antidotes to Irony," *New York Magazine* 17 (27 February 1984): 58–59.

62. Rosenthal, *Work Since 1974*, 65.

63. Silverthorne, "Jasper Johns," 86–87.

64. Hayum, *Isenheim Altarpiece*, 33.

65. Matthew 28, 4 and 5.

66. Deborah Solomon, "The Unflagging Artistry of Jasper Johns," *New York Times*, New York Times Magazine, 19 June 1988.

67. Luke 24, 49.

I.

1. Michael Brenson, "Hard Questions about Exhibiting U.S. Art Abroad," *New York Times*, 22 May 1988, sec.2, pp. 33, 44.

2. Tomkins, *Off the Wall*, 2–10.

3. Brenson, "Hard Questions about Exhibiting," 33, 44.

4. Michael Brenson, "As Venice Biennale Opens, Jasper Johns Takes the Spotlight," *New York Times*, 6 June 1988, section C, p. 15.

5. Jack Flam, "Around the Art World in One Day," *Wall Street Journal*, 2 August 1988, section II, p. 18.

6. Michael Brenson, "Jasper Johns Shows the Flag in Venice," *New York Times*, 3 July 1988, section II, pp. 27, 33.

7. Author's interview with Mark Rosenthal, New York City, 2 June 1995.

8. Amei Wallach, "Jasper Johns: On Target," *Elle* 4, no. 3 (1988): 152, 154, 156.

II.

9. John Russell, "An Englishman Looks at an American Painter: Jasper Johns," *Réalités* 251 (October 1971): 70–75.

10. Author's journal entry, April 1987.

11. *Ideas in Paint*, Tajada-Flores, field footage log.

12. Author's interview with Margaret Leng-Tan, Brooklyn, N.Y., 28 February 1991.

13. Author's conversation with John Cage, New York City, 1989.

14. Author's conversation with John Cage, New York City, 1989.

III.

15. Jasper Johns, "Sketchbook Notes," 0–9, *Art and Literature* 4 (Spring 1965): 185–92.

16. Rosenthal and Fine, *Drawings of Jasper Johns*, 286.

CHAPTER 4:
THE DIOSCURI
I.

1. Rosenthal and Fine, *Drawings of Jasper Johns*, 280.

2. In reproducing a musical score sheet, Johns refers to at least three artists he admires who included score sheets in their work: Picasso (e.g., *Violon et feuille de musique*, 1912); John Frederick Peto (*The Old Violin*, 1890); William M. Harnett (*My Gems*, 1888).

3. Rosenthal, *Jasper Johns: Work Since 1974*, 65.

4. Author's interview with Margaret Leng-Tan, 28 February 1991.

5. Ibid.

6. Calvin Tomkins, *The Bride and the Bachelors* (New York: Viking Press, 1965), 97.

7. Ibid.

8. Francis, *Jasper Johns*, 26.

9. Revill, *Roaring Silence*, 85.

10. Francis, *Jasper Johns*, 26.

11. Author's interview with Margaret Leng-Tan, 28 February 1991.

12. Tomkins, *Bride and the Bachelors*, 97.

13. Thomas S. Hines, "Then Yet Not 'Cage,' " in Marjorie Perloff and Charles Junkerman, eds., *John Cage: Composed in America* (Chicago: University of Chicago Press, 1994), 84.

14. François Fonvieille-Alquier, *André Gide* (Paris: P. Charron, 1972).

15. Stuart Timmons, *The Trouble with Harry Hay* (Boston: Alyson Publishers, 1990), 59.

16. Revill, *Roaring Silence*, 87.

17. John Cage, *Silence* (Middletown, Conn.: Wesleyan University Press, 1961), 127.

18. Ibid., 127.

19. Revill, *Roaring Silence*, 90.

20. Ibid., 110, 89.

21. Ibid., 113, 120.

22. Hines, "Then Yet Not 'Cage,' " 10.

23. Revill, *Roaring Silence*, 120.

24. Hines, "Then Yet Not 'Cage,' " 74.

25. Caroline A. Jones, "Finishing School: John Cage and the Abstract Expressionist Ego," *Critical Inquiry* (Summer 1993): 654–55, 652.

26. Revill, *Roaring Silence*, 158, 159.

27. Thomas E. Yingling, *Hart Crane and the Homosexual Text* (Chicago: University of Chicago Press, 1990), 26.

28. Hines, "Then Yet Not 'Cage,' " 6, 43, 98.

29. The lithograph *Face* derives from the cast of a face in a 1972 untitled work, which is recognizably a face; see Crichton, *Jasper Johns* (1994), pl. 168 and 205, and Richard S. Field, "The Making of *Foirades/Fizzles*," in *Foirades/Fizzles: Echo and Illusion in the Art of Jasper Johns*, edited by James Cuno (Los Angeles: Grünewald Center for the Graphic Arts, Wight Art Gallery, University of California, 1987), 102. Note that in his 1984 untitled, Johns has made a kind of vertically superimposed figure on his Grünewald tracing; below *Face* he "taped" *Knee* from the same series, and at the bottom of the picture—if turned one quarter—*Feet*. By means of a Magritte-like surrealistically dislocated body, Johns suggests a vertical whole figure, spanning the entire field of the diptych,

for the soldier whose face and helmet he obliterated with features of his own earlier work.

II.

30. David Bourdon, "I Never Sensed Myself as Being Static," *Village Voice,* 31 October 1977, p. 75.
31. Grace Glueck, " 'Once Established,' Says Jasper Johns, 'Ideas can be Discarded,' " *New York Times,* 16 October 1977, sec. 2. p. 1, 31.
32. Tomkins, *Off the Wall,* 109.
33. Author's interview with Rachel Rosenthal, Los Angeles, 4 February 1991.
34. Tomkins, *Off the Wall,* 112.
35. Ibid., 109–10.
36. From transcript of Fred Orton interview with Rachel Rosenthal, Los Angeles, 9 June 1992, p. 7.
37. Encaustic on canvas with glass and wood, now in the Menil collection.
38. Construction, oil and collage with plaster casts, now at the Smithsonian Institution, Washington, D.C.
39. Kotz, *Rauschenberg: Art and Life,* 71–76.
40. Jacqueline Lesschaeve, *The Dancer and the Dance* (New York: Marion Boyars, 1985), 39.
41. Ibid., 79.
42. Revill, *Roaring Silence,* 87.
43. Hines, "Then Yet Not 'Cage,' " 74, 70.
44. Lesschaeve, *Dancer and the Dance,* 33–34.
45. Walter Hopps, *Robert Rauschenberg: The Early 1950s* (Houston: Houston Fine Art Press, 1991), 65.
46. Ibid., 17.
47. Kotz, *Rauschenberg: Art and Life,* 82; and the author's 1995 conversation with Richard Shiff, who said that de Kooning had offered Robert Rauschenberg a drawing easy to erase, but Rauschenberg chose a difficult one.
48. Hopps, *Robert Rauschenberg,* 201.
49. Kotz, *Rauschenberg: Art And Life,* 72, 74.
50. Johnston, "World Outside His Window," 114–24, 183.
51. Barbara Rose, *Rauschenberg* (New York: Vintage Books, 1982), 72, 85, 114.
52. Author's conversation with Robert Rauschenberg, New York City, 14 March 1991.
53. Author's conversation with Robert Rauschenberg, New York City, 12 September 1990.

54. April Bernard and Mimi Thompson (interview), "Johns about painting, on . . . poetry, and himself," *Vanity Fair* 47 (February 1984): 65.

III.

55. Walter Hopps, "An Interview with Jasper Johns," *Artforum* 111, no. 6 (March 1965): 32–36.

56. Bernstein, *Johns' Paintings and Sculptures 1954–1974,* 34–35.

57. Ibid., 35–36.

58. Crichton, *Jasper Johns* (1994), 72.

59. Leo Steinberg, *Other Criteria* (London: Oxford University Press, 1972), 54.

60. Jonathan Katz, "The Art of Code: Jasper Johns and Robert Rauschenberg," in Whitney Chadwick and Isabelle de Courtivron, eds. *Significant Others* (London: Thames and Hudson, 1993), 173.

61. Eugene Victor Thaw, "Lust for Life," *New York Review of Books* 27, no. 16 (23 October 1980): 25–26.

62. Charles Harrison and Fred Orton, "Jasper Johns: 'Meaning What You See,' " *Art History* 7 (March 1984), 77–101.

63. Ibid., 81.

64. Bernstein, *Johns' Paintings and Sculptures 1954–1974,* 41.

65. Crichton, *Jasper Johns* (1977), 39.

66. Jonathan Katz, "Art of Code," 3.

67. Hilton Kramer, "Jasper Johns at Gagosian Gallery: Distinctly Comical, Pathetic Show," *New York Observer,* 20 March 1989.

68. Crichton, *Jasper Johns* (1977), 39.

69. Walter Hopps, *Robert Rauschenberg,* 64.

70. Bernstein, *Johns' Paintings and Sculptures 1954–1974,* 113.

71. Hilton Kramer, "Month in Review," *Arts Magazine* 33 (February 1959): 48–51.

72. Jasper Johns, letter to the editor, *Arts* 33, no. 6 (March 1959): 7.

73. Crichton, *Jasper Johns* (1977), 117.

74. Ibid., 117.

75. Perrone, "Purloined Image," 135–39.

76. Max Kozloff, "Art," *Nation* 198, no. 12 (16 March 1964): 274–76.

77. Fuller, "Johns Interviewed, Part I," *Art Monthly* 18 (July/August 1978): 6–12.

78. John J. O'Connor, "Jasper Johns: The Mystery of Simplicity," *New York Times,* 11 September 1989, section III, p. 20; *Ideas in Paint,* Tajada-Flores, field footage log.

79. Hilton Kramer, "Jasper Johns at Gagosian Gallery."

80. James E. B. Breslin, *Mark Rothko: A Biography* (Chicago: University of Chicago Press, 1993), 427, fn. 56.

81. Mark Stevens and Cathleen McGuigan, "Super Artist Jasper Johns, Today's Master," *Newsweek* 90 (24 October 1977): 66–68, 73, 77–79.

82. Barbara Rose, "Pop Art at the Guggenheim," *Art International* 7, no. 5 (1963): 20–22.

83. Max Kozloff, letter to the editor, *Art International* 7, no. 6 (1963): 88–92.

84. Kozloff, "Art," 274–76.

85. Stevens and McGuigan, "Super Artist Jasper Johns," 66–68, 73, 77–79.

86. Tomkins, *Off the Wall,* 260.

87. Moira Roth, "The Aesthetic of Indifference," *Artforum* 16, no. 3 (1977): 46–53.

88. Katz, "Art of Code," 194.

89. Martin Duberman, *Cures: A Gay Man's Odyssey* (New York: Penguin Books USA, 1991), 47.

90. Ibid., 79, 47.

91. Ibid., 47.

92. Ibid., 48, fn. 7.

93. Bryan Robertson, *Jasper Johns,* cat. (London: Hayward Gallery, Arts Council of Great Britain, Westerham Press, 1978), unpaginated.

94. Andrew Forge, "The Emperor's Flag," *New Statesman,* 11 December 1964, 938.

95. Harrison and Orton, "Jasper Johns: 'Meaning What You See'," 77–101.

96. Hughes, "Johns's Elusive Bulls-Eye," 21.

97. Roth, "Aesthetic of Indifference," **51,** 50.

IV.

98. Author's interview with Viola Farber, New York City, 24 October 1988.

99. Hopps, *Robert Rauschenberg,* 167–68.

100. Brad Gooch, *City Poet: The Life and Times of Frank O'Hara* (New York: Alfred A. Knopf, 1993), 259–60, 315.

101. Ibid., 33.

102. Ibid., 329.

103. Bernstein, *Johns' Paintings and Sculptures 1954–1974,* 79.

104. Marjorie Perloff, *Frank O'Hara: Poet among Painters* (Austin: University of Texas Press, 1979), 141.

105. Gooch, *City Poet,* 395.

106. Barbara Rose, "ABC Art," *Art in America* 53, no. 5 (1965): 59–69.

107. Perloff, *Frank O'Hara*, 167.

108. Ibid., 167.

109. Bernstein, *Johns' Paintings and Sculptures 1954–1974*, 87.

110. Nicolas Calas, "Icons and Images in the Sixties," in Nicolas and Elena Calas, *Jasper Johns: And/Or* (New York: Dutton, 1971): 72–82.

V.

111. John Unterecker, *Voyager: A life of Hart Crane* (New York: Liveright, 1987), 758.

112. Philip Horton, *Hart Crane: The Life of an American Poet* (New York: Viking Press, 1957), 302.

113. Crichton, *Jasper Johns* (1977), 50.

114. Yingling, *Hart Crane and the Homosexual Text*, 104.

115. Unterecker, *Voyager*, 73, 38.

116. Ibid., 542.

117. Gooch, *City Poet*, 285.

118. Unterecker, *Voyager*, 763.

119. Ibid., 534.

120. Horton, *Hart Crane*, 241.

121. Unterecker, *Voyager*, 538, 540.

122. Ibid., 567, 568, 571.

123. Ibid., 607.

124. Ibid., 27.

125. Ibid., 646, 666–67, 16.

126. Ibid., 758.

127. Peggy Baird, "The Last Days of Hart Crane," *Venture* 4, no.1 (1961): 21–46.

128. Unterecker, *Voyager*, 768.

129. Ibid., 756–57.

130. Waldo Frank, ed. *The Collected Poems of Hart Crane* (New York: Liveright Pub. Corp., 1946), xvii.

131. Ibid., 32.

132. Yingling, *Hart Crane and the Homosexual Text*, 209.

133. Ibid., 209.

134. Frank, *Collected Poems of Hart Crane*, 47.

135. Ibid., 31.

136. Yingling, *Hart Crane and the Homosexual Text*, 209.

137. Ibid., 213.

138. Frank, *Collected Poems of Hart Crane*, 39.

139. Ibid., 37.

140. Ibid., 34.

141. Yingling, *Hart Crane and the Homosexual Text*, 211.

142. W. H. Auden, *Collected Poems* (New York: Farber and Farber, 1976), 146–47.

143. Author's conversation with Bill Goldston, New York City, 4 October 1990.

144. Richard Shiff, "Anamorphosis: Jasper Johns," in Cuno, ed., *Foirades/Fizzles*, 158.

145. Yingling, *Hart Crane and the Homosexual Text*, 66.

146. Shiff, "Anamorphosis: Jasper Johns," 160–61.

147. Ibid., 149.

148. "My feeling about myself on the subjective level is that I'm a highly flawed person. The concerns that I have always dealt with in picture making didn't have to do with expressing my flawed nature or my *self*—I wanted something that wouldn't have to carry my nature as part of its message," Jasper Johns, quoted in Fuller, "Johns Interviewed, Part II."

CHAPTER 5:
THE GREAT MAN DISCOURSE
I.

1. Bryan Robertson, "Jasper Johns," *tate* 1 (London, Winter 1993), 41–47.

2. Fuller, "Johns Interviewed, Part II," 6–8, 10, 12, **10.**

3. Ibid., 10.

4. John Richardson, *A Life of Picasso*, vol. 1 (New York: Random House, 1991), 95.

5. Ibid., 33.

6. Ibid., 48.

7. Ibid., 51. Richardson recounts that Picasso's father, don José, asked his son to help him finish a painting of a pigeon. His eyesight was no longer sharp enough for the intricate bits, he said, so he chopped off the claws, nailed them to a board and set Pablo to paint them. When he returned from his evening stroll, he found that Pablo had painted the claws with such skill that, then and there, he handed over his palette, brushes, and paints to his prodigy of a son.

8. Ibid., 71.

9. Rosenthal and Fine, *Drawings of Jasper Johns*, 71.

10. Author's interview with Geraldine Lewis, Allendale, S.C., 12 April 1991.

11. Author's interview with Professor Edmund Yaghian, Columbia, S.C., September 1990.

12. Author's conversation with Jasper Johns, New York City, 1990.

13. James M. Saslow, *Ganymede in the Renaissance* (New Haven: Yale University Press, 1986), 51–53.

14. Richardson, *A Life of Picasso,* 157.

15. Bernstein, *Johns' Paintings and Sculptures 1954–1974,* 115.

16. Author's interview with Charles Shealey, first cousin of Jasper Johns, Batesburg, S.C., November 19, 1988.

17. Author's interview with Geraldine Lewis, Allendale, S.C., 12 November 1993.

18. Stevens and McGuigan, "Super Artist Jasper Johns," 66–68, 73, 77–79.

19. Robert Bly, *Iron John* (Reading, Mass.: Addison-Wesley Publishing Co., 1990), 42.

II.

20. Crichton, *Jasper Johns* (1977), 52.

21. Shiff, "Anamorphosis: Jasper Johns," 151.

22. Tomkins, *Off the Wall,* 129.

23. The original version was to be included in 137 numbered copies of the book, and were signed "Marcel déchivarit pour Robert Lebel."

24. Tomkins, *Off the Wall,* 125.

25. Joseph Mashek, ed., *Marcel Duchamp in Perspective* (Englewood Cliffs, N.J.: Prentice Hall, 1975), 158.

26. Jasper Johns, "Marcel Duchamp [1887–1968]," *Artforum* 7, no. 3 (November 1968): 6.

27. Jasper Johns, "Thoughts on Marcel Duchamp," *Art in America* 57, no. 4 (1969): 31.

28. Johns, "Marcel Duchamp [1887–1968]."

29. Kozloff, "Traversing the Field," 44–49.

30. Jennifer Gough-Cooper and Jacques Caumont, *Ephemerides on and about Marcel Duchamp and Rrose Sélavy,* edited by Pontus Hulten (Cambridge, Mass.: Massachusetts Institute of Technology Press, 1993), entry for 31 August 1936.

31. Bernstein, *Johns' Paintings and Sculptures 1954–1974,* 66.

32. Gough-Cooper and Caumont, *Ephemerides,* entry for 8 April 1959.

33. Gene R. Swenson, "Jasper Johns," interview, *Art News* 62, no. 10 (1964): 40–43, 62–67.

34. *Ideas in Paint,* Tajada-Flores, field footage log.

35. William Rubin, *Dada and Surrealist Art* (New York; Harry N. Abrams, 1968): 21.

36. Like Duchamp's *Nude Descending a Staircase* when it was refused in 1912 by

the Salon des Indépendants in Paris, *Fountain* was rejected by the Society of Independent Artists in New York, prompting Duchamp's resignation from the board of directors, other members of which were unaware that R. Mutt was a Duchamp alias.

37. Griselda Pollock, *Avant-Garde Gambits 1888–1893* (New York: Thames and Hudson, 1993), 14.
38. Ibid., 20.
39. Tomkins, *Bride and the Bachelors*, 10, 52.
40. Max Kozloff, "Johns and Duchamp," *Art International* 3, no. 2 (1964): 42–45.
41. Peter Higginson, "Jasper's Non-dilemma: A Wittgensteinian Approach," *New Lugano Review* 10 (1976): 53–60.
42. Johns, "Marcel Duchamp [1887–1968]."
43. John Coplans, "Fragments According to Johns: An Interview with Jasper Johns," *Print Collectors Newsletter* 3, no. 2 (1972): 29–32.

III.

44. John Cage, *A Year From Monday* (Middletown, Conn.: Wesleyan University Press, 1967), 78.
45. Johns, "Marcel Duchamp [1887–1968]."
46. Gough-Cooper and Caumont, *Ephemerides*, 18 March 1912.
47. Arturo Schwarz, *The Complete Works of Marcel Duchamp* (New York: Harry N. Abrams, 1969), 16.
48. Tomkins, *Bride and the Bachelors*, 22.
49. Amelia Jones, *Postmodernism and the En-gendering of Marcel Duchamp* (Cambridge, Mass.: Cambridge University Press, 1994), 174.
50. Johns, "Marcel Duchamp [1887–1968]."
51. Tomkins, *Bride and the Bachelors*, 26.
52. Jones, *Postmodernism*, 37; Tomkins, *Bride and the Bachelors*, 27.
53. Gough-Cooper and Caumont, *Ephemerides*, 4 November 1912.
54. Ibid., 18 March 1912.
55. Ibid., 9 November 1959.
56. Ibid., 19 November 1961.
57. Bernstein, *Johns' Paintings and Sculptures 1954–1974*, 68.
58. Gough-Cooper and Caumont, *Ephemerides*, 16 April 1968.
59. Revill, *Roaring Silence*, 213.
60. Moira and William Roth, "John Cage on Marcel Duchamp," *Art in America* 61, no. 6 (Nov–Dec. 1973).
61. Tomkins, *Bride and the Bachelors*, 66.

62. Rosalind Krauss, "Jasper Johns," *Lugano Review II*, 1, no. 2 (1965): 84–114.

63. Christian Geelhaar, *Jasper Johns Working Proofs*, cat. (Basel: Kunstmuseum Basel, 1979), 56.

64. Wallach, "Jasper Johns: On Target," 152–56.

65. Author's conversation with Barbara Rose, 5 November 1988.

66. Gough-Cooper and Caumont, *Ephemerides*, 5 February 1923.

67. Ibid., 31 November 1927.

68. Rosenthal and Fine, *Drawings of Jasper Johns*, 274.

69. Gough-Cooper and Caumont, *Ephemerides*, 25 August 1912.

70. Ibid., August 7, 1912.

71. Ibid., January 13, 1913.

72. Ecke Bonk, *Marcel Duchamp: The Box in a Valise*, David Britt, trans. (New York: Rizzoli International Publications, 1989), 214.

73. Roni Feinstein, *Robert Rauschenberg: The Silkscreen Paintings 1962–64* (New York: Whitney Museum of American Art in association with Bulfinch Press, Little, Brown and Co., 1991), 88 (emphasis added).

74. Paul Matisse, "Some more Nonsense about Duchamp," *Art in America* 68, no. 4 (1980).

75. Jones, *Postmodernism*, 33.

76. Bernstein, *Johns' Paintings and Sculptures 1954–1974*, 59–60.

77. Gough-Cooper and Caumont, *Ephemerides*, 10 August 1916.

78. Jones, *Postmodernism*, 178.

79. Tomkins, *Bride and the Bachelors*, 49.

80. Ibid., 45.

CHAPTER 6:
THE EVOLUTION OF MONTEZ

I.

1. Louis Arthur Searson, *The Town of Allendale* (Columbia, S.C., 1949), 64.

2. *Spanked Child*, dated 1952, was a gift from Jasper Johns to Augusta Young Burch in 1952, when the artist was serving in the U.S. army at Fort Jackson, S.C. Augusta Burch was director of the culture center at Ft. Jackson, a program for enlisted men to participate in art, music, or drama. Pvt. Johns was on her staff as head of the art department. He taught art to other soldiers, and showed work at the Ft. Jackson gallery. When Augusta Young died in 1983, *Spanked Child* passed to her son, Bruce Lamar Burch Jr. It was sold to a European collector in 1988.

3. Bernstein, "Jasper Johns and the Figure: Part One, Body Imprints," *Arts Magazine* 52 (October 1977): 142–44.

4. Crichton, *Jasper Johns* (1977), 20.

5. Told to author by anonymous source.

6. Edmund White, "Enigmas and Double Visions," *Horizon* 20 (October 1977): 48–55.

7. Rosenthal and Fine, *Drawings of Jasper Johns*, 152.

8. Judith Goldman, *Jasper Johns: 17 Monotypes* (West Islip, N.Y.: Universal Limited Art Editions, 1982), unpaginated.

   In a lithograph, *Savarin*, of 1977–81, Johns introduced a blood-red impression of his right forearm and hand in a kind of predella underneath a rendition of a Savarin coffee can full of artist's brushes. The initials E.M., standing for Edvard Munch, appear in the same color red as Johns's forearm in the "predella." Johns's reference was to a *Self-Portrait* by Munch, of 1895, showing a skeletal arm and hand lying along the bottom edge of the picture, underneath Munch's representation of his head and visage. In 1982, Johns made 17 monotypes from 27 extra proofs of the lithograph.

9. Rosenthal *Jasper Johns: Work Since 1974*, 62.

II.

10. Author's interview with Charles Shealey, 19 November 1988.

11. *Citizen Leader*, Allendale, S.C., 26 April 1989.

12. Author's interview with Mary Young, Allendale, S.C., 19 September 1990.

13. Author's conversation with Owen Lee, Jasper Johns's half-sister, Edisto Island, S.C., 11 June 1989.

14. Author's interview with Charles Shealey, 19 November 1988.

15. *The People's Sentinel*, 15 September 1927.

16. Author's interview with Geraldine Lewis, 12 April 1991.

17. Bernstein, *The Seasons*, 9.

18. *Mirror's Edge*, 1992, painting by Jasper Johns.

19. Author's interview with Geraldine Lewis, 12 November 1993.

20. Author's interview with Mrs. Ernie Stevenson, Allendale, S.C., 12 April 1991.

21. Author's journal, 18 September 1990.

III.

22. Edward J. Sozanski, "A Peek at Jasper Johns," *Philadelphia Inquirer*, 23 October 1988.

23. Richardson, *A Life of Picasso*, vol. 1, 317, 228.

24. Ibid., 216.

25. Perrone, "Purloined Image," 135–39.

26. Jasper Johns has used these as "logos" for his note paper.

27. Helen Dudar, "Enigmatic, distant, Jasper Johns is at the top of his form," *Smithsonian* 2, no. 3 (June 1990): 57–60, 62, 64, 65–66, 68.

28. Vivien Raynor, "Conversation with Jasper Johns," *Art News* 72 (March 1973): 22.

IV.

29. *Citizen Leader,* 26 April 1989.

30. Author's interview with Charles Shealey, Batesburg, S.C., 10 November 1993.

31. *Citizen Leader,* 26 April 1989

32. *Ideas in Paint,* Tajada-Flores, field footage log.

33. Author's interview with Mary Young, 19 September 1990.

34. Author's interview with Geraldine Lewis, 12 April 1991.

35. Author's interview with Charles Shealey, 10 November 1993.

36. Author's interview with Katherine Grubbs, Allendale, S.C., 19 September 1990.

37. Dudar, "Enigmatic, distant," 57–60, 62, 64, 65–66, 68.

38. Crichton, *Jasper Johns* (1977), 20–21.

39. Jasper Johns, *A Calendar for 1991* (London: Anthony d'Offay Gallery, 1991).

40. Jasper Johns, untitled 1990 watercolor and pencil on paper.

41. David Douglas Duncan, *Picasso's Picassos* (New York: Harper and Brothers, 1961), 111.

42. Author's interview with John Duff, New York City, 12 February 1991.

43. Rosenthal, *Jasper Johns: Work Since 1974,* 67; Riva Castleman, *Jasper Johns: A Print Retrospective* (New York: Museum of Modern Art, 1986), 45.

44. Rosenthal and Fine, *Drawings of Jasper Johns,* 42–43.

45. Wallach, "Jasper Johns: On Target," 152–56.

46. Two of Picasso's mistresses, Marie-Thérèse Walter and Dora Maar.

47. John Yau, "Proofs Positive: The Master Works," *Art News* 87, no. 7 (September 1988): 104–106.

48. Rosenthal and Fine, *Drawings of Jasper Johns,* 304, 306, 308.

49. Steven Naifeh and Gregory White Smith, *Jackson Pollock* (New York: Clarkson N. Potter, 1989), 604.

50. Paul Brach, "Auditioning for Posterity," *Art in America* 79, no. 1 (January 1991), 110–13, 153.

51. Yau, "Proofs Positive," 104–106.

I.

1. Rosenthal, *Jasper Johns: Work Since 1974,* 43.
2. Between 1981 and 1983 Johns made three big paintings called *Between the Clock and the Bed* after the title of an Edvard Munch painting of 1940–42.
3. Kenneth Bendiner, "Robert Rauschenberg's *Canyon,*" *Arts* 56, no. 10 (June 1982): 57–59.
4. Author's interview with Jim Self, 14 April 1990.
5. Author's interview with Richard Elovich, New York, 15 June 1990.
7. Crichton, *Jasper Johns* (1994), 62.
8. Barbara Rose, "Jasper Johns *The Tantric Details,*" *American Art* 7, no. 4 (Fall 1993): 47–71.
9. Rosenthal and Fine, *Drawings of Jasper Johns,* 252.
10. Ibid., 252.
11. Shapiro, *Jasper Johns: Drawings 1954–1984,* 39.
12. Eve Kosofsky Sedgwick, the gay theoretician, uses the term "closet-in-view" in her classic *Epistemology of the Closet* (Berkeley: University of California Press, 1990). Another suggested term is "hidden in plain sight."
13. Johnston, "World Outside His Window," 114–24, 183.
14. Rose, "Jasper Johns *The Tantric Details,*" 47–71.
15. Crichton, *Jasper Johns* (1994), 62.
16. Ibid., 62.
17. Ibid., 62.
18. Author's interview with Richard Elovich, 15 June 1990.
19. Fuller, "Johns Interviewed, Part II," 5–7.
20. Riva Castleman, *Jasper Johns: A Print Retrospective,* cat. (New York: Museum of Modern Art, 1986), 34.

II.

21. Author's interviews with Mark Lancaster, Folkestone, England, 19 April 1988, and New York, 26 September 1994.
22. Author's interview with Mark Lancaster, 26 September 1994.
23. Author's correspondence with Christian Geelhaar, June–July 1990.
24. Author's interview with Mark Lancaster, 19 April 1988.
25. Author's correspondence with Christian Geelhaar, June–July 1990.
26. Author's interview with Jim Self, New York City, 13 November 1992.
27. Rosenthal and Fine, *Drawings of Jasper Johns,* 36.

28. Randy Shilts, *And the Band Played On* (New York: Penguin Books, 1987), 49, 50.

29. Ibid., 87.

30. Ibid., xxi–xxii.

31. The author made some attempts to talk to women who have either claimed some intimacy with Johns or have been said to have had such encounters. The names themselves seemed unimportant. The accumulation of them, through claim or rumor, indicates a "phase" that was significant in the artist's life and work at that time.

32. *American Image* 24, nos. 1 and 2 (Spring/Summer 1967), 98–128.

33. Author's interview with Richard Elovich, 15 June 1990.

34. Author's interview with Jim Self, New York, 13 November 1992.

35. Author's interview with Jim Self, New York, 28 September 1994.

III.

36. Mario Amaya, "Jasper Johns, Greene Street, New York," *The Times*, London, 26 April 1984.

37. Ann Morris Reynolds, "Jasper Johns," *Arts Magazine* (April 1984): 7.

38. Carter Ratcliff, "The Inscrutable Jasper Johns," *Vanity Fair,* 47 (February 1984): 60–64.

39. Jennifer Allen, "Jasper Johns's Beautiful Banalities," *New York Magazine* 17, no. 8 (February 1984): 32.

40. Kay Larson, "Antidotes to Irony," *New York Magazine* 17, no. 9 (February 1984): 58–59.

41. Jill Johnston, "Tracking the Shadow," *Art in America* 75, no. 11 (1987): 128–43.

42. Philip Larson, "Famous Artist Bottoms Out in Love Nest with Own Shadow," Print Collectors Newsletter (July/August 1990).

43. Tim Marlow and Bryan Robertson, "Jasper Johns," *tate-the art magazine,* 1 (Winter 1993): 40–47.

44. Crichton, *Jasper Johns* (1994), 72.

45. Ashbery, "Tortoise among Hares," 81.

46. Crichton, *Jasper Johns* (1994), 72.

47. Ibid., 72.

48. Ibid., 72.

49. Ibid., 72.

50. Shapiro, *Jasper Johns: Drawings 1954–1984,* 45.

IV.

51. Rosenthal and Fine, *Drawings of Jasper Johns*, 69–83.

52. Deborah Solomon, "The Unflagging Artistry of Jasper Johns," *New York Times*, New York Times Magazine, June 19, 1988.

53. Salvatore Settis, *Giorgione's Tempest: Interpreting the Hidden Subject*, trans. Ellen Bianchini (Chicago: University of Chicago Press, 1990).

BIBLIOGRAPHY

Adam, Judy, ed. *Dancers on a Plane: Cage, Cunningham, Johns*. New York: Alfred
    A. Knopf, 1990.

Alpers, Svetlana. *Rembrandt's Enterprise: The Studio and the Market*. London: Thames
    and Hudson, 1988.

Balmary, Marie. *Psychoanalyzing Psychoanalysis: Freud and the Hidden Fault of the Fa-
    ther*. Translated by Ned Lukacher. Baltimore: Johns Hopkins University
    Press, 1982.

Berkson, Bill, and Joe LeSueur, eds. *Homage to Frank O'Hara*. Berkeley: Big Sky,
    1978.

Bernstein, Roberta. *Jasper Johns' Paintings and Sculptures 1954–1974: The Chang-
    ing Focus of the Eye*. Ann Arbor, Mich.: University of Michigan Research
    Press, 1985.

———. *Jasper Johns's The Seasons: Records of Time*. Catalogue. New York: Brooke
    Alexander Editions, 1991.

———. *Jasper Johns*. New York: Rizzoli International Publications, 1992.

Bly, Robert. *Iron John: A Book About Men*. Reading, Mass.: Addison-Wesley Pub-
    lishing Company, 1990.

Bonk, Ecke. *Marcel Duchamp: The Box in a Valise*. Translated by David Britt. New
    York: Rizzoli International Publications, 1989.

Boudaille, George. *Jasper Johns*. New York: Rizzoli International Publications, 1989.

Bowness, Alan. *The Conditions of Success: How the Modern Artist Rises to Fame*. New York: Thames and Hudson, 1989.

Breslin, James E. B. *Mark Rothko: A Biography*. Chicago: University of Chicago Press, 1993.

Brown, Norman O. *Love's Body*. New York: Vintage Books, 1968.

Brundage, Susan, ed. *Jasper Johns/35 Years/Leo Castelli*. Catalogue. New York: Leo Castelli Gallery, 1993.

Cage, John. *Silence*. Middletown, Conn.: Wesleyan University Press, 1961.

Castleman, Riva. *Jasper Johns: A Print Retrospective*. Catalogue. New York: Museum of Modern Art, 1986.

Chadwick, Whitney, and Isabelle de Courtivron, eds. *Significant Others*. London: Thames and Hudson, 1993.

Cohen, Janie, ed. *Picasso: Inside the Image*. New York: Thames and Hudson, 1995.

Crichton, Michael. *Jasper Johns*. New York: Harry N. Abrams, 1977.

Crichton, Michael. *Jasper Johns*. Revised and expanded edition. New York: Harry N. Abrams, 1994.

Daix, Pierre. *Picasso: Life and Art*. Translated by Olivia Emmet. New York: HarperCollins, 1993.

Duberman, Martin. *Black Mountain: An Exploration in Community*. New York: E. P. Dutton & Co., 1972.

———. *Cures: A Gay Man's Odyssey*. New York: Penguin Books USA, 1991.

Feinstein, Roni. *Robert Rauschenberg: The Silkscreen Paintings 1962–64*. Catalogue. New York: Little Brown, and Co., Bulfinch Press, 1990.

Ferguson, Russell, ed. *Hand-Painted Pop: American Art in Transition 1955–62*. Catalogue. Los Angeles: Museum of Contemporary Art, 1992.

Field, Richard. *Jasper Johns: Prints 1960–1970*. Philadelphia: Philadelphia Museum of Art, 1970.

Foirades/Fizzles: Echo and Allusion in the Art of Jasper Johns. Catalogue. Los Angeles: University of California, Wight Art Gallery, 1987.

Francis, Richard. *Jasper Johns*. New York: Abbeville Press, 1984.

Frank, Waldo, ed. *The Collected Poems of Hart Crane*. New York: Liveright Publishing Corp., 1946.

Freeman, Judi. *Picasso and the Weeping Women*. New York: Rizzoli International Publications, 1994.

Freshman, Phil, ed. *Jasper Johns: Printed Symbols*. Catalogue. Minneapolis: Walker Art Center, 1990.

Gilot, Francoise, and Carlton Lake. *Life with Picasso*. New York: Doubleday, Anchor Books, 1989.

Glimcher, Arnold, and Mark Glimcher, eds. *The Sketchbooks of Picasso*. Boston: Atlantic Monthly Press, 1986.

Goldman, Judith. *Jasper Johns: 17 Monotypes*. West Islip, N.Y.: Universal Limited Art Editions, 1982.

Gooch, Brad. *City Poet: The Life and Times of Frank O'Hara*. New York: Alfred A. Knopf, 1993.

Gruen, John. *The Party's Over Now*. New York: Viking Press, 1972.

Guilbaut, Serge. *How New York Stole the Idea of Modern Art*. Translated by Arthur Goldhammer. Chicago, University of Chicago Press, 1983.

Haskell, Barbara. *Charles Demuth*. Catalogue. New York: Whitney Museum of American Art and Harry N. Abrams, 1987.

Hayum, Andrée. *The Isenheim Altarpiece: God's Medicine and the Painter's Vision*. Princeton: Princeton University Press, 1989.

Hickey, Dave. *The Invisible Dragon: Four Essays on Beauty*. Los Angeles: Art Issues Press, 1993.

Hopps, Walter. *Robert Rauschenberg: The Early 1950s*. Houston: Houston Fine Art Press, 1991.

Huffington, Arianna Stassinopoulous. *Picasso, Creator and Destroyer*. New York: Simon and Schuster, 1988.

Hulten, Pontus, ed. *Marcel Duchamp: Work and Life*. Cambridge, Mass.: Massachusetts Institute of Technology Press, 1993.

Johns, Jasper. *A Calendar for 1991*. London: Anthony d'Offay Gallery, 1991.

Johns, Jasper. *Retrospective of Jasper Johns Prints from the Leo Castelli Collection*. Catalogue. Gainesville, Ga.: Brenau College, 1991.

Jones, Amelia. *Postmodernism and the En-Gendering of Marcel Duchamp*. Cambridge, Mass.: Cambridge University Press, 1994.

Kaplan, Louise J. *The Family Romance of the Impostor-Poet, Thomas Chatterton*. New York: Atheneum, 1988.

Kotz, Mary Lynn. *Rauschenberg: Art and Life*. New York: Harry N. Abrams, 1990.

Kozloff, Max. "The New American Painting Post-Abstract-Expressionism: Mask and Reality," in Richard Kostelanetz, ed., *The New American Arts*. New York: Horizon Press, 1965.

Krauss, Rosalind E. *The Originality of the Avant Garde and Other Modernist Myths*. Cambridge, Mass.: Massachusetts Institute of Technology Press, 1986.

Kuenzli, Rudolf, and Francis M. Naumann, eds. *Marcel Duchamp: Artist of the Century*. Cambridge, Mass.: Massachusetts Institute of Technology Press, 1989.

Lebel, Robert. *Marcel Duchamp*. New York: Grove Press, 1959.

Lesschaeve, Jacqueline. *The Dancer and the Dance*. New York: Marion Boyars, 1985.

Lubin, Albert J. *Stranger on the Earth: A Psychological Biography of Vincent van Gogh*. New York: Holt Rinehart Winston, 1972.

Masheck, Joseph, ed. *Marcel Duchamp in Perspective*. Englewood Cliffs, N.J.: Prentice-Hall, 1975.

McGoldrick, Monica, and Randy Gerson. *Genograms in Family Assessment*. New York: W. W. Norton and Co., 1985.

McQuillan, Mellisa. *Van Gogh*. London: Thames and Hudson, 1989.

Mellinkoff, Ruth. *The Devil at Isenheim: Reflections of Popular Belief in Grünewald's Altarpiece*. Berkeley: University of California Press, 1988.

Monick, Eugene. *Evil, Sexuality, and Disease in Grünewald's Body of Christ*. Dallas: Spring Publications, 1993.

Monk, Ray. *Ludwig Wittgenstein: The Duty of Genius*. New York: Free Press, 1990.

Morse, Samuel French, ed. *Poems by Wallace Stevens*. New York: Random House, Vintage Books, 1959.

Naifeh, Steven, and Gregory White Smith. *Jackson Pollock: An American Saga*. New York: Clarkson N. Potter, 1989.

Naumann, Francis M. *Jasper Johns: According to What and Watchman*. New York: Gagosian Gallery, 1992.

————. *New York Dada 1915–23*. New York: Harry N. Abrams, 1994.

O'Neill, John P., ed. *Barnett Newman: Selected Writings and Interviews*. New York: Alfred A. Knopf, 1990.

Orton, Fred. *Figuring Jasper Johns*. Cambridge, Mass.: Harvard University Press, 1994.

Perloff, Marjorie. *Frank O'Hara: Poet Among Painters*. Austin, Texas: University of Texas Press, 1979.

Perloff, Marjorie, and Charles Junkerman. *Johns, Cage: Composed in America*. Chicago: University of Chicago Press, 1994.

Pollock, Griselda. *Avant Garde Gambits 1888–1893: Gender and the Color of Art History*. New York: Thames and Hudson, 1993.

Revill, David. *The Roaring Silence, John Cage: A Life*. New York: Arcade Publishing, 1992.

Richardson, John. *A Life of Picasso*. Vol 1. New York: Random House, 1991.

Rose, Barbara. *Rauschenberg*. New York: Random House, Vintage Books, 1987.

Rosenthal, Mark. *Jasper Johns: Work Since 1974*. Philadelphia: Philadelphia Museum of Art, 1988.

Rosenthal, Nan, and Ruth E. Fine. *The Drawings of Jasper Johns*. Washington, D.C.: National Gallery of Art, 1990.

Sandler, Irving. *The New York School: The Painters and Sculptors of the Fifties*. New York: Harper and Row, 1978.

Sartre, Jean-Paul. *The Family Idiot: Gustave Flaubert 1821–1857*. Vol. 1. Translated by Carol Cosman. Chicago: University of Chicago Press, 1981.

Saslow, James M. *Ganymede in the Renaissance*. New Haven: Yale University Press, 1986.

Sedgwick, Eve Kosofsky. *Epistemology of the Closet*. Berkeley: University of California Press, 1990.

Selz, Jean. *E. Munch*. Translated by Eileen B. Hennessy. New York: Crown Publishers, 1976.

Settis, Salvatore. *Giorgione's Tempest: Interpreting the Hidden Subject*. Translated by Ellen Bianchini. Chicago: University of Chicago Press, 1990.

Shapiro, David. *Jasper Johns: Drawings 1954–1984*. New York: Harry N. Abrams, 1984.

Shattuck, Roger. *The Banquet Years*. New York: Random House, Vintage Books, 1967.

Shiff, Richard. *Cézanne and the End of Impressionism*. Chicago: University of Chicago Press, 1984.

Shilts, Randy. *And the Band Played On*. New York: St. Martins Press, 1987.

Simon, Marc, ed. *Complete Poems of Hart Crane*. New York: Liveright Publishing Corp., 1993.

Solomon, Alan R. *Jasper Johns*. Catalogue. New York: Jewish Museum, 1964.

Steinberg, Leo. *Jasper Johns*. New York: George Wittenborn, 1963.

———. *Other Criteria: Confrontations with Twentieth-Century Art*. New York: Oxford University Press, 1972.

Timmons, Stuart. *The Trouble with Harry Hay: Founder of the Modern Gay Movement*. Boston: Alyson Publications, 1990.

Tomkins, Calvin. *The Bride and the Bachelors*. New York: Viking Press, 1965.

———. *Off the Wall: Robert Rauschenberg and the Arts World of Our Times*. New York: Doubleday and Company, 1980.

Unterecker, John. *Voyager: A Life of Hart Crane*. New York: Farrar, Straus and Giroux, 1969.

Varnadoe, Kirk. *Cy Twombly: Retrospective*. Catalogue. New York: Museum of Modern Art, 1994.

White, Edmund. *Genet: A Biography*. New York: Alfred A. Knopf, 1993.

Whitney, David, ed. *Jasper Johns: The Seasons*. Catalogue. New York: Leo Castelli Gallery, 1987.

Wittgenstein, Ludwig. *Notebooks 1914–1916*. Translated by G.E.M. Anscombe. Chicago: University of Chicago Press, 1979.

Wolfe, Tom. *The Painted Word*. New York: Farrar, Straus and Giroux, 1975.

Wood, Mara-Helen, ed. *Edward Munch: The Frieze of Life*. Catalogue. London: National Gallery Publications, 1992.

Yakush, Mary, ed. *ROCI: Rauschenberg Overseas Culture Interchange*. Catalogue. Washington, D.C.: National Gallery of Art, 1991.

Yingling, Thomas. *Hart Crane and the Homosexual Text*. Chicago: University of Chicago Press, 1990.

INDEX